French and Germans, Germans and French

Richard Cobb (1917–1996) was one of the foremost modern historians of France. He served as an interpreter with British forces in France and Belgium from 1944 to 1946 and remained in France until 1955 researching his doctoral thesis, which became *The People's Armies*. He subsequently taught at the University of Wales, Aberystwyth, Manchester University and Leeds University. He spent the rest of his life at the University of Oxford, ultimately becoming Chair of Modern History. As his entry in the *Dictionary of National Biography* states: 'his idiosyncratic character, unrestrained opinions, strong likes and dislikes, and fondness for liberal, noisy entertainment gave him something of a legendary reputation among students and colleagues'.

His major works include *The Police and the People* (1970), *Paris and its Provinces* (1975) and *Death in Paris* (1978). He also wrote a sequence of memoirs, *Still Life: Sketches from a Tunbridge Wells Childhood* (1983) being a startling celebration of oddness. Perhaps above all it is as a uniquely brilliant writer of essays that he will always be valued, some of which are gathered in *Paris and Elsewhere*.

He won the Wolfson History Prize in 1979, and was made Commander of the British Empire and chevalier of the Légion d'Honneur.

RICHARD COBB

French and Germans,

Germans and French

A Personal Interpretation of France
under Two Occupations, 1914–1918 /
1940–1944

PENGUIN BOOKS

PENGUIN CLASSICS

UK | USA | Canada | Ireland | Australia
India | New Zealand | South Africa

Penguin Books is part of the Penguin Random House group of companies
whose addresses can be found at global.penguinrandomhouse.com.

First published in 1983
First published in Penguin Classics 2018
001

Copyright © Richard Cobb, 1983
Translations copyright © Penguin Random House, 2018

First published for Brandeis University Press by the University Press of New
England as a volume in the Tauber Institute for the Study of European Jewry
series

Published by arrangement with the University Press of New England

The moral right of the author has been asserted

Set in 11.25/14 pt Dante MT Std
Typeset by Jouve (UK), Milton Keynes
Printed and bound in Great Britain by Clays Ltd, Elcograf S.p.A.

A CIP catalogue record for this book is available from the British Library

ISBN: 978-0-241-35131-4

www.greenpenguin.co.uk

In memory of my friend
Christopher Lee,
poet, teacher and man of peace

Guten Tag, *Fritz* – *Bonjour, monsieur* – Kalt – *Ya, pas chaud* – *Et tes officers?* – *Quand il fait froid, officiers ne sont pas là; ils boivent du champagne* – Böse Krieg! – *Et pas finie!*[1]

(Franco-German conversation piece, winter 1916, from *Vie et mort des Français*, Ducasse, Meyer and Perreux)

Je dois avoir six ans, c'est en 1917. Je suis avec Roger, mon grand frère. Des hommes en bleu, rien que bleu, des soldats, un régiment qui passe. Ran! Ran! sur les pavetons les godillots. Je tiens Roger par la main, il la serre fort, ma petite pogne. On suit les poilus jusqu'aux maisons là-bas, ran! jusqu'à ce qu'ils s'évanouissent au loin. Pour n'en jamais revenir, ranranplan! à la riflette ils barraient ces pauvres mecs.
Avec Roger on a fait un dernier signe, et par les rues bordées d'arbres, vides à nouveau, on est rentrés . . .[2]

(Robert Lageat, *Robert des Halles*)

Where indicated, German and French translations appear at the end of the text.

Contents

Preface

In January 1920, when I was about two and a half, my mother started what she called a 'Book of Richard' in a small notebook with hard black covers, which I found among her papers after her death at the age of eighty-five, in 1962. It is a very private chronicle of no literary pretension and little general interest, devoted as it is to most of the things that a mother might note about a small child: the struggling, squeaky beginnings of speech and of counting, the appearance of first teeth, then their loss, the first visit to a dentist, the recurrence of coughs, colds and tummy troubles, the tantrums provoked by the onset of some awful children's party (a form of torture common in middle-class circles in southern England in the 1920s), the first departure for school, the first time on a train, and the growing evidence of naughtiness (though I was glad to note that my *worst* crime – the havoc caused by my air gun to some forty windows – each still had a white circle of paint in the middle, as if in invitation to target practice – in a block of new houses and to the green buses of the Autocar company, and the consequent loss of a Kruger sovereign – had remained undetected).

From my Book I learn, among other matters of private interest, that in May 1924, at the time of my seventh birthday, while staying with my uncle, a doctor in Chelsea, having noticed 'Made in France' on the back of a dinner plate, I remarked, at table: 'the lavatory was made in the Midlands' (this rather acute social observation referred undoubtedly to Royal Doulton's standard pan, 'Golden Flush', in willow-pattern blue on a white background – I think most children would be attentive to the colour, design, and wording of the interior of a lavatory pan).

Now for *teeth*. I had eight at nine months, and lost my first tooth in gingerbread in June 1923. I had already had my first visit to the dentist two years earlier. But there is no more about teeth. Alas! I could fill in the missing chronicle of dental decay, extractions, the drill, agonizing fillings, even more agonizing killing of nerves with a squiggly instrument, for teeth have provided me with the most reliable and consistent private calendar. *All* the most important events of my career have been marked and emphasized by the accompaniment of agonizing toothache: my award of a scholarship to Oxford in December 1934, and, above all, what should have been the happiest day of my life, my release from the British army and my return to a civilian status, longed for every day of the previous four-and-a-half years. (I used to say to myself that, if I ever returned to civilian life, I would never, never complain, and that I would remind myself, if things seemed particularly gloomy, that at least I was no longer in uniform: a therapy that has worked wonderfully well for the last thirty-eight years even though, after all these years, I still have recurrent nightmares in which I am remobilized.) In September 1946, the complicated process of demobilization, spread over from Iserlohn, via Münster, Harborn – where we were disarmed (and how infinitely glad I was to see my sten go!) – and Hull, to the demobilization camp at Guilford, took, in all, just over a week, but the joy of escape from uniform and of survival was marred by continuous jagged pain, day and night, and only slightly checked by regular intakes of schnapps. The very first act of my free life as a civilian was to have myself driven by taxi to a dentist in the Edgware Road – the taxi driver assured me he was cheap. Smelling of whisky, this very drunken Scot injected me with a dirty needle – I had noticed him wiping it on his blood-stained white (or once white) coat, and had been past caring (it was too late anyway) with the result that, on my second day as a free civilian, my gum swelled up with pus, causing a second visit, this time to a more reputable dentist, on Mount Ephraim, Royal Tunbridge Wells, who set about draining my gum.

Earlier, before my release from military servitude, while in Iserlohn, I had had recourse to a German (civilian) dentist, in an impeccably clean white coat – a very rare article in the Ruhr in 1946 – whose assistant provided the power for the drill by riding a bicycle contraption – and whom I paid, most gratefully, in cigarettes. Earlier still, while in a sealed camp in May 1944, I had had a tooth extracted by a Cypriot dentist who sweated in the effort. In a very long chronicle of pain, set like background music – a sort of dental obligato – to public events, one occasion springs out as agonizingly and unrelentingly as the week-long top-jaw throb of demobilization. I had had a nerve killed on one of my visits to the dentist on Mount Ephraim. I had then started to walk home across Tunbridge Wells Common when, all at once, the nerve started on a prolonged death agony during which I lay writhing on the ground, looking at the 1916 tank which used to stand, throughout my childhood – it was removed, for some reason, at the beginning of the Second World War – outside the General Post Office on a little triangle of grass. Oh yes! I could fill in *that* chronicle all right! indeed, I think perhaps the *third*-happiest – the *second*-happiest would be the birth of my little boy, William, in April 1980 – day of my life, (but, of course, not comparable to the joy and relief of becoming a civilian and of regaining freedom and privacy) was when I got rid of the last six or seven of the wretched things in 1973.

I had a special word for soldiers in 1918, when I was just over a year and when the First World War still had six more fright-ful months to run before the Armistice. This is not surprising because they must have been very much in evidence both in Colchester, a garrison town and the home of my grandparents, and in Frinton, near where there were coastal artillery batter-ies on the Naze. I cannot actually remember any individual soldiers, but what I can still recall is the presence of the colour of khaki, at eye level, to the left of my pram and moving along with it. Just a khaki blur, floating along like a cloud; but also the smell of Brasso – I identified that particular army smell much later – and of tobacco. My nanny, Kate Scurrell, was, though rather sharp-featured, quite a good-looking girl, her face reddened by the east winds off the German Sea. Anyhow, the walking khaki blur and the cloying smell of Brasso seemed to accompany me in my pram rides more often than not, com-peting with the east wind, the changing texture of the sea, the brightness of the East Anglian skies, and the rich, lush colour of the Greensward, as claims on my earliest sensations of colour and smell.

We moved to Tunbridge Wells in May 1920, when I was just four. I don't remember the move, but the date is in my 'Book'. There was no hint at all of a khaki presence in the Royal Bor-ough, much too respectable a place to tolerate the presence or even the proximity of a garrison. (Poor Tunbridge Wells was later punished by becoming, in 1940, the headquarters of South-eastern Command: I date its social decline from then.) Men in civilian clothes – sometimes, in the summer, not in very many of them – would suddenly appear, as on a prearranged signal, during my walks with my nanny on the Common. I quite wel-comed these intruders, as they generally gave me sweets and told me to be a good boy and to stay put and not to wander off, as, singly, they went off among the tall ferns with Kate for a few minutes. The man who kept the antique shop on Mount

Pleasant was called Major Morland; there was also a Colonel Howarth – rather distant echoes of a military society. And, on our walks, I would look out for the wooden shacks and stove-pipe chimneys of the half-dozen local hermits, on wasteland, in boggy fields, or in thick undergrowth. There was also one living in a small tent in a field on the north side of the town. He wore greying cricket trousers, held up by a red and black boy scout belt with a serpent clasp – the serpent biting its own tail – dirty gym shoes, and an old blazer. He was bearded, long-haired, wild-looking and well spoken (generally while talking to himself out loud); and he went from door to door selling boot brushes, boot polish and yellow dusters, and, sometimes, just boxes of matches. My mother told me that I must be nice to him, as he was 'shell-shocked'. I think perhaps all the other local hermits were, too. Whether they had also been the pathetic débris of the officer corps I could not tell, for I never heard them speak, though it was said of the one who lived in a cave half-way down the rocks of Happy Valley that he had 'a good accent'. Such were their independence, their ability to rough it, even through the long wet winters, and their ingenuity in constructing for themselves ramshackle retreats that had some modest pretensions to a sort of bizarre elegance, that I think, in retrospect, that they *must* have been former officers, for ordinary soldiers would not have opted for such intense discomfort but would have got their feet under the table in some warm kitchen. Other 'temporary gentlemen' survivors went in, like the father of the war poet Keith Douglas, for chicken farming in the neighbourhood of the town; my parents said that they nearly always went bankrupt within a matter of months. Perhaps the next stage from there would be a leafy wooden hermitage with a roof of corrugated iron held down by large stones.

These were the only visible débris of the war. There were no one-legged men to be seen; indeed, in a community so middle-class, their presence would not have been appreciated. Such people should be shut away somewhere where 'they would be properly looked after'. There could be flag days for the blind, but the blind themselves would remain as unseen as unseeing. I tended to regard them as somehow unreal, a strange, alien collectivity, almost as a concept, about whom grown-ups talked obliquely, in low voices and with pity. They did not seem to have any reality.

It is strange that, through all my years at school – kindergarten, prep school, Shrewsbury – and at Oxford, I never came across any boy who had had a father killed in the war. My own father had spent the war (reluctantly, so my mother told me, and I must say I found such reluctance pretty silly; surely any sane person would have been happy to miss the war?) in the Soudan. Only my Chelsea uncle had served as an army doctor; but he never referred to his years in uniform and earned my intense and early admiration by referring to his neighbour in the village of Etchingham as 'Mr Rudyard Bloody Kipling'. Of course, there was a war memorial as well as the tank. On November 11th there would be a Two Minutes' Silence; from thirteen onwards, I would regard it as a matter of honour to talk loudly through it. At school, and in books written for boys, one was so constantly reminded that we had won the war that my school friends and I found our curiosity excited by those who had lost it. Losing seemed much more original and stimulating than winning, and one got so fed up with all the smooth-faced subalterns who outwitted the entire German fleet or who captured a secret zeppelin. I think that by about thirteen I had already come to recognize what should be a golden rule for any historian: 'Let us assume that our own country is *always* wrong' – certainly an excellent starting point. In my 'Book', under June 1933, my mother has written: 'Began to wish to get rid of law and order! and war.' No doubt a middle-class parental oversimplification on the subject of law and order, but certainly a fair comment on my attitude, at sixteen, to the last. Most of my close friends at Shrewsbury shared such views; we were appalled by bayonet practice on dummies in sacking. I even went to the extent of failing – with some difficulty, though I made sure that I got every answer wrong – Certificate A, known among ourselves as 'the Death Certificate'. I did not wish to become a subaltern, which would mean leading my platoon out of the trench, holding my little swagger stick. Of course, we were all thinking in terms of the previous war: bayonets, swagger sticks, the endless lists on the school war memorial, Lewis guns that invariably jammed, Four O'Clock Bushy-Topped Tree (the method used to direct the fire of light or medium artillery). So were those who tried to train us.

At Merton College, Oxford, the prospect of war dominated our thoughts and occupied much of our private conversations through the night. There seemed little doubt, between 1935 and 1938, that it would come. What were we to do? We came up with various solutions. One of my friends set about learning Swedish and putting money away regularly in a Stockholm bank. He was convinced that there would be sufficient advance warning to get out of the island before the government started introducing exit permits. He actually spent the war in Sweden, and got a decoration for services rendered to intelligence. Most of my friends opted for conscientious objection on religious grounds, not because they were religious, but because it was the only way to become an officially recognized CO. I spent a lot of time going to Oxford Town Hall, where the CO tribunal met, to attest to my friends' deep and lasting attachment to this recognized religion or that (Buddhism would not have washed). As my mother lived in the most middle-class town in England and played tennis and croquet at the Nevill Club and bridge at the Kent and Sussex Club, I could not possibly have become a CO. It would have distressed her much too much. There were also in my College a few young bloods, including Leonard and Charles Cheshire, who *longed* for war; but they were not among my friends. Most accepted the inevitability of war with reluctance, while recognizing that it might be necessary. It would be a war against fascism. If only we could be sure of getting the Red Army as our allies! I daresay a few never even gave a thought to the war, but I never met them. There was one undergraduate who had an artificial leg that he took off at night. *He* did not have to worry!

The Munich crisis found me in Paris. I was a one hundred percent *munichois*, immensely and quite physically relieved (it was perhaps one of the rare happy events in my life not to be marred by toothache). It might give me – who knows? – another six months in the Archives. I would never have dared count on another whole year of peace. I remember explaining my reactions to an American friend, as we crossed the pont d'Arcole in September 1938. I said my priority was to get on with my research. 'I would feel like a rat,' he observed, at the revelation of such single-minded selfishness. I did not mind feeling like a rat.

My position at the time was reasonable, if not elevating. I thought a war against Hitler was necessary, but I did not myself want to take part in it. The two things did not seem incompatible. 'Suppose everyone felt as you do,' someone objected; I argued that this would not happen, as most people were not such extreme individualists as myself. I wrote to my history tutor at Merton to express my profound relief at Munich and got a letter back from him in which he stated that I was the most selfish person he had ever encountered and that I thought myself the centre of the earth. I certainly thought that – well, wasn't I?

Matters were for a time taken out of my hands. I returned to

England in August 1939 feeling extremely ill. X rays revealed that I had pleurisy, with a largish spot on one lung. I remained ill till the end of the year, attending my army medical board in December, when I was found temporarily unfit for service in the forces. I was so pleased that I took a friend out to a grand dinner at the Calverley Hotel the night of my return from Maidstone.

It was a reprieve. But I could not count on a second one; and every day my health was getting better. I spent January and February 1940 writing to British consuls in neutral countries in search of a job that would take me out of Britain and her dependencies. I acquired a great many exotic stamps in pretty colours, but no job. However, some time in the spring of that terrible year, I was interviewed in London by the British Council and offered a job as a teacher of history, French and English at a preparatory school for the sons of the employees of Callender's Cables at Carcavelhos, between Lisbon and Estoril. I even signed a contract. It seemed an ideal job. I bought myself a *Teach Yourself Portuguese*, in its bright yellow cover, in an effort to come to terms with that strangely nasal and half-swallowed language. I also organized a farewell dinner at the Café Royal with my closest friends, promising to send them postcards from Portugal at regular intervals. I then took my passport and my contract to the passport office in order to apply for an exit permit. To my fury, it was refused me by the Ministry of Labour. My fury was further fuelled by my meeting, in a queue, a school friend of mine who triumphantly brandished a brand new green Irish passport that he had just obtained, which enabled him to pass the rest of the war in Dublin. I had never realized that he was even remotely Irish. The state had got the better of me.

But I was not regraded medically for a further eighteen months, and meanwhile I secured an Air Ministry assignment teaching English to Polish and Czech air crew. At the same time, I volunteered for, and was accepted by, the Free French. If I had to serve in an army, it would be much more interesting to do so in a foreign one; there could indeed be no better way to get inside a foreign society. It even seemed worth the extra risk, for it was unlikely that there would be any quiet berths in an army as small as the *FFL*. It was certainly pushing francophilia rather far, but my enthusiasm was genuine.

At much the same time, I was medically regraded. A little later, before I was actually in the *FFL*, I received an OHMS envelope containing a mobilization notice, a transport voucher, a postal order and a photograph of George VI telling me: 'We welcome you into Our Army.' But I did not want to be in their army, so I sent the travel warrant, the mobilization order, the postal order, and the photograph and welcome back, with a polite and patient letter in which I explained that I had already been accepted for service with the Free French. I received three more similar missives with the same contents, which I likewise sent back. The trouble was that the Free French could not actually admit me until they had received a clearance from the Ministry of Labour, and this my old enemy would not grant. It was a prolonged and obstinate rearguard action in the course of which I enlisted the help of two MPs, while my mother actually managed to beard the Minister of War, Sir Edward Grigg; she had the persistence and assurance of a Victorian middle-class background. But, of course, blind bureaucracy won in the end. I was arrested and spent the inside of a week in Tunbridge Wells gaol awaiting the arrival of my military escort, both Londoners, who had used the occasion to stop off for a few nights at their homes. They turned up in the end; but when we reached Paddington, it was discovered that there was no train to Chepstow, the training camp, for about six hours. They had spent all their money and did not know what to do with the unexpected – but apparently useless – bonus of six extra hours in the metropolis. I pointed out that, in the sealed OHMS envelope containing the contents of my pockets and my braces, there was also a sum of a little over £6. I suggested that this should be used on food and drink for the three of us. After a short debate, they agreed that the envelope should be opened, the money recovered, and the envelope then resealed. We spent the rest of the day drinking, and I was able to get my escort, a staff-sergeant and a corporal – with the active help of two sailors who took the legs while I took the arms – onto a midnight train. They at once fell asleep lying in the corridor, and we overshot Chepstow, my escort not waking up till Swansea. By the time we got back to Chepstow, it was past eleven, and we all agreed that drinks were called for. We eventually reached the gates of the camp a bit after three, arm in arm and singing. The escort and myself were put in the guardhouse to cool off. My escort were both stripped, and the next day I was brought before the adjutant, who asked me if I were prepared to 'soldier'; on my assuring him I was, he released me for ordinary duties. The circumstances of my arrival had by now reached my fellow recruits, who treated me with a mixture of awe and puzzled admiration. I felt that my entry into His Majesty's Forces had a Švejk-like quality. But, unlike Švejk and his creator, I never deserted, never even contemplated desertion. Like Švejk, I was a reluctant and untidy soldier, but I soon discovered that the army was not nearly as bad as I had feared, that one could enjoy very good company in it, and that I was only rarely in positions of physical danger. I was also very lucky in all my postings.

The origins of the present study are both accidental and varied. Ten years ago, while walking on Zooma Beach with a graduate pupil of Eugen Weber from the University of California, Los

Angeles, I was told by the young man that he intended doing research on civilian life in occupied France during the First World War. Did I have any ideas about possible sources? All I could come up with at the time were the novel, *Invasion 14*, by Maxence van der Meersch, the newspaper, *La Gazette des Ardennes*, and such personal memoirs as he could lay hold of. I also suggested that he should interview people living in the Nord or elsewhere behind the Front who had been children in 1914–18. Some years later, I enquired of Eugen Weber about the progress of the young man's research. He told me that he had indeed gone to Lille, but that, once there, he had abandoned historical research for the teaching of English in a commercial school, that he had married a girl from Béthune, the daughter of a Polish miner and a Frenchwoman, and that he had settled in the Nord. It seemed to me that he had taken the better course.

In the summer of 1979, I was asked by Professor Geoffrey Best of the University of Sussex if I would like to take part in a series of lectures to be given in the autumn on the general theme of 'Occupier and Occupied'. I agreed to give a lecture on occupied France, 1914–18. At much the same time, the late Lord Boyle, Vice Chancellor of the University of Leeds (where I was once a lecturer and where I met my wife when she was a student there) invited me to give one of the public winter lectures organized by the university, and I chose as my subject Vichy France, as viewed primarily from the Northeast. The same winter, I was asked by my good friend and former pupil, Professor Bernard Wasserstein, if I would be prepared to give two or three of the Helmsley Lectures at Brandeis University in the spring of 1981. To this I agreed most readily. At Brandeis I lectured on both occupations of France, as well as on those of Belgium, and gave seminar talks on the French records and on the Thermidorian régime. In the course of the academic year,

I gave four lectures on the first occupation, four on Vichy, and sixteen on Paris collaborationism, the origin of the two chapters devoted to that subject.

I am not a military historian, and this is neither the work of a specialist nor the product of original research, though, in the past, I have undertaken detailed research, in the French and Belgian records, on the relations between *occupants* and *occupés* in the nine *Départements Réunis* (the present-day Belgium) from 1795 to 1807, so that the general nature of the subject is not unfamiliar to me. I also discovered, much to my surprise, that little work had been done on civilian life behind the Front in the occupied Northeast during the First World War. My study is more an essay in interpretation and a very tentative approach to the elusive problems of the relations between soldiers and civilians, *occupants* and *occupés*, both seen as individuals rather than as collectivities. I make no apology for relying heavily on literary sources, on works of imagination, on my own explorations into necessarily tentative and groping interpretations – for history at this very often private, intimate level is not easily documented – as well as on my own personal experience, working as a soldier in close contact with civilian authorities and with individual families in France, Belgium and Germany, from July 1944 to September 1946. I hope that some at least of my suggestions may prove fruitful and illuminating to those who might wish to take them a stage further; but my main concern is that the present study – one as much of individuals as of groups – should make enjoyable reading.

I would like to have been able once more to thank the late Louis Guilloux for having told me so much about his own experiences in Paris and in Saint-Brieuc between 1939 and 1944, when I met him in July 1966. (I wish I could thank him too, in person, for having included me – so flatteringly, almost as if I had entered French literature, *par la grande porte*, rue

Sébastien-Bottin – in the second volume of his *Carnets*, published posthumously in April 1982.) During a recent visit to Paris, I was given a graphic account by my old friend Arthur Birembaut, who was nine when his part of the Pas-de-Calais was invaded, of his childhood experiences in Hénin-Liétard and in and around Bapaume, between 1914 and 1917. He described to me two rows of men, the one red and blue, the other field grey, facing one another across a field of sugar beet, a strange and constant whooshing noise, like a long-sustained sigh, coming between them, as if arising from the ground; he had felt no sense of danger as he eagerly watched the peculiar scene from a balcony of his grandmother's farm, for he could not imagine what two groups of coloured men lined up in rows could be doing lying in the beet in the hot sun. It seemed an odd sort of game. He graphically communicated his sense of amazement when, on being 'repatriated' to unoccupied France via Switzerland in 1917, he had arrived in Bâle and seen the streets of the Swiss town crowded with young men. He had not up till then been aware of the negative fact of their absence from his visual world. Nothing can replace the acuity of a child's observation; and he managed to recreate, for my benefit, some minor military engagement in the early stages of the war, in August/September 1914, in all its visual inconsequence as viewed by a child.

I have greatly profited from many conversations, most of them in Worcester Garden, with Mike Weaver, Reader in American Literature at Oxford, on the subject of Jacques Benoist-Méchin, the first translator into French of Ezra Pound. My friend and colleague, Hartmut Pogge von Strandmann, Fellow and Tutor in History at University College, Oxford, has rendered valuable assistance by translating for me passages of Bavarian slang from the *Liller Kriegszeitung* and by having made me a present of an illustrated edition of *La Gazette des Ardennes* of 1st August 1916. He was also kind enough to put me in touch with Professor Umbreit, of the University of Freiburg-im-Breisgau, who gave me valuable information on the subject of German military legislation for the period of the second occupation. My friend and successor at Balliol College, Oxford, Dr. Colin Lucas, very kindly gave me his copy of the memoirs of Paquis, which I have used extensively. My greatest debt is to my friend and colleague, Wilfred Halls, of the Oxford Institute of Education, the author of a brilliant study of the youth policies of the Vichy régime, who has been tirelessly generous in opening to me his considerable archive, mostly derived from normally closed sources in Lille and in Paris. If, as he claims, I encouraged him in the early stages of his work, I can say the same for what he has done for me. I have been very lucky to have a friend in such close proximity whom I could consult, at any time, on Vichy educational and religious matters. I have also profited from conversations with Roderick Kedward, of the University of Sussex, on the early period of Vichy, the subject of his excellent book. Professor Michael Marrus, of the University of Toronto, has been generous with unpublished information about the fate of the Belgian Jews during the second occupation. I would also like to thank my faithful and eccentric lecture audience (including the city planning officer of Los Angeles) who have sat out my Guinness-aided (a pint a lecture) lectures on Paris collaborationism, and who have not appeared to wilt under my sometimes lengthy quotations in direct French speech, including a good deal of Paris slang. From start to finish, this has been very much a *spoken* book (this is how it grew and grew) and if my readers can actually hear the speech, I shall have achieved one of the things that I set out to do.

I would like to thank the members of the History Department and the Tauber Institute at Brandeis for having given me such a tremendous welcome and for having made my stay there so enjoyable. And, above all, my warmest thanks go to Bernie Wasserstein for a fine combination of persistence and patience in nudging me slowly forward towards the completion of this book. He is not, however, to be blamed for any of its mistakes or imperfections. These are mine, and mine alone.

Glossary

ajiste   (n.m.): Member of the youth organization, *Auberges de Jeunesse*. From the abbreviation *AJ*.

apache   (n.m.): Roughneck from an eastern district. Paris slang, pre-1914.

arpète   (n.f.): A shopgirl. Paris slang.

attentisme   (n.m.): Sitting on the fence, siding neither with collaboration nor with resistance during the Occupation.

bandes amarantes   Members of the German general staff. From the maroon stripes down the sides of the trousers that designated staff officers.

barrer   To rush. Slang.

barrésien   (n.m.): Someone influenced by Maurice Barrès.

la Bastoche   The Bastille quarter. Paris slang.

BEF   British Expeditionary Force, the official title of the British divisions sent to France in 1939.

belge	(as in *fumer du belge*): Belgian tobacco or cigarettes.
BHV	Bazar de l'Hôtel de Ville, a celebrated general store.
blaquaoute	(n.m.): Blackout. Paris slang.
blette	(n.f.): Beet.
boueux	(n.m.): Dustman, garbage collector.
brown book	British soldier's paybook and identity book.
Bureau Central	Directing body of the French Communist party.
cabas	(n.m.): Black shopping bag.
capote	(n.f.): French army greatcoat.
la Carlingue	The Gestapo. Paris slang.
la Carrière	The French diplomatic service.
ceinture	(n.f.) *rouge*: Belt surrounding Paris made up of mostly Communist municipalities.
CGT	Confédération Général du Travail, the leading French trade union, associated with the *PCF*.
chantiers	(n.m.pl.) *de la jeunesse*: Vichy youth organization entailing forms of compulsory service in the open air.
cheminot	(n.m.): Railwayman, employee of the SNCF.

chleuh — (n.m.): German. Second World War slang. Originally the name of a warrior tribe in the Atlas Mountains of Algeria.

chtimi — (n.m.): Inhabitant of the Nord or the Pas-de-Calais. Slang.

ci-devants — (n.m.pl.): 'Has-beens'. Originally applied to members of the former nobility during the Revolution, and so here used in the more general sense.

CNE — *Comité National des Ecrivains*, an inquisitorial body set up by a group of writers after the Liberation.

condé — (n.m.): Permit or pass, and so the more general sense of clearance, politically or morally. Paris slang.

contrepèterie — (n.f.): Form of French humour based on the inversion of syllables; spoonerism.

corbeau — (n.m.): Writer of letters of delation. Literally, crow.

cordée — (n.f.): Group of mountain climbers roped together. *Premier de la cordée*: Leader of the group.

coron — (n.m.): Back-to-back, slum, in Roubaix or elsewhere in the Nord or the Pas-de-Calais.

côte — (n.f.): Standing in the stock market.

cothurnes — (n.f.pl.): High-heeled, wooden-soled sandals in use during the Occupation as a result of the shortage of leather.

décade   (n.f., as in *fumer sa décade*): Tobacco or cigarette ration.

déveine   (n.f.): Bad luck. Slang. Opposite of *veine*: good luck.

doryphore   (n.m.): German. Second World War slang. Literally, Colorado beetle.

drapeautique   (a.): Jingoistic, flag-waving.

la drôlette   The 'phoney war' of September 1939–May 1940. Paris slang for *la drôle de guerre*.

embusqué   (n.m.): Shirker in the military sense, someone in a 'cushy' job well away from the front line. Military term dating from the First World War.

enceinte   (n.f.): Enclosure in a fortification.

l'Epuration   The political purge of 1944–45.

estaminet   (n.m.): Café. Northeastern French regionalism.

Etappen   (Ger., n.f.pl.): Military supply and provisioning centres, good places for *embusqués*. From French *étapes*.

l'Exode   (n.m.): The collective panic of May–June 1940.

l'Expo   (n.f.): The international exhibition held in Paris in 1937.

Feldwebel   (Ger., n.m.): Army rank of sergeant-major, senior-sergeant.

félibrige   (n.m.): Poet writing in Provençal; follower of Mistral.

la Fête de l'Huma   The annual party given in September in the suburbs of Paris by the Communist daily, *L'Humanité*. Abbreviation of *la Fête de L'Humanité*.

FFL   *Forces Françaises Libres*, the London-based Free French army.

fibrane   (n.f.): Ersatz clothing material made out of wood fibre.

Fichier Central   Central identity register established in the prefecture of police in Paris.

filature   (n.f.): Woollen mill.

FLN   Front de Libération Nationale, Algerian resistance group.

fortiche   (a.): Strong, cunning. Paris slang.

franc-garde   (n.m.): Privileged member of the fascist *Milice* of Darnand.

francisque   (n.f.): Double-headed axe that was the emblem of Vichy. *Porteur de francisque*: Person officially authorized to wear the badge to indicate loyalty to the Vichy regime.

franc-tireur   (n.m.): Partisan or terrorist not in uniform. Literally, sharpshooter.

fretin   (n.m.): Fry, young fish. *Menu fretin*: Small fry.

fridolin   (n.m.): German.

fritz   (n.m.): German.

frizou   (n.m.): German.

galéjade   (n.f.): Tall story. Marseilles regionalism.

gaspard   (n.m.): Rat. Paris slang.

gaule   (n.f.): Fishing rod. Hence the significance of carrying two fishing rods in public during the Occupation: *deux gaules*.

Gefreiter   (Ger., n.m.): Army rank of corporal.

genièvre   (n.m.): Type of gin much appreciated in the Nord.

gestapette   (n.f.): Nickname of Abel Bonnard, Vichy Minister of Education. Combination of *Gestapo*; and *tapette*: pederast.

godillot   (n.m.): Boot. Military slang.

gouaille   (n.f.): Parisian impudence.

Guesdiste   (n.m.): Partisan of Jules Guesde, the doctrinaire Marxist French socialist leader.

la Guille   A quarter of Lyon. Hence *la Guillotière*.

HBM   Habitations Bon Marché, subsidized municipal housing in Paris.

HLM   Habitations aux Loyers Modérés, much the same as the *HBM*, but of rather better quality.

l'Hexagone   France.

hirondelles   (n.f.pl.): Nocturnal bicycle police. Paris slang.

l'indignité nationale   The deprivation of all civil rights as a punishment for collaboration.

insoumis   (n.m.): Young man who failed to report for compulsory labour service (*STO*).

internat   (n.m.): Boarding school.

interne   (n.m.): Houseman, intern.

jalon   (n.m.): Pick used in mountaineering for attaching the rope. Hence *poser des jalons*.

JC   *Jeunesses Communistes*, French Communist youth section.

jociste   (n.m.): Member of the *Jeunesses Ouvrières Chrétiennes*, a Catholic youth organization particularly strong in the Northeast of France.

JP   *Jeunesses Patriotes*, French fascist group.

jules   (n.m.): Procurer, gigolo. *Le Jules, le grand Jules*: The Boss.

lapalissade   (n.f.): Statement of the obvious. From *les vérités de Lapalisse*.

lazaret   (n.m.): Military hospital.

LRT   Lille-Roubaix-Tourcoing.

Liste   Otto: List of French books prohibited by the Germans.

LVF   *Légion des Volontaires Français*, Vichy volunteers for the Eastern Front.

manger ses tickets   To use up one's rations well in advance. Literally, to eat one's ration tickets.

marbre   (n.m.): Type. Printing term.

maréchaliste   (n.m.): Vichy conformist, partisan of Pétain.

marollien   (n.m.): Patois spoken in les Marolles, a poor quarter of Brussels beneath the Palais de Justice.

maurrasisme   (n.m.): Any muddy 'thought' associated with Charles Maurras.

mec   (n.m.): Chap, fellow. Slang.

midinette   (n.f.): Shopgirl.

la Milice   The fascist police formed by Darnand. Hence *milicien*.

Moâ   Nickname of actor Sacha Guitry. Evokes his constant reference to himself, *Moi-je*: I myself.

moco   (n.m.): Southerner, an inhabitant of Marseilles. Breton nationalist slang.

môme   (n.m.&f.): Kid, urchin. Paris slang.

montante   (n.f.): Prostitute, woman who goes upstairs. Northern French slang.

l'Occupance   (n.f.): The Occupation. Paris slang.

OHMS   On His (or Her) Majesty's Service, the initials designating an official letter from a British government department.

outre-Quiévrain   Beyond Quiévrain, the Belgian side of the Franco-Belgian border; thus Belgium.

OVRA   Mussolini's secret police.

parigot   (n.m.): Inhabitant of Paris; the Parisian manner of speech. Paris slang.

PCF	*Parti Communiste Français*.
pédalo	(n.m.): Pedal boat. Also pederast (slang), hence *il est de la pédale*.
pépée	(n.f.): Girl. Slang.
pétanque	(n.m.): French bowls, played with metal balls.
PJ	*Police Judiciaire*, the French equivalent of Scotland Yard, its headquarters 39 quai des Orfèvres.
PMU	*Pari Mutuel Urbain*, municipal tote.
PNB	*Parti National Breton*, a pro-German separatist movement with links to the IRA.
poujadiste	(n.m.): Literally, follower of Pierre Poujade. Hence anti-intellectual, lower middle-class, small shopkeeper.
PPF	*Parti Populaire Français*, the fascist movement led by Jacques Doriot.
PQJ	*Police aux questions juives*, Police for Jewish Affairs.
la Préfectance	The prefecture of police. Paris slang.
Pruscot	(n.m.): Prussian. Slang, 1870.
PSF	*Parti Social Français*, a fascist group associated with de la Rocque.
PSU	*Parti Socialiste Unifié*, a left-wing breakaway group from the *PCF*.
pythonisse	(n.f.): Female fortune-teller.

le Quai	The French Foreign Office, quai d'Orsay.
rafle	(n.m.): Round-up by police.
raté	(n.m.): Person who is a failure. *Le ratisme*: The cult of failure.
la Relève	The movement, set up by Laval, to volunteer for work in Germany in exchange for French prisoners of war.
riflette	(n.f.): War, massacre. Paris slang.
RNP	*Rassemblement National Populaire*, a fascist organization formed by Marcel Déat.
la Royale	*La Marine Royale*, the French navy, especially as described by those serving in it.
salopard	(n.m.) *en casquette*: Worker. Term used in right-wing circles in the 1930s.
Section Spéciale	Anti-Communist, antigaullist section of the French police formed under the Occupation.
le sieur de Gambais	Landru, the murderer of refugee widows from the Occupied Departments during the First World War.
Signal	The weekly illustrated magazine published, with a French edition, by Goebbels's ministry.
smokeleer	(n.m.): Black marketeer. Belgian slang, also used in the Northeast; derived from smuggler.
SNCF	*Société Nationale des Chemins-de-fer Français*, the French state railways.

Soldatenheim   (Ger., n.f.): Military leisure centre, hostel, restaurant, provided for soldiers in the German army.

souris grise   Member of the German army women's services, referring to their grey uniform.

Stanislas   *Collège Stanislas*, a leading Catholic school in Paris, thus indicating someone who has had a Catholic education and clerical associations.

STO   *Service du Travail Obligatoire*, compulsory labour service in Germany for young Frenchmen.

strapontin   (n.m.): Folding seat in a theatre or cinema.

la Sûreté Nationale   The French antiespionage police.

truand   (n.m.): Villain, criminal.

tsouin-tsouin   (a.): Delicious, tasty. Feminine language of love.

U-bahn   (Ger., n.f.): *Die Untergrundbahn*, the Berlin subway system.

verts-de-gris   (n.m.): German. Second World War slang.

viandox   (n.m.): Brand of meat extract cube. *Faire viandox*: To make dead meat, to be dead.

VNV   *Vlaamsch National Verbond*, a collaborationist Flemish nationalist organization linked with the IRA and led by Staf de Clercq.

Glossary

vouloir du linge	To lust after a woman, to want a woman. (*Linge* in the sense of feminine underwear.)
VVVF	*Vlaamsch Verbond voor Frankrijk*, a pro-German Flemish separatist group led by the *abbé* Gantois in the Nord.
zazou	(n.m.): Long-haired youth. Paris slang during the Occupation.
la zone	The area surrounding Paris once covered by the old fortifications. Hence *un zonier*, an inhabitant of *la zone*.

I

The First Occupation, 1914–1918

I.

Occupants *and* Occupés:
The Département du Nord

... *le régiment s'achemina vers Noyelles-sur-Mer pour s'y embarquer en chemin de fer pour destination officiellement inconnue, mais tous avaient le pressentiment qu'on allait à Verdun ... à 7 heures du matin, nous passâmes au Bourget. A midi, nous étions à Sézanne, en Champagne, et nous marchions toujours vers l'est. A 4 heures du soir, le train entrait en gare de Vitry-le-François. A ce point, on ignorait encore notre destination mais on allait être bientôt fixés si le train prenait la direction de Châlons, c'était aller en Champagne très calme en ce moment; si l'on continuait vers l'est, plus de doutes possibles, on allait à Verdun. Hélas! c'était bien là que nous allions et à la tombée de la nuit nous débarquions à la gare de Revigny ...* [3]

... *2 kilomètres après Lamotte-Buleux, la route bifurque d'un côté vers Noyelles-sur-Mer, notre gare d'embarquement, et de l'autre vers les plaines du Ponthieu; on s'expliquera les efforts que nous faisions le lendemain pour surveiller la direction qu'allait prendre la tête de la colonne à cette bifurcation. Nous poussâmes un soupir de soulagement en constatant que l'avant-garde tournait le dos à Noyelles; on n'allait donc pas embarquer, on ne partait pas pour Verdun, dont le seul nom nous glaçait d'épouvante. Toute autre destination nous était indifférente et aussitôt la joie et la gaieté se répandirent dans les rangs sous forme de chants, rires, lazzis et conversations animées . . .*[4]

(*Les Carnets de guerre de Louis Barthas, tonnelier, 1914–1918*)

. . . Dans le silence, au milieu d'une paix nocturne fugitive, montait un roulement sourd, plus tragique encore que tout le reste, le roulement des trams, des camions, des trains s'en allant vers le front porter leurs charges d'hommes ou ramener des blessés et des morts tandis que Roubaix dormait. Les Allemands cachaient les mouvements de troupes à la population. On écoutait cela avec angoisse . . .[5]

(Maxence van der Meersch, *Invasion 14*)

There is a passage in the novel *Invasion 14* which describes the terrible winter of 1917/8, the fourth, the longest, and possibly the coldest of those bitter winters of the First World War. It is the fourth, too, of German occupation, in the industrial belt of the Northeast of France, up against the Belgian frontier: the triple textile towns of Lille, Roubaix and Tourcoing and their sprawling suburbs, spilling over into Belgium at some thirty frontier posts, the coal basin of Valenciennes and Anzin, the towns of Douai and Cambrai, Maubeuge and Béthune. All were within the almost constant sound of the guns on a largely immobile Front nowhere more than twenty miles away, a geography that, after four years, had become part of daily existence, and apparently frozen into permanence by the steady growth of a railway network backing the line of the Front, and creeping down from Lille to Valenciennes, from Valenciennes to Charleville-Mézières, and thence all the way down to Bâle, as well as inland to Brussels, Liège, Cologne, the Ruhr and the Rhineland. In German plans, railways and war had grown up together, like spoilt twins; and as the war dragged on, so they went on growing, new lines being constructed by gangs of forced labour – young men and girls from the industrial towns of the Nord, aged sixteen and over, picked up, street by street, in the course of night swoops carried out by the *Feldgendarmerie*, the feared and detested *diables verts*, recognizable from the tall green collars of their tunics, always accompanied by their huge Alsatians. Other gangs gathered in by similar swoops and housed in rickety huts in the rear areas of the Front, were engaged, for periods of six months or more, in laying out barbed-wire entanglements and field telephone wires, in digging deep gun emplacements and ammunition dumps. Others again, of both sexes, were carried off to bring in the harvest in the villages of the southern Ardennes. After the construction of each new line, the rolling stock, drawn from the many-doored *réseau du Nord*, from Belgian State Railways, or from the Kaiser's own favoured network, formed into trains made up of goods and passenger waggons, would ease their way gingerly over a track balanced precariously over shell holes, almost tipping into the troughs of a lunar landscape, and travelling only very slowly, very quietly, as if holding their breath, in the dead of night, relentlessly moving through the night hours, from midnight to four in the morning. Hardly even the wild shriek of a whistle, just a dull rumble in the frozen stillness of the arctic night.

In the quartier de l'Epeule, a slum area near the Roubaix station, whole families huddle together on the floors of their little brick houses, under whatever covers they have been able to retain or to collect: old overcoats, filthy blankets, torn and blood-marked *capotes* of faded blue, taken off dead French soldiers, scrounged off the Bavarian supply services, in semi-clandestine exchange operations, and now offering a minimal warmth to French civilians. Mattresses and bedding have gone long ago, most of it requisitioned systematically by the implacable *Feldgendarmerie*, in house-to-house searches, in the course of the first winter of the War. The beds themselves have been burnt up for firewood in November/December 1917, internal doors, bannisters, even stairs, cupboards, wardrobes, tables, chairs, kennels, pigeon-houses soon following, reducing whole families, or what is left of them, in the absence of most adult males between the ages of eighteen and forty-five, to a mainly horizontal existence, on the upper floor because it is of wood – the ground floors generally being stone – though, in some houses, even the upper floor has gone. By this time, February/March 1918, the tiny houses of the *corons* consist of little more than outer walls and roofs – the windows papered over on the inside with back copies of the *Gazette des Ardennes* and *Le Bruxellois*, even German propaganda enlisted in the desperate fight against the cold – mere shells of houses, the stair replaced by a ladder.

The family, minus its adult menfolk but enlarged by nephews and nieces, uncles and aunts and cousins brought in, some from the bombarded quarters of Lille, some from neighbouring villages, spends much of the day, as well as the long winter night, thus prone on the floor, getting up briefly only at sixish, when the stove is lit with newspaper covered in tar, and the single daily meal is cooked.

Thanks to the Americano-Hispanic Commission for Relief to Belgium, set up in 1916 under the aegis of the future President Hoover, and, since 1917, administered under the patronage of Alfonso XIII (as if Spain had at last returned to Flanders, in a strange reversal of historical narrative) basic foodstuffs were available to the occupied French as well as to their Belgian neighbours, though much of such relief was diverted into other channels, through black market operations carried out jointly by French and Belgian *smokeleers* and by accommodating and interested members of the Bavarian supply services and *Etappen*.

After the daily meal, lit by a candle and accompanied by watered-down beer or by acorn coffee, there was not much for the family to do but get down on the floor again and see it out, clinging together for the long hours of the night. By February/March 1918, with the freeze still holding fast and cracking doorsteps, the nights were strangely silent, even the *diables verts* staying indoors; and the silence seemed sinister as much to shivering civilians as to warmer soldiers. For if the guns were silent, something was afoot, or would soon be afoot, once the thaw came. Possibly, *occupant* and *occupé* might have differing views as to the desirability of a thaw that surely must come soon, for even *this* dreadful winter must at some stage give way to a pale spring. For the soldier, now warm in his quiet billet, it might suggest a rapid approach to death, at the end of a short and hesitant railway line. For the able-bodied civilian, it might at least offer the resumption of work and of a limited movement within the confines of the city.

As February gave way to March, the silence of the night was succeeded by a dull, steady, implacable rumble: the sound of trains, moving very slowly, only feet apart, with an increasing reverberation as each went under the road arch near the main station, and making a tuneful clatter as each crossed the metal bridge over the frozen canal. The lines from Courtrai and Audenarde, from Menin, to Lille, went right through the centre of the town, the railway gulleys marking the frontier between Roubaix and its twin, Tourcoing. By the eve of the fourth spring of occupation, even the children of the quartier de l'Epeule could interpret the dull music of the night, the low rumble of iron wheels, a *berceuse* that brought some reassurance to those who knew that they would probably stay put and whose existence had been reduced to the primary task of *waiting*. To stay put, even in a house that was no more than a shell, was to keep out of danger. Danger resided in movement, particularly by night train. Waking up fitfully to the continuous rumble, they would guess, from the experience of previous late winters (and by then the *Roubaisiens* had become very acute train-listeners) that an offensive – yet another offensive, and judging from the intensity of the rumble, lasting over several weeks, an offensive of unparalleled size and organization – would soon get under way.

Then, in due course, in late March and throughout April and much of May, the same rumble would be heard, but from a different quarter, and carried by a different wind, the reverberation from the road bridge, the clatter from the metal railway bridge, coming in reverse order, and so moving in an opposite direction, eastwards, towards Mouscron, Herseaux and Wattrelos, and the great lime pits in the quarries of the open plain. Other trains, or indeed the same trains, mostly long lines of cattle trucks, moved, equally gingerly, equally unhurriedly, equally stealthily, as if ashamed of their cargo, eastwards: bodies, stripped naked and tied together, like faggots, with strong industrial wire heads to feet, in fours, their uniforms and underclothes, socks, boots, helmets, paybooks, personal possessions, identity discs removed previously, and deposited in neat heaps further up the line. The offensive was now under way.

What went on in the minds of the inhabitants of l'Epeule, as, waking in the arctic night, in February/March, or in the warmer ones of April/May, they half-listened to the regular rumble, first in one direction, and then in the other, a rumble that was perhaps even reassuring because it suggested continuity and regularity, in the way that what has become a habit is always reassuring? The war had been going on for so long, it was hard here to imagine any other form of existence. *On s'installait dans la guerre*, and even the dreaded *diables verts* had become familiar figures, with names and nicknames; there were even *estaminet* songs about them, sung in the black market establishments near the station. For, whichever Germans moved, the *Feldgendarmerie* did *not* move – they too had become part of the urban landscape. Perhaps, as they listened to the trains, they may have reflected that, even in their Asian condition of having to recline, day and night, on the ground, to see the winter out, under the now totally familiar humiliation of *occupés*, they were still marginally better off than those who did the silent travelling, sitting up or standing up packed tight together, due west, southwest, or northeast, during the hours supposed to be reserved for sleep. At least they, the waiting ones – and by the spring of 1918, they would hardly know what they were waiting for, certainly not for the war to end, for that seemed totally improbable – could turn over in the warmth of an embrace inspired by necessity rather than by affection, in the knowledge that they would all be there in the grey, dull dawn. And they were certainly much better off than those who travelled, four by four, in wired-up industrial embrace in the opposite direction.

There was much to be said for such enforced immobility. A home was still a home, even if stripped down to the rudiments of a brick box. Each box was surrounded by boxes exactly similar, and the familiar pattern of the streets, marked by tramlines and uneven in huge rounded *pavé*, still offered the reassurance of a known world and of familiar dangers and vexations. The Germans, who had done so much to make themselves comfortable in the place – striking clocks and feather mattresses and eiderdowns, *buffets Henri II* – had at least not bothered to change the names of the streets and squares, for Roubaix did not carry the prestige of an old fortress town such as Lille. It might be a topography of deprivation, but at least it was recognizable. What is so terrible, almost unbearable, is the sheer contiguity of civilian and soldier – as the former crouches at home, the latter often a few yards' distance from the *coron*, cut off by the railway gulley, is edged, locked in, very slowly, even gently, to avoid noise, not to save him from jolts and sudden swerves, on the uneven track, towards the dreadful terminus, the end of the line. This, perhaps more than anything else, is what is so terrible, so inadmissible about a railway war, as the fodder of offensive and counteroffensive are shunted this way and that, eastwards and westwards, across vast night land-scapes, through sleeping cities, almost touching sleeping houses, their ends cut off to meet the dictates of the iron stra-tegic lines. They pass the occasional yellowish light of the night-watcher and the sick, the coloured signals of approaching stations, across the whole of the Second Reich, from Brest-Litovsk and Bucharest, to Lille and Saint-Quentin. It is the realization of a nightmare *Mitteleuropa* of rumbling wheels spelling out, at every join of the line, the German word for death: the music of the darker poems of the First World War and of the evocative and compassionate novels of Heinrich Böll in the Second. What is so terrible is the uncrossable divergence of fates, as between German soldier and French civilian.

In consolation, let us believe that, very occasionally, it had been possible to cross such a chasm. Roubaix was a big, sprawl-ing city, and even the *Feldgendarmerie* cannot have penetrated every labyrinthine *coron* of Wasquehal or the rue aux Longues Haies. It is not just a novelist's compassionate fancy that sug-gests that a few ingenious Germans at least managed to see out the war in this urban setting either as deserters or as well-established, well-protected *embusqués*, relatively safe in the fastnesses of the comfortably immobile *Etappen*, the military institution that came nearest to the civilians. By the spring of 1918, *occupants* and *occupés* had grown closer together, had, as we shall see, developed a peculiar sort of lingua franca of basic communication, a mixture of Bavarian or Saxon, and of *chtimi*, a wry shared humour on such well-worn themes as the endlessness of war, the powerlessness of individuals caught up in it, the imbecilities of official propaganda, the gulf between the front line soldier and the luxury-loving gentlemen of the *Etappen* and the *Feldkommandantur*, the loneliness provoked by nearly four years' absence of menfolk or womenfolk. By the beginning of 1918, soldiers and civilians were even beginning to look alike, as the uniforms of the former became increasingly tattered, stitched, stained and ill-fitting, as if to match the bizarre objects with which the inhabitants of Roubaix were now covering themselves: bits of camouflaged tenting filched from a ruined *filature*, rotting sacking taken from coal barges, *louis-philippard* topcoats reemerging, from many years in camphor, from once rural *garderobes*. The outer physical frontier had even been crossed, at least by the more ingenious or the better placed, once *Roubaisiens* who had regular dealings with the supply services or who were in touch with local farmers began to appear in very roughly dyed German military topcoats and perfectly recognizable top boots, while soldiers emerged muffled up in scarves and helmets in poor quality wool that, far from coming in family parcels from somewhere in the depths of the Reich, had been knitted by not indifferent hands in l'Epeule. Coming out of the endless winter of 1917/8, *all* looked as if they had been participating in a polar expedition. The Germans even began to walk like civilians: shuffling along wearily in the deep snow or brownish slush, bent against the bitter east wind off the Mont Cassel and the canal. And, like civilians, they had become collectively silent, while individually and in private more verbose: no more marching songs, indeed no more bands – perhaps even the trumpets, the bugles and the trombones had become frozen up, or had been melted down, perhaps the drums had burst. No more *Gloria, Victoria,* endlessly reiterated, as if in defiance of a dragged-out war. What was the point? There was no fooling the *Roubaisiens* and the *Lillois*, who, from day to day, had watched, with some compassion, the gradual transformation of the proud, arrogant, insolent, impeccable, shining soldiers of October 1914, into the cynical, fatalistic, resigned and listless *occupants* of 1918. In this respect, relations between civilian and military went in reverse order to what was to happen in the Second World War. The longer the Occupation lasted, the closer became French civilians and German military. Most of the atrocities and signal brutalities had been committed, in the full flood of early military successes, in August/September 1914. In 1944, the German forces proved themselves the most ferocious while in retreat from the Southwest of France, where, previously, they had had little contact with the local population.

Occupants and *occupés* were by now drawing closer together also as far as predominant age groups were concerned. Elderly soldiers do not generally make ferocious occupiers, being more concerned with their home comforts. Very young soldiers are likely to be objects of pity to female civilians of an age to be their mothers. In the Nord, there were few adult Frenchmen between eighteen and fifty or so still around in 1917; and, by then, many children of school age had been 'repatriated' to what was euphemistically described as 'France', thanks to the good offices of the Swiss and Spanish authorities, via the Ardennes and Bâle, only to find that, at the receiving end, their compatriots treated them with suspicion, calling them '*les boches du Nord*'. Now the age structure of Germans and *Roubaisiens* became interrelated. These were Germans who could not be hidden away in closed night trains: units of artillery, horse-drawn, moving west through the town, towards Croix and Lille, were seen to contain a high proportion of grey heads, of men walking with difficulty, not much better off than their scraggy horses, and of pale, stumbling youths, in trailing great-coats, their sleeves hiding their hands, aged fifteen, sixteen, and seventeen.

Of course, in many instances, the *inner* physical frontier had been crossed long before 1918, perhaps as early as the very first winter of the Occupation, when it had become apparent, both to the *Lillois* and the *Roubaisiens*, and to the Bavarian soldiers of the army of Prince Rupprecht, that the war would not be a short one, and that French and Bavarians were no doubt going to have to live together for a considerable time. A great many women of Roubaix and Lille had seen their husbands, brothers and sons go off to the French army between August and October 1914; this had been made possible thanks to the confused military situation in and around the two towns between the outbreak of hostilities and the second week of October 1914. German patrols had reached the Grand'Place of Lille in August, but had then withdrawn, after suffering some losses. The French garrison had then been reinforced, though it had long been decided that neither Roubaix nor Lille could be held for any length of time. A last stand had been made in October, enabling most of the garrison, as well as most *Lillois* and *Roubaisiens* of military age, to leave the two cities, either by train, for Dunkirk, or on foot. It was in this way that, in this part of the Nord at least, most of the *classes* liable to mobilization were able eventually to reach the French army, though some were killed during the bombardment of Lille, and rather more were massacred when one of the last trains out of Lille was attacked by German units. Once the German occupation really set in, after October 10th, most adult Frenchmen of military age had got away, an indication that there had been as much confusion on the part of the German high command as there had been, between August and October, on that of the French headquarters and the general in charge of the Lille garrison. Ever since

October, the women of the three towns, Lille, Roubaix and Tourcoing, had had to cope on their own. There was no means of their knowing whether their absent men had been killed in one of the great offensives of the early years of the war, though, if they had been taken prisoner, their names would have been published in the German-controlled newspaper, *Le Bruxellois*, a paper that was, for this reason, eagerly scanned in the occupied areas, the newsboys in Lille going round the streets, before the curfew, shouting: '*Le Bruxellois*, dernière liste des prisonniers de guerre du Nord.' This would be the *only* form of private news of concern to families divided for the previous two or three years that was likely to get across the great divide provided by a more or less stable, and apparently permanent Front, a breakdown in communications that, as it may be recalled, provided the ingenious murderer Landru with a dozen or so convenient victims from among the female refugees from the *Départements Occupés*. For four years, the existence of the Front impeded the normal course of French justice in cases that took the form of *recherches dans l'intérêt des familles*, an exceptional wartime situation that would offer particular advantage to the bigamist and to the adventurer.

When such places as Nesle or Roye were liberated by the French or Allied armies, great piles of mail were discovered addressed by women of the occupied departments to their absent husbands or sons, who, in many cases, having been killed in the meantime, would never have received them. This was perhaps often just as well, as many of these letters brought news of the birth of a child eighteen months or two years after the departure of the husband, or referred to the kindness of a Bavarian or Saxon soldier who had helped out the family from his own meagre ration or who had lent a hand on the farm or even in the absent man's trade. Even the rather unimaginative Poincaré, on one of his tours of the liberated areas, declared himself to have been moved by the evidence of so much human misery and fragility. The *corons* were not all *that* impenetrable, however distant and infinitely desirable they must have seemed to the poor soldier sealed off in his train in 1918. There were no barracks in Roubaix – though there were plenty in Lille – and soldiers, as well as officers, had from the start been billeted *chez l'habitant*, the officers in Boulevard de Cambrai and Parc Barbieux, the other ranks in rue aux Longues Haies, Wasquehal, quartier de l'Epeule, as well as in the inns, *estaminets* and farms of the surrounding plain. Some agricultural technicians spent the whole war as advisors, directing the exploitation often of hundreds of hectares of good land. This could have advantages as well as disadvantages to both parties, though this is an area of Franco-German history which, for obvious reasons, largely eludes the historian, even if it may force its way into a discreet *état civil*, listing the children born between 1915 and the spring of 1919 under the title *'né de père inconnu'*. Unknown officially, no doubt, but at once identifiable by neighbours, both in urban and rural settings, equally closely and uncharitably observed. The *filles à boches* were above all the object of jealousy on the part of neighbouring wives who had been without news of their husbands often since October 1914, and because they obtained many material advantages and privileges as a result of their connection with a member of the occupying forces. To have both a man *and* better rations and more freedom of movement was not unnaturally gall and brimstone to women not similarly privileged. A majority of the anonymous letters, addressed daily – an average of twenty a day – to the *Kommandantur* brought to the attention of the German military command the existence of such *ménages*. It should be added that liaisons of this kind do not seem to have much concerned the *Kommandantur*, as long as no possibility of a breach of security could arise. In this respect, the Germans were a good deal more liberal in their attitude to the civilian population than they were to be in the course of the second occupation. As we shall see, even the official army newspaper, the *Liller Kriegszeitung*, in its conversation pieces, took it for granted that German soldiers were likely to engage in conversation *Lilloises* at least of the working class. Apart then from the vigilant jealousy of female neighbours, there were no insuperable obstacles to prevent the crossing of sexual national barriers. German soldiers do not appear to have illustrated prejudices of racial superiority, and, after more than three years of occupation and consequent daily coexistence, the working-class elements at least of Roubaix had become much less chauvinistic than at the giddy outbreak of the war. Proud gestures of anti-German disdain were mainly reserved to the *notables*. I do not suggest that such *ménages* were especially common, but that, with each year of occupation, they were becoming both commoner and more readily tolerated.

With so few adult Frenchmen around there could often be little doubt as to the nationality of the father. Each such birth at least represented a small, pathetic victory for life, in a dark universe of all-enveloping death; and, as such, it must command a tiny spark of joy on the part both of the novelist and of the historian, who can only rejoice at the spectacle of the unnatural priorities of military life and war being thus met with temporary defeat just at that very linkage which always constitutes the most vulnerable area in the institutional Moloch of a war machine. War is an unnatural state from which any soldier will endeavour to escape, given the slightest opportunity. Military commanders and men of war generally would no doubt prefer campaigns always to be confined to the emptiness of steppe or desert, so as to remove altogether the civilian element. But, in the First World War, the areas to the rear of the Front were heavily populated industrial conurbations from which it would have been impossible to remove the whole of the civilian population. This was quite out of the question, as much on practical as on humanitarian grounds. The Germans needed all the able-bodied civilian labour, both male and female, that they could lay hands on, in order to keep at least some of the mills open and for semimilitary work behind the lines; and Germany itself was suffering from such acute food shortages by the spring of 1918 that any sort of massive deportation would have strained resources unbearably. So the risk of such individual contacts between soldiers and local women had to be run, a minor victory for human nature that, because it represents at least a temporary escape from the awful masculine collectivity of military life, has nearly always provided tempting material for the novelist, especially one who has himself been a combatant. One recalls the war novels of Jules Roy, *Le Navigateur* and *Vésuve*, both on this theme of temporary escape through love. There could be no more insidious enemy of Ludendorff and Hindenburg than the well-scrubbed kitchens of the Roubaix *corons*, the table covered with a red and white chequer-board cloth. And, on the Allied side, too, writers such as Blunden or Lucien Descaves will pause in wonder at the spectacle of the main room in a French farmhouse, still intact, its family photographs, its calendar, its palm leaves, its crucifix and its cluttered *buffet Henri III* proclaiming the survival of a civilian world still undisturbed by the noise and horror of a few miles' distance. All recall, even into their eighties, the fresh looks, the winning smile, the powerful but graceful legs, the pale blue eyes covered with long dark eyelashes of some Picarde girl, *fille de ferme* or merely *serveuse d'estaminet*, moving about with natural grace and engaged in the daily chores of washing or housework: a quiet sylvan glade, a place to rest, in a nightmare landscape of churned-up mud and stumps of trees. In most cases, merely a fleeting memory of visual happiness, a very brief shaft of beauty, conserved in human memory, over all these years, like a pressed flower. But this, of course, was the experience of front line troops only briefly taken out of the line. It was quite a different matter as far as the supply services and the soldiers stationed in such bases as Lille, Roubaix, Tourcoing, Douai and Valenciennes were concerned. They were the lucky and envied ones in the unequal lottery of military society and war. Even Hitler, a signals runner, it may be supposed, must have enjoyed a few such moments of human respite. It has even been suggested that one such moment may have had human consequences.

Just what became of these infants is again beyond the records of public history, though, judging from what happened in the same area during the second occupation, a great many of the poor mites must have eventually been placed in the Bon Pasteur of Lille, confined to the none too tender care of the nuns, or in similarly sparse and grim charitable institutions. A few may later have been adopted, but most would have grown up in those grim institutional surroundings provided by a relentless French state, before being placed as apprentices, farm labourers or domestic servants. One would like to think, too, that a number had been kept by their mothers, and that – is it too much to hope? – in a few instances, after a decent interval and once national tempers had been cooled, the *father* may have turned up again, out of the depth of Germany. This again is an area of social history that has only recently been investigated, in the context of the Second World War.

Such intimacies, not yet described derisively, as in the Second World War, as *collaboration horizontale*, could take place between Frenchwomen of all classes and German officers and other ranks. But it is likely to have been much commoner among working-class and peasant women and German soldiers and NCOs than among the rather pious, priest-ridden wives of the *lainiers*, and German officers, much more cut off from the civilian population both by the pride of rank and by the existence of comfortable messes (*Kursäle*) which would be likely to provide, as well as an excellent cellar and a high-class *cuisine*, the services of semiprofessional *demi-mondaines*. The professionals, described in this part of France as *montantes*, need not detain us. Every now and then, they were rounded up by the German medical authorities and sent off to the hospital in Tourcoing known as *les Princesses*, a nickname that was soon given to its present or its former inmates. In Douai, the German authorities even went one better, collecting some two hundred *filles de joie*, and 'repatriating' them to France, via Switzerland. What sort of reception they received in Lyon we are not told.

Let us then give a thought to the Roubaix working girl: *fileuse*, *cardeuse*, servant in an *estaminet*, or to the peasant girl from Leers or Hem, who, for one reason or another, in March 1918 is sleeping with a member of the German forces, preferably one in the supply, medical or *Kommandantur* services, because they are likely to stay put, or so it would seem from the experience of the previous three years. Here she is then, either merely a *fille à estaminet*, with nothing much to lose, certainly not a reputation, or the mother of a family, or a single girl, waking up in the night beside her sleeping Bavarian, Prussian, Saxon, Swabian, Rhinelander, even Berliner, demilitarized in his nudity – or in the woollen pyjamas or nightshirt of the absent husband – his leather belt (with *Gott Mit Uns* clasp), uniform and side arms laid out on a chair (for there still would be a chair in a house enjoying such valuable protection) and perceiving, half-awake, the continuous rumble. She has noticed that, in recent weeks, her German has become moody, reticent, has lost his appetite and has been plunged into long periods of silence. The relationship, in any case so tenuous, so constantly threatened from outside, can be snapped in a moment, perhaps at the bidding of a paper brought by the dreaded *Feldgendarmerie*, enemies of civilian and soldier alike (who, the lucky ones, never move, till, in October 1918, they can be seen quietly and unhurriedly cycling away eastwards, accompanied still by their huge dogs). The German has been good to her children, has shown her photographs of his own, or she is pregnant by him, her child due in the summer or autumn of 1918 (in the latter case, it could not have been worse timed, as events were to turn out). The man is able to sleep heavily, having stoked up, the night before, on *Goldwasser*, the name given by the *occupants* to the rough and dangerous *genièvre* of the Nord and the Pas-de-Calais. There are frontiers within frontiers. Next door to a black marketeer or to a whole family of mill workers, their children absent from school because of the cold, there is a well-furnished house, carpeted, full of shining brass pots, giving every appearance of a permanent and comfortable home, even of that heavy, but peaceable, *confort belge*, a German calendar – brought back from leave, a romanticized Prince Rupprecht or a pencilled All-Highest under storm clouds, the proud eagle – replacing the unobtainable *calendrier des PTT*, but quite as threatening as to what lies ahead, *März* being as baneful as *mars*. As likely as not, the sleeping man will not see out the end of the month.

I have concentrated so far exclusively on *private* history and on a *private* vision of war and occupation, as illustrated in a novel of no great literary merit and frequently interrupted by gushes of *démochrétien* moralizing and grace. I have squeezed the novel dry, have indeed gone far beyond it, on my own even less permissible flights of fancy in pursuit, above all, of an elusive but reassuring dialogue, a flickering but tender *vie à deux*.

There is a single sentence in van der Meersch on the subject of the rumble of the trains in the spring of 1918. On this I have built a whole edifice of supposition and fancy, pushing further and further into the intimacy of the sleeping *coron*, of the closed room, and emphasizing what, so it seems to me, should always be emphasized when describing that most horrific of all states: *war* – the cruel contrast between those who sleep in their beds in the still night, even those who sleep on the floor, but at least in the shared warmth of their own people, and those, poor souls, who travel, already mentally disembodied, and awaiting mutilation or death, just ahead of them, in slow-moving trains through the night, indeed a *voyage au bout de la nuit* more terrible than anything the cruel Céline could think up.

Perhaps I have romanticized some Franco-German *ménages*; but such personal evidence as I acquired, in the same place, after another war, would suggest that such *ménages* could, briefly, be exceedingly happy, and that, on rare occasions, they could have subsequently acquired a permanent status. One has only to recall that the German military governor of Belgium and northern France, von Falkenhausen, returned to Brussels, in 1952, in order to marry his Belgian mistress, a lady of considerable volume who spoke with the succulent *accent bruxellois*.

In my account there is no record of a patriotic French girl stabbing to death a monocled German officer with a hairpin or a kitchen knife; nor have I encountered the Roubaix equivalent of '*Boule de suif*' or '*Mademoiselle Fifi*'. The worst the Roubaix prostitutes ever did to the German soldiers was to give them the pox. I would not dispute the accuracy of Maupassant's tales of war in his native Upper Normandy in 1870/1. He was there, after all, and may have seen and heard some such things. Some German soldiers, it is true, *were* murdered in Roubaix during the first occupation. But they were not murdered by women; they were killed in drunken *estaminet* brawls, either by fellow soldiers, or by the local *mauvais garçons*.

There did exist, it is true, both in Lille and in Roubaix, patriotic girls who smuggled out news to the Allies, or who managed to cross the electrically wired frontier between Belgium and Holland, at Axel. And there were many acts of heroism carried out by civilians: wine merchants, schoolteachers, mill owners, priests, several of whom were shot in the citadel of Lille.

My main reason for concentrating so heavily on what might be described as the private chronicle of war and occupation is that, in most histories, especially military and official, it is omitted entirely or earns only a passing reference. It is also a matter of choice, because, if war can be domesticated, if the soldier can be accommodated into the welcoming kitchen, his feet firmly planted under the table, his nostrils taking in the northern aroma of coffee cum chicory as it boils on the stove, then the triumph of civilian priorities and virtues over military ones has been asserted. War, like revolution, is not a natural state, and so, mercifully, it can never be permanent, though, in 1918 or in 1943 it must often have seemed likely to be so. At least it can be tempered, if not killed, by kindness and intimacy. Both in October 1918 and in September 1944, British soldiers very rapidly acquired at least a mental demobilization by gaining their welcomed entries to the Roubaix *corons*. And they were certainly welcomed much more warmly than their predecessors had been, the working-class population of the Nord being traditionally anglophil, and the Germans having been especially brutal in 1915 and in 1944.

But there did exist another dimension of Franco-German relations, and one that is even revealed, rather surprisingly, in the official *Liller Kriegszeitung*, a newspaper published by two officers of the Lille high command, Hauptmann D. L. Hoecker, and Rittmeister Freiherr von Ompteda, in 1915, 1916, and 1917.

The paper is conventionally anti-French in certain respects. There is, for instance, an article entitled *'Die Apachen in der franzoesischen Armee'* which is the work of a certain Marie Luise Becker, no doubt *orfèvre en la matière* and a specialist on *apache* matters, and from which we learn that the French army had been recruited heavily from the gutters of Toulon and Marseille, from the *Jules* of the two ports, as well as from la Villette and the other *'Pariser Vororten'*. These slouching bad lads in their velvet trousers and long-peaked caps, their ratlike faces *à gueules de raie* (to use Robert Lageat's splendid phrase) had been gathered in by police with revolvers, on the orders, odd though it may seem, of Aristide Briand. And, of course, they were assigned to such special operations as rape and plunder, or for use as *francs-tireurs*, an old favourite dating from the Franco-Prussian War. If the *Lillois* had read the paper that bore the name of their city, they would no doubt have recognized some of their own antimeridional prejudices in this description of the *souteneurs* of Marseille and Toulon. And, of course, there are numerous references to the Senegalese and to their savagery.

The paper cannot refrain from a good laugh on the subject of some of the names that patriotic French parents have been giving their newborn children: France, Joffrette, Marne, Marnette, Marnon, Fochette, all of which were in fact regular favourites. Why not these then, the paper goes on to suggest: Nikolausine, Poincarline, Nowo-Georgette, Brest-Litowska, Armentière (really rather a good suggestion), Perenchisse, and Dardanelly?

Under the heading *'Das deutsche Fräulein in Lille'* we have a piece very revealing of Wilhelmian class distinctions and containing a by no means inaccurate description of the meanness and selfishness of a family of the *haute bourgeoisie lilloise*, the head of which, a mill owner, Monsieur R., had fled in panic at the time of the bombardment, at the beginning of October 1914, not stopping till he had reached Bordeaux, with Madame R.

and their three children, aged nine, twelve and thirteen, leaving the servants behind in the house in la Madeleine in which the author of the piece, a German officer, was subsequently billeted. The young German girl of the headline had been taken on as a German teacher; but she had also been employed, so we gather from the officer's indignant account, as nanny, seamstress, typist, secretary, tennis instructor, washerwoman, cook, translator, runner of errands, and so on, all for forty francs a month (whereas Lille cooks received from sixty to seventy francs, housemaids fifty). She had lunch with Madame R. but the evening meal with the servants, and slept in a tiny attic, inspected by the officer. He also questioned the housemaid. 'Oh, elles sont très habilles, ces allemandes freulaïns,' she is quoted rather Germanically, as saying. The ill-treated girl, he adds, had a father who was 'Seminardirektor in Sued-Deutschland', her brother was an officer, another brother was a 'Chemielehrer an einer Hochschule', and the ill-used girl had herself obtained her 'Lehrerinnen-Examen'. And with all this, to have been treated worse than a housemaid! The officer's indignation seems perfectly genuine. The behaviour of the family too seems quite in character.

But the paper does not display a similar hostility to the population in general of Lille. Nor does it advocate nonfraternization, providing, on the contrary, often quite hilarious sketches of Bavarian and Saxon soldiers attempting to make themselves understood in French and to carry on conversations with *Lilloises*: 'Madame, du lait!' – 'Ah, nix du lait, messieurs, nix lait, nix beurre, nix fromage, nix oeufs, *rien, rien, rien!*' The same theme is maintained in a short guide to French under the heading: *'Essen, Trinken, Pferdefutter'*, listing the key words phonetically: 'Duelae, duepaen, manscheh, charkuterie, pommdeterr, asiett, aen kutoh, furschett, der sarg, tihrbuscho [one can indeed wonder if this rendering would have ever got a bottle open], estamineh, ohdevih', then, in one word, 'aenverrdoe-likehr', before coming onto the equine needs for 'doelawoan'. One can almost hear poor Sepp, the Bavarian soldier, with his squiggly pipe, struggling with the unfamiliar vowels and consonants: 'Manscheh.'

The subject of war can be tricky; and the paper contains a warning under the dramatic heading: *'Spion'*. Watch out, it says, for anyone who uses the telltale phrase: *la guerre, un grand malheur, pour nous, pour vous, pour tout le monde*, and then report it. Anyone who speaks in this way is either an Allied agent or a defeatist.

The paper provides for another traditional soldiers' need, a need that no doubt becomes more insistent on the eve of an offensive, by obligingly reprinting from the *Bulletin de Lille*, the official gazette put out on Tuesdays, Thursdays and Sundays by the *Kommandantur*, the list of Lille female fortune-tellers (*die Wahrsagerinnen von Lille*): '. . . Madame de Bergerac sagt nur die Wahrheit, empfaengt rue . . . Freitags, Samstags, Sonntags und Montags.' Other recommended ladies include Madame Airam (*célèbre voyante*), Madame Léa, de Paris (*liseuse de pensées*), Madame Henriette (*la grande cartomancienne*), and Madame Marie-Jeanne (*cartomancienne diplômée, 9 à 12, 2 à 6*). Were it not for the fact that the list is published in a paper of such vouched-for respectability and under the aegis of two Prussian officers, one of them monocled (the paper has a drawing of the two of them, bent over their sheet apparently in an editorial briefing), one might have suspected that ladies with names so evocative had more than one string to their bow, and that, far from just providing for the soldiers' needs about the future, both immediate and more distant, they also had more to offer in terms of immediate personal comforts. Madame Valérie, Madame Marie-Jeanne, above all Madame Léa have been encountered before, in garrison towns, in houses down discreet streets, sitting at their cashboxes, dressed in dark red silk. One way or another, these ladies cannot have done badly out of the German occupation of Lille. The war ended, the city liberated by the British, trade must, on the contrary, have fallen off, Tommy being less concerned with his immediate future when it really was '*après la guerre finie*'.

Much of the rest of the *Liller Kriegszeitung* for the years 1915 to 1918 is taken up with more edifying patriotic literature: poems about the homeland, notices about the heroic deeds of the fallen, set pieces to mark the birthdays of the All-Highest, the King of Saxony, the King of Bavaria, Prince Rupprecht and the *Kronprinz*, poems about the U-boats, sentimental pieces about Christmas in the homeland. But both the contents and the concerns of the paper do indicate at least a permitted level of contacts with the civilian population, as well as guided tours of the Lille museums and art galleries (there is a drawing of a group of soldiers being shown a piece of statuary by a teacher at the Ecole des Beaux Arts, under the heading '*Die Barbaren*', a reference to the rather more inept forms of Allied propaganda), and one or two rather ponderous excursions into the history of French Flanders, indicating the many links with a Germanic past and the common stems of German and Flemish, though the Flemish theme only rarely appears; clearly it was not a priority with the two officer editors. Jeanne Hachette gets a mention; so, more predictably, does Joan of Arc. There are jokes about the toughness of the steaks served at the Hôtel Métropole. If the conversation pieces are mainly confined to the promising subject of food, drink and tobacco there is a poem entitled 'Maedchen von Lille' that is not uncomplimentary to the subject to which it is addressed.

And we are shown photographs of civilians, the men bowler-hatted or in caps and mufflers, the women hatted and mostly in black, listening in rapt attention to German military bands playing on the Grand'Place, and of little boys and girls running to keep up with detachments of infantry and artillery as they march through the town. The trams, carrying their advertisements (*Bières Lilloises*), appear to be working as usual, but there is a row of ruined houses in the neighbourhood of the Bourse and the Comédie. The Gare Centrale, with its facade from the original Paris Gare du Nord, is intact; but it carries only military traffic, and there has been no train to Paris for over three years. It is the ghost of a station, an elaborate facade, carrying the coats of arms of Paris and of the cities of the northeast: Amiens, Arras, Abbeville, Valenciennes, Douai, Cambrai, Bapaume, Béthune, Albert, Lens, Laon, Saint-Quentin, Roye, Noyon, Beauvais, Nesle, heraldic reminders of an ancient and lost topography, now cut through by the curling chasm of the Front. One is reminded of the game played by Edward Spears and the other young staff officers of the British liaison to the French high command when they were in Arras, or what was left of it: '. . . Then we would go to the station, where only the ticket office remained standing, and stamp ourselves tickets to Lille, Cambrai and other places on the German side of the line' – in fact, playing at peace. Perhaps young German officers in the Lille garrison amused themselves in a similar manner, stamping themselves tickets to the elusive Paris (which should have been reached by the third week of August 1914) or to Bailleul, Haig's headquarters. Inside Lille station, there were still posters of the Chemins de Fer de l'Ouest, inviting the *Lillois* to enjoy the sun and sand of Houlgate, Cabourg, Dinard, Deauville-Trouville, Paramé, Saint-Malo, and les Sables-d'Olonne.

The public record is much more familiar and need detain us only briefly. In the course of four years, some twenty French departments, or parts of them, came under temporary or permanent German occupation, bringing under German military rule from two and a half to three million civilians, at least in the autumn of 1914. For, thanks to fairly steady 'repatriation', organized through Switzerland by the Red Cross, the numbers were being reduced as the war dragged on, the German authorities being concerned to get off their hands as many unproductive civilians as possible: children under sixteen, men and women over sixty. (In Douai, they managed to return to France the prison population, the vagrants, and, as we have seen, most of the local prostitutes.)

The Germans brought with them no overall plan for the administration and exploitation of the area that fell under their control, improvising often contradictory policies as month followed month. Had their military plans been successful in August 1914, much of the Northeast of France would no doubt have been detached from the French Republic, to form some sort of buffer state, perhaps with Belgium and Luxembourg. But, with the settling down of the Front, they found themselves in control of a truncated area of industrial and agricultural territory of no natural unity. The whole was placed under the high command in Brussels. But von Bissing, the governor of Belgium, himself did not follow any consistent policy and does not seem to have had any long-term aims. Even his Flemish policies were vague and inconsistent.

In the Nord and the Pas-de-Calais, policies seem to have been directed towards the immediate satisfaction of short-term needs: vast indemnities, the removal of crops and fodder, the requisitioning of metal goods, bedding, linen, even of factory equipment – in short, a war economy of pillage, practised, at first, at every level. As in 1870, the German soldier might be seen returning eastwards loaded with striking clocks and eiderdowns, driving cattle and sheep ahead of him. Horses, bicycles, telephones, wirelesses and carrier pigeons (the pride and joy of the Roubaix mill workers) were requisitioned during the first weeks of the Occupation.

In the Nord, the greatest brutalities were committed very early on, immediately after Lille had been captured in October 1914, the Germans, not without reason, accusing the civilian authorities of having attempted to organize military resistance even after the French garrison (a colonial regiment) had been withdrawn and Lille had been declared an open city (its fortifications had been finally destroyed in 1910). The prefect, Trépont, and the secretary-general, Borromée, narrowly escaped lynching at the hands of infuriated German soldiers, in the same month; and they were both deported in 1915, returning at the end of the year, following insistent *démarches* on their behalf by Alfonso XIII.

From the beginning, the population was subjected to a number of vexations, some of which seem to have been dictated uniquely by the desire to humiliate, but all of which were aimed at reducing the movement of civilians to a minimum: the imposition of a strict curfew, the requirement of a *passe* even for a journey from one quarter to another, the prohibition of any journey beyond the municipal limits. Even funeral convoys had to be accompanied by armed escorts. Most public buildings and the most comfortable private dwellings were requisitioned for billets, though one-third of the Lille schools were reopened at the end of 1914. Civilians had to salute members of the German forces; and certain areas of pavement were forbidden to them, shut off by white barriers. Rationing was introduced at once, followed immediately by the development of a profitable black market jointly administered by the *Etappen* and by French or Belgian intermediaries. German civilian technicians, in uniform, were placed in the railways and in all the technical services; and even farms had to take mobilized German *agronomes*. Every French farrier or blacksmith found himself with a German working alongside him. Such cooperation was not necessarily unfriendly.

When the war was going well, the Germans treated the *Lillois* and the *Roubaisiens* better, no doubt on the assumption that they would eventually be included either in the Reich or in a satellite state. And so when the war went badly, requisitions, deportations and humiliations would be showered down. The worst year for the levies of forced labour was 1915; but in 1917, faced with the threat of a strike in the Anzin coalfield, the military authorities sent the *Feldgendarmerie* into the *corons*, and the miners returned to work. There was one important difference between the first occupation and the second. In the first, there were no labour deportations to Germany, the levies of forced labour being used either on agricultural work or in areas behind the Front. The first occupation was more onerous, vexatious and humiliating than the second, though there were many fewer executions. There was also much less resistance; indeed, in this war zone, there was little possibility of any resistance, though a priest set up a clandestine transmitter in Lille, and some Allied agents from Roubaix managed to reach Holland. There were one or two cyclostyled newssheets, but their circulation was minimal. On the other hand, the population as a whole was more patriotic than in the second occupation, lining up behind the *notables*, who led official objections to German demands.

The period of German rule had some interesting and even lasting consequences, at least in the Nord and the Pas-de-Calais. As the French government was an enemy one, the Germans would not recognize any authority emanating from Paris, thus eliminating not just the prefects, subprefects and *secrétaires-généraux*, but also minor officials like tax inspectors, managers of local branches of the Banque de France, officials of the Eaux et Forêts, and railway inspectors. On the other hand, educational personnel, though state employees, were maintained; and once the schools reopened, the teachers continued to use the same textbooks, which, in history, were decidedly anti-German. In

Lille English was being taught again as early as Christmas 1914. The Germans do not seem to have had any consistent cultural policies and they hardly interfered with educational processes. They had other, more immediate priorities and no doubt thought that the French were unlikely to be won over in any case.

What this meant in practice was that such prefects and subprefects as were not deported – and most were, at one time or another – were left completely powerless, as well as homeless, the prefectures and subprefectures being taken over by the military administration. In short, the only authority recognized by the *occupants* was the municipal one. And municipalities, generally under the *maires* who had been elected in the 1914 elections, remained the sole channel of communication between the military and the population though the Germans also worked through the chambers of commerce and approached individual mill owners. These too would be motivated by purely municipal loyalties. In so far as some semblance of normal life was maintained during these years, it was due entirely to the efforts of urban and rural *maires* and *conseillers municipaux*, though they also occupied a seat of danger, for they were generally sought out for deportation in the event of their commune being in arrears for one of the huge forced loans imposed, at regular intervals, by the rapacious military authorities. (The municipalities even had to pay for enjoying the privilege of the German presence, all the costs of occupation having to be met by them.) As the Banque de France was unable to function and as its notes did not circulate in the Occupied Zone, each municipality had to organize its own finances. (The municipal authorities of Douai, significantly, looked to the neighbouring kingdom to meet the burden of the German forced loans by running up gigantic borrowings from the *Société Générale de Belgique*, an initiative no doubt adopted by other municipalities and that once more underlines the similarity of the experiences of the two neighbouring countries.) Each municipality had to print its own money (metal, tin or cardboard tokens, *bons municipaux*) fixed to the exchange rate of the mark imposed by the *occupants*, in order to meet the German levies, municipal costs, and the running of essential services. The German indemnities had to be paid in gold, mostly from private accounts, another instance of the *notables* taking the full weight of the burden of occupation. Rural *communes* came into the area of circulation of the *bons de trésor* of the nearest town. By 1918, the cities of the occupied areas had run up debts of billions of francs, many of them on the Brussels market.

This municipalization of civilian authority was an arrangement that well suited the Germans, anxious to fragment French administration as far as possible and to avoid its acquiring even a regional polarization. (Though French and Belgian *communes* came under the ultimate authority of the governor of Belgium in Brussels, the Germans were careful to differentiate between French *maires* and Belgian *bourgmestres*, even though, at one time, they had abolished the customs barrier between the two countries.) But it also suited the ingrained habits and traditions of French Flanders, Artois and Picardy (as well as of Belgium, where each *bourgmestre* reigned like a monarch from the *maison communale*) – all regions in which 'municipalism' and 'communalism' had been firmly rooted in history, and in which municipal loyalties had remained stronger than in any other part of France. The *Lillois* were the first to remind anyone interested that they had defended their city from enemy attack in 1793, repulsing the invader with their own national guard, an episode of municipal prowess that, oddly, the authors of the *Liller Kriegszeitung* thought worthwhile recalling to its soldier readers, though the adversaries then had been the dukes of Brunswick and York. Perhaps, in their view, the one eliminated the other. At the best of times, it would have been difficult to get Lille to cooperate with Roubaix, or Roubaix with its twin, Tourcoing, or Douai with Valenciennes.

Now each town became a sort of sovereign state, subject only to German control and demands. Much the same applied to village *maires*, who, entrusted with the task of designating the quota set aside for forced labour service, found themselves with unprecedented powers, which they often abused, though if things went wrong – for instance in the event of an assault on a member of the German armed forces – they would be the first to be sought out as hostages.

The experience of four years' complete municipal autonomy and of total separation from the rest of France and from the national experience of other Frenchmen and Frenchwomen had a double effect. It greatly increased the sense of a municipal collective identity, firmly embedded in the memory of the sufferings of each such urban community during the hard years of occupation, and the sense of a regional apartness, making the inhabitants of the Nord feel separate from the more fortunate national unit that had not only managed to live without them, but in fact given them little enough thought. Poincaré, an easterner, who had the experience of knowing that his parents' house – or what was left of it – had come under enemy occupation, was an exception. It was only the deputies and the senators of the Nord who had managed to reach Paris who were concerned to point out to the government the difficulties under which their constituents were living, and to put pressure on the national authorities to intervene with Alfonso XIII on behalf of those *notables* who had been deported to Germany, a lengthy and roundabout process that brought results only after months of delay. (It says something, however, for the conditions under which the First World War was conducted, that such diplomatic *démarches* would eventually meet with a measure of success.) But of such interventions, the inhabitants of the Nord, cut off from most French or Allied sources of information, would generally have remained unaware. It was hardly surprising that, left to their monthly and daily *tête à tête* with the Germans, the *chtimis* should often have felt that the only persons who appeared to take a direct interest – and that hardly a benevolent one in their plight – were the members of the *Kommandantur* of the various towns and of the German high command in Brussels. This sense of apartness was felt even more acutely by those fortunate people who managed to reach France, through Switzerland, under a repatriation agreement, only to discover that, on arrival in the redistribution centre at the Parc de la Tête d'Or in Lyon, they were considered almost as foreigners, as *les boches du Nord*, as if they had somehow been contaminated by their contacts with the *occupants:* a sense of bitterness and alienation well expressed in a recent article in the *Revue du Nord* on Douai between 1914 and 1918: 'L'union sacrée se forgeait face au Midi bavard et exploiteur d'un Nord travailleur et silencieux.' This feeling would be further aroused by the awareness that most French people were indifferent to their sufferings, and that life in Paris was not only normal but a good deal more carefree than usual. Those from the Nord who managed to visit Paris during the war years came away with a sense almost of moral outrage. They had tried to convey to the Parisians what life had been like in the dark, beleaguered, frozen towns on the Belgian frontier, during the terrible winters of the Occupation. Oh yes, replied the Parisians, they too had suffered, they too had been bombed, Paris had been in the front line, but it had *held*. Some *Lillois* came away with the impression that the Parisians actually believed that they were in the process of winning the war.

And who, in the spring of 1918, in Lille or Roubaix, would have believed that those derisory posters hanging torn in the Gare de Lille were still active holiday resorts for Parisians and for the inhabitants of other areas of France, that people actually *went* on holiday, and that young officers on leave could put on tennis clothes and play mixed doubles on the fashionable courts of Deauville? It was perhaps as well that such things could not even be imagined, and that, in the Siberian wastes of the wool towns of the Northeast, Provence and the seaside towns of the Côte would have become mere place-names, as unreal and as exotic as Sorrento or Seville.

For four years, the *Roubaisiens* and the *Lillois* had been forced to turn in on themselves, mentally and even physically, being seldom allowed even to go beyond their city limits. If they had managed to survive, it was thanks to their own ingenuity and cunning, to their own initiatives, and to the help coming from the Americano-Spanish Committee for the Relief of Belgium. For, when help came, it had come in this form, from Holland and from Brussels. And when liberation came, it came from the British Army. In the circumstances, it was not surprising that an experience so different from that undergone by the rest of the population should have reinforced regional prejudices and suspicions both of Paris and of the South that had already acquired deep historical roots. We can witness here the beginnings of what might be described as *le problème du Nord*, a problem that became even more acute as a result of the second occupation, and under rather similar administrative conditions (with rule once more from Brussels) during 1940–44.

If the inhabitants of such places as Lille and Roubaix, Valenciennes and Douai, regarded themselves as particular victims of the war, they had not in fact been as unfortunate as those of towns such as Arras, Bapaume, Albert, Saint-Quentin, or Noyon, which had been largely destroyed, and which had changed hands more than once. These were the real *villes martyres*. And if the Germans had been relatively decent in places well behind their lines, they reserved all their savagery and ingenious beastliness for towns and territories that they had been forced to abandon. Poincaré and Spears describe the scene of desolation left by the Germans in retreat: every tree sawn down by the roadside, fruit trees systematically destroyed, houses blown up, women's underwear, defiled with excrement, hanging invitingly in trees (a *carte de visite* often left behind in Norman villages too, in the summer of 1944, every lavatory chain wired to a mine or to some ingenious explosive device). In September 1918, in a massive operation carried out in conditions of chaos, the German command had forcibly evacuated most of the population of Douai to Mons and to Brussels. The town was then thoroughly pillaged by the fleeing German troops and by the remaining inhabitants.

From Lille and Roubaix, on the other hand, the Germans retreated, often in revolutionary disorder and completely drunk but without further damage to the locals. Some regiments, indeed, could be seen moving off, in October 1918, in perfect order, the men in fours, bands playing, officers and NCOs to the front and on their flanks. It was only in Brussels that something like a revolutionary situation developed, with soldiers trundling up cannon to shell the hotels in which the staff were located, place de Brouckère.

The *chtimis* could then look back at the ordeal that they had been through with a considerable measure of pride. Their main concern throughout had been to retain their nationality, their main fear that, in the event of a German victory, they would be annexed. Once again, they had proved themselves to have been the most patriotic of Frenchmen and Frenchwomen. A few of them were even, rather grudgingly, decorated. But the Nord obtained its reward in another, more concrete shape, in the form of enormous war indemnities, eventually payable by the Germans, while, in Lucien Loucheur, the minister of *les Régions Dévastées*, the inhabitants eventually could count on a friend in high places, one of their own, a man who could understand their grievances. Of course, the war indemnities did not always go to the right people: a great many racketeers were rewarded for services rendered as much to the Germans as to their compatriots. A man who in 1914 had two taxis in service outside Roubaix station ended up, in 1919, with a fleet of Dodge trucks, obtained, as war compensation, from the American base. Some mill owners who had closed their mills had to start from scratch; others, who had worked for the German market, were able at once to continue production. But, as there had been hardly any collaborators, the transition from occupation to liberation was carried out with a minimum of violence and injustice. The *Feldgendarmerie* were remembered with fear and hatred, so generally were the *Kommandanturen* and the *Etappen*. The German soldier was recalled with a lingering respect. The inhabitants of the Nord are hard-working people; and they had been enormously impressed by the magnificent capacity of the German army for detailed planning and for organization. But they were glad to see the Germans go, gladder still to welcome the British. October 1918 represented another, and decisive, stage in the tradition of anglophilia so firmly rooted in the Nord from the 1870s and 1880s.

II

The Second Occupation, 1940–1944

2

Vichy and the Nord

There was a dark stain on the wall of the village schoolroom where the portrait of Marshal Pétain had been for the previous four years. But the poster bearing the Marshal's new year address to the schoolchildren of France dated 1st January 1944, though somewhat tattered, was still up on the wall beside the blackboard, as though, in this Norman village, the authorities were still undecided as to the future in immediate political terms, and, in typical Norman manner, were keeping all their options open. Or perhaps no one had thought of taking the message down. And so there it continued to address itself, in somewhat querulous terms, to an empty, indifferent, dusty room, the July sun lighting up oblique shafts of rising chalk. Classes had been interrupted, presumably since D Day, and the Marshal's ancient voice spoke into emptiness, over one of those huge chasms that, every now and then, mark the broken progress of French history, from regime to regime.

There is always something rather pathetic about the tattered relics of defeated regimes, rather like the brutally scattered intimacies that lie about on recent battlefields: postcards of French villages with German writing on them, and strands of blood-stained clothing that caught the eye of Poincaré, when, in September 1914, he was visiting the site of the Battle of the Marne. The poster headed with the double-bladed *francisque* spoke of hopes that seemed incredibly ancient and of a paternalism that had lost its relevance, as if France had outgrown the stress on redemption and atonement that had been Pétain's particular message ever since the terrible summer of 1940. It seemed indeed as impossibly dated as the letter, written in green ink on squared school exercise book paper, in Slovak, some of the writing dissolving in blotches of water, the paper covered in mud, that had been brought to me by an eager local: a message, apparently addressed to a wife or to a mother in some Slovak village that had never reached its destination.

I can remember to this day the gist of the Marshal's message, and even more its tone, almost as if one could hear the old man's rather halting speech, as, patiently and didactically, he spelled out what he wanted to say to his little friends:

Mes chers petits *amis*, à cette époque de l'année, et chaque année [and this would indeed have been the fourth time] ma pensée va vers vous. Mes meilleures années sont celles que j'ai passées sur les bancs de l'école [and a village school, too, somewhere in the Pas-de-Calais]. Mes chers petits amis, ne copiez pas, ne trichez pas, nommez entre vous un chef de classe, constituez dans chaque classe un comité d'honneur[6]

and so on and so on, ending on the injunction: 'ce qu'il faut à la France, à notre cher pays, ce ne sont pas des intelligences, ce sont des caractères', a message the gist of which would have seemed entirely familiar to any English public schoolboy brought up in the early thirties. It was as if one had come in at the tail end of an act witnessed many times before. Until that day in early July 1944, I had tended to regard Philippe Pétain almost as evil incarnate, certainly more wicked, because more damaging, than Pierre Laval. Now he seemed to have borrowed both the language and even some of the clothing of a French Baden-Powell. One almost expected to see him on the lawn outside the Hôtel du Parc, wearing shorts, displaying nobbly knees, in an effort, rather touching, to bridge the gap of seventy-odd years that separated him from his dear little friends, the hope of the future, the guarantors of France's moral regeneration. It is hard to think of an old man who spoke in such genuine and clearly deeply felt grandfatherly tones as a politician of consummate wickedness who had anaesthetized and deceived his people into semicollaboration. There was a tired candour about the old man's nostalgia for a very, very distant youth (after all, when *he* had been sitting on the hard school bench, it would not have been very long after the Franco-Prussian War, as if this Picard peasant had been destined to experience three wars in the most war-torn area of France). And in this candour there was no doubt an element of loss and compensation. Like so many childless people, Philippe Pétain delighted in the company of little boys and little girls, to whom he could address himself at their own mental level. So many of the Marshal's speeches seem to have been drawn heavily from the uplifting sayings of *L'Almanach Vermot*, and even his conversations were peppered with *lapalissades*, as if he had been a military Monsieur Prudhomme. 'Alibert, parle-moi des Chinois, ils sont jaunes, n'est-ce pas? Je n'aime pas les jaunes.'

Of course, this childlike stance could be combined with an elephantine memory for slight and with an anti-English bias that dated back to Doullens. Yet, undoubtedly, an important element in the public style and language of *l'Etat Français* is its archaic dottiness. 'Labourage et pâturage sont les deux mamelles de la France,' as proclaimed on the Vichy banknotes, would hardly seem relevant to the priorities of a regime very largely run by technocrats and high-ranking civil servants, at last released from the trammels of parliamentary control and free to plan the immediate future without interference from troublesome deputies. Perhaps, though, it did vaguely reflect the rural values of an Auvergne all at once promoted to the status of the centre of political patronage and influence.

There was much that was dotty about Vichy, particularly in its period of *relative* innocence and hope, in the period 1940–41, when the regime has been described as *la république flottante*. It was certainly not a republic, and, in the end, it did not float, leaving, on the contrary, the main elements of the French Mediterranean fleet at the bottom of Toulon harbour. But, as long as Darlan was prime minister as well as minister of the interior, local administration was given over to landlocked naval officers, with *amiraux* and *vice-amiraux* as prefects, *capitaines de vaisseau* as *sous-préfets*, indeed a unique example in modern French history of the navy, *la Royale*, being put to some use, even if that use was fairly detestable. For naval officers eagerly led the crusade against Jews and Freemasons, serving as the zealous executants of Vichy's anti-Semitic and anti-Masonic legislation that, incidentally, owed absolutely nothing to German prompting, the German authorities, both in Vichy and in Paris, being perfectly happy to let the French get on with whatever form of persecution they wished to inflict on their compatriots. *La république flottante* was, in historical terms, the most anti-British regime France has ever possessed. It was a bitter disappointment to Darlan that he was cheated of the opportunity of actually going to war with Britain.

Vichy has also been described, at least in its initial stages, as *la république des recalés*, a regime of dunces, representing, in educational terms, what was so clearly spelt out in the Marshal's new year message of 1944. Of course they were not *all* dunces, for Vichy put in positions of unrestricted power technocrats and civil servants of great experience, specialists like the father of the historian Le Roy Ladurie, syndicalists like Belin, financial experts like Bouthillier. But the entourage of the Marshal at least up to November 1942 was drawn from Stanislas and from *l'enseignement libre*. As the French hierarchy was quick to realize, and to rejoice, moral values would mean a Moral Order, putting the clock back on Ferry and on sixty years of *laïcité*. *Instituteurs* and *professeurs de lycée* were in for a rough time, and the way was open for clean living, the open air, the hewing of wood and the drawing of water, songs round the blazing campfire set in the midst of the forest, a minister of youth, as well as a minister of sport (both offices, incidentally, inherited from the hated Popular Front) and much public official concern for the problems of youth – though, by 1943, under overwhelming German pressure, that concern would often take the form of helping with the deportation of young men over eighteen to work in German war factories. The *STO* certainly stripped bare the equivocations of Vichy youth policies and lost the regime the support of middle-class parents. Even so, any regime that places character and honour at a higher priority than intelligence is fairly eccentric.

Because of the terms of the Armistice and thanks above all to the initiative of Pierre Laval, who, as well as having been *député-maire* of Aubervilliers, was the *châtelain* of Châteldon, twelve kilometres from Vichy, and already by the end of 1940, linked to the new capital by a macadam road, Vichy France at once emerged as a geographical object of wonder. It was as if *l'Hexagone* had been turned upside-down, with, for the first time in history, the capital of France placed in a watering-place in the underprivileged and backward Massif Central. In historical terms, the geographical aberration that was Vichy could be described as *la revanche du Midi* and, indeed, as the temporary solution of what generations of southern politicians have described as *le problème du Midi*, even if that problem was of their own making or existed only in the imagination of poets and *félibriges*. It is not surprising that, even forty years on, Vichy should be recalled as a lost golden age in places like Clermont-Ferrand, Thiers, Vichy and Moulins, and among the rural population of the Auvergne and the Bourbonnais. It is true that, in intent at least, it was as highly centralized as had been the Third Republic; but the centre was not in Paris, temporarily disinherited, cut off from favour and patronage, and merely the capital of anti-Vichy collaboration – in intent, at least, because in practice, thanks to the Germans, the writ of Vichy did not extend very far, being largely confined to the land-locked, truncated territory of *la France Non-Occupée*, and almost completely excluded from the industrial area extending from the Belgian frontier to the course of the Somme.

What the French of my generation are most likely to recall about the Vichy interlude, whatever their political affiliations, is its bizarre and recalcitrant geography, its many, and dangerous, frontiers and the relative impenetrability of the five distinct regions into which France was now divided: a geography of fear and danger that made of once sleepy little provincial towns like Niort, Orthez, Moulins, Montluçon, perilous *passages de ligne* where the traveller had to run the gauntlet of the watchful double filter of the *gendarmerie* and the *Feldgendarmerie*, both forces working in harmony and both employing well-tended Alsatian dogs. A geography that made of each of the Paris termini the potential end of the line for the *résistant* and for the Allied agent, as well as for the black marketeer. A geography that, till 1942, established a militarily patrolled frontier along the course of the Somme, cutting off the Nord, the Pas-de-Calais and much of the Somme from the rest of France, while, at the same time, removing the frontier that divided the Nord from Belgium. A geography that made any coastal area inaccessible to the ordinary traveller, that took the Haut- and Bas-Rhin and the Moselle out of France altogether, to form a new *Gau* of the Third Reich, and that placed the southern Alpine departments under Italian military occupation. So much of the literature of the Vichy period relates to the anxieties of a midnight *passage de ligne*, in the inexorable silence of a stationary train that seems unlikely ever to get up steam again; and to be crawling on hands and knees through the undergrowth, in dread fear of the sudden yellow probe of the tentative finger of a searchlight. By multiplying the internal frontiers, the Germans had multiplied the internal dangers of travel and had deliberately set about isolating the French from one another.

The result is that it is almost impossible to write the history of Vichy for France as a whole (and, for Alsatians and German-speaking Lorrainers, it is not even French history; for the inhabitants of the Nord and the Pas-de-Calais, the occupation years related much more to the history of Belgium than to that of France). Just as the Marshal, in his initial appeal, had sought to rebuild a shattered and humiliated France on the basis of the family unit, the Germans had ensured that the experience of occupation should differ radically from place to place. As it turned out, the Normans, at least the Lower ones, got off rather lightly, indeed often did quite well out of the German occupation; the *Auvergnats* too prospered, but the *Marseillais* and the *Niçois* starved. In Paris, social life went on with a gay intensity, reaching a climax of inventiveness in 1943, when, among other works, one of Sartre's plays had its highly successful premiere in the presence of *le Tout-Paris* and the leading literary lights of the German military hierarchy. There were areas of resistance and areas of *attentisme*. Toulouse went one way, Bordeaux the other, as if in conformity to some well-tried historical law governing the always contrary attitudes of the inhabitants of the two southwestern towns.

If Vichy remained, predictably, *vichyssois*, Montpellier never was. Both the history of collaboration and that of resistance can be studied only in local or, at most, regional terms. In Paris, in the summer and winter of 1940, the working-class population of the northeastern *arrondissements* could be seen fraternizing with the German soldiers, sitting with them on the café terraces of Belleville and Ménilmontant, while the western *arrondissements* remained shuttered and silent at least till September 1940, when social life started to pick up once more. But, after June 1941, there would be no more fraternization in the XVIIIme, the XIXme and the XXme. Between June 1940 and June 1941, the highly intelligent young men in charge of German occupation in the Nord and the Pas-de-Calais, in the textile and mining towns, made a point of making contact with Communist trade union officials of the *CGT*, while by-passing the official Vichy *syndicat unique* imposed by Belin, because they were concerned to get the population back to work, the mills and mines reopened. But, of course, all that too changed overnight in June 1941.

Of all the areas of a fragmented France, the one that remained the *most* impenetrable to Vichy persuasion and influence was the Northeast. This was as much the result of historical experience as of deliberate German policy. The Germans, from the time of the Armistice in June 1940, placed the Northeast under the military governor of Belgium, von Falkenhausen, creating a new unit under the denomination of Belgium and Northern France. There may have been annexionist *arrière-pensées* in thus differentiating between Belgium and the Northeast, and the rest of France. Certainly this was the view of the inhabitants of the Nord. Or the Germans may simply have decided to do in 1940 what they had done, in Lille, Roubaix, Tourcoing, Douai, Cambrai and Valenciennes in 1914, when the Occupied Departments had been placed under the authority of von Bissing, the military governor in Brussels. Certainly there was a degree of continuity in German policy. For instance, the *Kommandantur* of Roubaix appointed in 1940 was the nephew of the one appointed in 1914. What is more, he arrived fully provided with his uncle's *fiches*. Those who had been arrested and deported in 1915 or 1916 were redeported in 1940. These included the *maire*, a veteran *Guesdiste*, Jean Le Bas, who had been released, at the insistence of Alfonso XIII, in 1916, and who died in Mauthausen in 1943. It was much the same in Lille, Douai and Valenciennes. The Germans had long memories; so did the *Roubaisiens* and the *Lillois*; and each lived up to the historical expectations of the other, though the Germans were not quite so brutal and rapacious in the second occupation as they had been in the first.

The Nord was the only part of France in which the Germans were referred to exclusively as *les boches* in the Second World War as well as in the First. Here, no *fridolins*, no *verts-de-gris*, no *chleuhs*, just the old, familiar *boches*. Perhaps, among the garrison troops of Lille, there was even a return of the Bavarians, familiar uniforms there from 1914 to 1918, though they would no longer have been distinguishable to the civilian population. Perhaps, in 1940, *occupant* and *occupé* resumed a tentative, all-purpose dialogue composed of *chtimi* and South German slang? Certainly one of the leading German officials in Lille, Carlo Schmid, director of the *OFK* 670, was bilingual, with a French mother, and strong sympathies for the type of Christian socialist currents that had long existed among the Catholic working classes and *patronat* of the wool towns of the Franco-Belgian border; Schmid had direct access to the local Catholic hierarchy, and was able to induce some local leaders of what had been Catholic boy scout movements to moderate the *gaulliste* fervour of *Boulonnais lycéens*. Another German, General Bertram, at one time garrison commander of Lille, was the brother of the Cardinal-Archbishop of Breslau; and, in his relations with the powerful and enormously respected Cardinal Liénart, this stood him in good stead, in an area of France in which the clergy were especially influential, even among a section of the working class.

It is hard to know what the Germans had in mind for the future either of Belgium or of French Flanders and French Wallonia. In the Nord, they seem to have given little encouragement to *l'abbé* Gantois, *curé* of Watten, the leader of a pan-Flemish separatist movement, the *Vlaamsch Verbond voor Frankrijk*, though he got some financial assistance from Ribbentrop's people. Certainly they treated the Belgians much better than they did the French, so that in 1944, as I was able to experience, conditions were far better *outre-Quiévrain* than on the *LRT* side of the frontier. It is likely that the main concern of the military authorities in this absolutely vital area of supply and communications was to keep the trains running, the factories open, the coastal defences in the making supplied with a work force, and the movement of troop trains concealed from Allied agents. Above all, at least up till 1942, they managed to keep Vichy emissaries at arm's length, so that the *préfet du Nord*, Carles, found himself much of the time in an administrative vacuum.

In this, the Germans were no doubt helped by the attitude of the inhabitants, for many of whom Vichy would have seemed a complete irrelevance, even though Pétain, like de Gaulle, was an *enfant du pays*. In both wars, the *chtimis* had had the disagreeable experience of having been treated almost as foreigners, as *les boches du Nord*, not only by southerners and people from central France, but also by Parisians. And both wars greatly strengthened this sense of apartness, even of rejection. Had the *Lillois* not been told that, were it not for their beastly frontier and their silly tradition of patriotism, dating from 1793, there would never have been a war in the first place, and that both wars had been *their* wars? As refugees returned to the Nord, after *l'Exode*, in the summer and autumn of 1940, they were able to see on the ground the evidence of the hardness of the fighting in the summer; burnt-out tanks and scout cars, German as well as French, abandoned guns, all witnessing to the intensity of the fighting rather than to the suddenness of total collapse.

It was widely held, in the Nord, in the summer and autumn of 1940, that the Armistice had been concluded at the instance both of southern politicians and of southern public opinion, in order to save the Midi from becoming a battleground; and from this it was an easy step to go on to suggest that at the time of the Armistice, military victory had been just round the corner, and that France had been cheated of such a victory by the selfishness and the cowardice of Laval and other *Auvergnats*, of Marquet and other *Bordelais*. And it followed from such convictions that, as France had fought well, there was no need to drape her in sackcloth and to wallow tearfully in atonement. Even Pétain, the *sauveur* for so many Frenchmen living far from the frontiers, would seem a very distant, and, indeed, somewhat irrelevant, saviour. And whom was he going to save them from? Certainly not from the Germans, very much back again, and here to stay, settling in, even requisitioning the same buildings and houses as in 1914. And here too, as in 1916 and 1917, were the Germans building new railway lines, tying the Nord more intimately to Brussels, to Liège and to the Rhineland, as well as to the Ardennes, Luxembourg and Alsace, as if they were planning for a distant, but stable, *après-guerre* of permanent occupation or annexation. New lines did indeed seem to spell an unshakable confidence in some sort of pan-German New European Order. People who felt that they were likely to have to go, cutting their losses, taking what they could away with them, stripping the place, as they had done in the first months of war, in the summer and autumn of 1914, would not have taken the trouble to have new lines constructed.

And of course there were other, more familiar patterns of German behaviour: the confiscation of carrier pigeons, in an urban zone in which every miner and every mill worker would be a *colombophile*; the confiscation of wireless sets; the increasing collusion between the German armed forces and the development of a black market, based largely on tobacco smuggling from Belgium (though, in both wars, smuggling might as readily lead to resistance as to economic collaboration); and two generations of *horizontales* (some perhaps the daughters of the first lot) who, in 1918 and 1944, might suffer the same humiliating fate of having their heads shaven, generally by *patriotes* and *résistants* of the eleventh hour, the octobrists of 1918, the *résistants de septembre* of 1944. In this area of France there had grown up a sort of intimacy between *occupant* and *occupé* based on long familiarity and, in 1917/8, common privations, on a peculiar blending of mutual loathing and mutual respect, a *pas de deux* that would exclude a third party, and that, in physical terms, resulted, in both four-year cycles, in the birth of an unknown number of small Franco-Germans, their origins hidden under the merciful veil of the formula: *né de père inconnu*. Certainly there were plenty of these among the orphans kept by the Bon Pasteur in Lille in 1944/5. Vichy would not understand such particular problems. And the enemy presence would still be more familiar than an inhabitant of Marseille or of Perpignan. The *chtimis* derived a sense of identity from their exclusion from what had been the common national experience in both wars. They *knew* their Germans, knew too, in a way that Laval and many of the Vichy ministers did not, that there was not a deal to be done with the Germans. It was a matter as much of hard experience as of patriotism.

Then there was, at least in the Nord and the Pas-de-Calais, if not in the more rural Ardennes, the tradition of anglophilia dating back at least to the 1870s and 1880s, and extending from the factory owners to the professional and working classes. Roubaix is the only place in France in which I have encountered Frenchmen speaking English either with a Bradford accent or with an Australian one. Over the interwar years, a steady stream of mill owners' sons from Roubaix-Tourcoing had been sent to the Bradford Institute of Wool Technology for their professional training, while a number of purchasers had been despatched down under. Roubaix was the second town in France – le Havre was the first – to form a football club (*Le Racing Club de Roubaix*), association football having been brought there, in 1877, by two Yorkshire textile engineers; the game then spread gradually inwards from the Channel coast. In 1939, the trainer of the *stade* was a Lancashire man. Again, from the 1880s, the prestigious Faculté des Lettres de Lille, a showpiece of secular education, emerged as the principal centre in France for English studies, exporting to Paris and to Lyon a string of celebrated *anglicistes*, while retaining, in the Lycée Faidherbe, the best teachers of English in the country. When, in the winter of 1914, the Germans authorized the reopening of about half of the Lille schools, the first subject on the programme to be reestablished was English. I don't know what the Bavarian command made of that! It was the same in Douai, when, with the reestablishment of the *école technique* in the winter of 1916, English and typing were the first subjects to be reintroduced. All French educational institutions existing in England and in Scotland still form part of the Académie de Lille.

This tradition of anglophilia, at first professional and educational or deriving from common habits of leisure, was given a much more intimate, concrete, and indeed, physical form, from the autumn of 1918 and much of 1919, and often resulting in intermarriage between Thomas Atkins and Mlle. from Armentières (or from Lille, Hem, Loos, Douai, Bapaume, Albert, Béthune) in 1919 and 1920, disproving the gist of the famous song: 'Après la guerre finie, soldier anglais parti.' An unknown number stayed, never returning to England, blending into the general population in the course of the next twenty years, many of them by 1940 grandfathers, and speaking an odd blend of English and *chtimi*. Most such marriages concerned soldiers of working-class origin and represented for the husbands often considerable social advancement; some married into family occupations – an *estaminet*, a garage, a grocery, a butcher's – other became football coaches, a few worked in the mills. It was a phenomenon exclusive to the working class, illustrating, once again, the greater adaptability of the other ranks than of the officer corps to the standards of foreign communities. There were many similar marriages, in this part of France, in 1944/5, when, again, most of the British husbands stayed on in the Nord.

The British were back again, with the BEF, in large numbers and with plenty of money, during the period of the 'phoney war', their presence certainly welcomed by the keepers of *estaminets* and by the younger feminine population. According to a local historian, there was a massive increase both of venereal diseases and of alcoholism in Douai, inducing the prefect to limit the opening hours of drinking establishments. It was no doubt the same in Lille and in other towns in the British area. But there was more to it than such basic commercial considerations. (It should be added that advantages enjoyed by the British troops hardly endeared them to the poorly paid French servicemen stationed in the same area.) British soldiers and airmen were still being hidden both by farmers and townsmen as late as June 1941, a year after Dunkirk, despite the execution of several people caught housing Allied personnel or passing them on down the line of escape routes towards the Midi and Spain.

The population of the Nord was not as massively anglophil as it had been in 1918 and 1919. This time, anglophilia was tempered by subtle class distinctions, the professional and working classes looking to Britain for deliverance as early as the winter of 1940, when the BBC was listened to with pathetic regularity by the textile engineers and the mill workers of Roubaix. But the *patronat*, the peasantry, and the Catholic hierarchy displayed a more ambivalent attitude, and one often receptive to the endearments of Vichy's Moral Order and to the regime's emphasis on discipline, authority and atonement. Both Liénart and Dutoit were sympathetic to *la Révolution Nationale*, both had been personally acquainted with Pétain from a very early age; both failed to come out openly against the *STO*, thus alienating many of the young. Both signed the famous open letter, organized by van Roey in 1943, on the subject of the bombing of open cities. Whereas, in the First World War, the lead had been taken by the *notables*, including the *lainiers* of Roubaix-Tourcoing, some of whom had been deported in 1915, in the Second, it was taken by the railway workers, the miners, the mill workers, the *jocistes* (a group of Belgian inspiration), many urban and country *curés* (several of whom were either shot or deported), the occasional *pasteur*, the schoolteachers and the textile engineers. The experience of the *Front Populaire* had left deep scars in this part of France, leading part of the *patronat* into instinctive anti-Communism. The Germans also offered many economic inducements to those mill owners who were prepared to work for the German domestic market. It should be added, in their defence, that they were also concerned to see that their work force was employed and that those thus employed might escape the *STO*.

There were more early *gaullistes* here than in any other part of France, not just because de Gaulle was a *Lillois* and his wife a *Calaisienne*, but because *gaullisme* was early identified, no doubt wrongly, with British fortunes. Nor was it an empty anglophilia, consisting of graffiti on *lycée* walls and similar gestures. From 1943 onwards, and above all between April and

July 1944, an immense amount of information reached Britain from this crucial area of France, especially from railway engineers and *cheminots*, relating to German troop movements from the Pas-de-Calais to Normandy, and to what was going on in Watten (where the *abbé* Gantois must have been a very lonely voice among his parishioners). In such a heavily populated area, large-scale military forms of resistance were impossible. But information was much more valuable than random attacks on military personnel. The *Lillois* and the *Roubaisiens* considered it their natural reward that they should have been liberated, in September 1944, by the British. They had never expected any other outcome. In this sense, popular attitudes corresponded much more closely to those of the Belgians than to those of other parts of France. The Belgians, too, looked to London, where their government in exile had been established in December 1940; and the Belgians had the advantage of not having been faced with a Vichy-type alternative and the apparent promise of safeguarding at least some tatters of national sovereignty. Leopold III was no Pétain. Walloon Belgium at least had displayed an equally firm and touching anglophilia, in both wars, even if the Flemish population, led by their clergy, had been less enthusiastic, if not openly hostile. Many Belgian children born between 1900 and 1910, had spent the whole of the First World War with English foster parents, returning home in 1918 as lifelong anglophils.

In social terms, the frontier had always been nonexistent, merely an invitation to a mutual concern with contraband and to the development of a common *esprit fraudeur*. People from both sides of the frontier had long been in the habit of congregating, at weekends, in the *zone neutre* for cockfights, illegal in both countries. In retrospect, it would seem that the Germans had committed a serious error, both times, in thus grouping together two areas, the populations of which had so much in common in terms of urban occupations, social attitudes, Christian socialism and leisure enjoyments, the pigeons of working-class *colombophiles* making regular weekend flights, in peacetime, over a frontier which divided houses, cafés, *estaminets* and *tavernes*. Of course, the Germans were concerned to fragment French unity; and, had they been victorious, it is likely that both Belgium and the French departments under Brussels military rule would have formed a satellite state under the aegis of the Third Reich.

For all these reasons, the echoes of Vichy propaganda were very muted in the Northeast, while much Vichy legislation remained there *lettre-morte*. Few Vichy ministers or notabilities were ever seen in the Nord, the Germans often denying them entry. Pétain never visited his native department. The prefect, Carles, spent much of the period in an administrative vacuum and in 1941 he often had the greatest difficulty in forming the *délégations spéciales*, made up of personalities known for their sympathy for the *Révolution Nationale*, that were to replace the elected municipalities of 1939 (most of which were dominated by the *SFIO* and by the *PCF*). The Nord was an area of traditional municipalism, and during the first occupation, as we have seen, it was the municipalities that had managed more or less to keep some sort of life going for the civilian population, printing their own money, and constituting the only French authority that the German military command had been prepared to recognize. A northern *maire* was perhaps a greater personage than in any other part of France, indeed more equivalent to a Belgian *bourgmestre*. And some *maires* had very long runs: Augustin Laurent, in Lille, 40 years, Victor Provo, in Roubaix, ever since the Liberation; and such interference from Vichy met with much local resentment. In times of crisis, each town, each *commune*, had been driven back on its own resources and had been in the habit of taking its own initiatives.

Even the anti-Semitic legislation was applied here in a

piecemeal fashion, and many Antwerp Jews were passed down the lines of escape through the Nord. A joint operation was carried out on 15th September 1942 by the *Feldgendarmerie* and four French *agents de police*, using lists drawn up two years earlier by the French authorities (prefects and subprefects and local *commissariats*), in which 516 Jews were rounded up in the Nord and deported to Auschwitz (only 25 returned). The Jewish population of the department had in fact been much in excess of this figure; and many municipalities had 'lost' the lists drawn up in accordance with the Vichy anti-Semitic legislation of the summer of 1940. And the *étoile jaune*, so prominent in Vichy, was hardly ever seen here before 1944.

The Germans also saw to it that Vichy youth organizations, the *chantiers* and so on, should not be allowed to develop in an area in which there remained a large pool of available manpower in the eighteen to thirty-five age group. The Germans, under the impetus of the Sauckel Organization, which recruited French labour for war work in Germany, had their own notions as to how French youth could be best employed, and in the Northeast, Vichy's much publicized concern for the so-called sacrificed generation would have appeared as a hollow mockery. In his pioneering study based on the correspondence between the prefect Carles and successive Vichy ministers of youth and education, Bill Halls, an English historian, has shown how totally irrelevant to conditions existing in the Nord were the directives pouring out from the provisional seat of government. Nor was there the possibility, in this heavily populated area, of forming a maquis composed of *réfractaires* from the *STO*. At best, the only positive response to Vichy youth policies came from the hierarchy.

Darlan's own brand of anglophobia had small appeal to a population that had never contributed, in significant numbers, to the recruitment of the French navy; and, in the summer of 1940, Abrial, the furiously anglophobe naval commander of

Dunkirk, had himself set up in Vichy, along with Platon, back from Oxford.

But Paris was equally unsuccessful. In Douai, a town of 40,000 inhabitants, the figures for the membership of collaborationist organizations are derisory: the *RNP*, 4 members; the *Milice*, 1; the *LVF*, 2; the *PPF*, 80, many of them ex-Communist militants; the *VVVF*, 4, all of them apparently drawn by the promise – unfulfilled – of German rations: a total of 120 collaborators, of whom one, a doctor, a correspondent of the *SS* Racial Institute in Berlin, was shot in July 1946. Here, out-and-out collaboration was suspect as being either Parisian, or of southern origin, or both (as in the case of Brasillach and Montherlant). Even Gantois had to admit, in 1943, that 'Dietsland' had little appeal, and that only a complete recolonization of French Flanders and the expulsion of the francophone majority would have made the formation of a Greater Flanders viable. Indeed, the greatest fear felt by the inhabitants of the Nord during the occupation years was that, in the event of a German victory, they would all be uprooted and transported to central France, where their sudden and massive arrival would be bound to be resented by the local population. They knew, from previous bitter experience, that refugees from the Nord would encounter little sympathy and much hostility from the peasants of the *Nivernais*, the *Mâconnais*, the *Bourbonnais* and the *Beaujolais*.

It could of course be argued – and Gantois argued thus – that, in linguistic terms, even de Gaulle was of Flemish origin; but the origin was a very long time ago; and it would have been hard to convince every inhabitant of the Nord whose surname began with de or with van that he was, in some vague way, not really French, and that he should learn what was proclaimed as his native language, Flemish. Furthermore, in this industrial area, there was considerable sympathy for the Soviet Union, and the *LVF* was hardly likely to find many recruits in the

Anzin coal basin or in Hénin-Liétard, places in which the cadres of the *PCF*, underground since 1939, had managed to subsist, with much support from the local population. Thorez, though in exile, was after all himself an *enfant du pays*. The strength of the clandestine Communist party may be gauged from the severity of the judicial repression meted out to its militants by the French courts. The *Section Spéciale* of the Douai Appeal Court, set up in September 1941, tried nearly two thousand (1,966) suspected party members, 1,706 men and 260 women, condemning five of them to the guillotine, for alleged acts of terrorism.

Of course, in this industrial area, there was plenty of economic collaboration, and, as during the previous occupation, there existed an ill-defined nether zone in which black marketeers, *smokeleers* and members of the supply services of the German army met in shady places – in Roubaix, mostly in the *estaminets* near the station – to carry out mutually profitable transactions. The German military authorities themselves directly contributed to the vast growth of the black market in cigarettes and tobacco by removing, for the period 1940/2, the customs barrier between France and Belgium, though it was later reestablished. Common shortage of raw materials inspired the inventiveness of Roubaix mill owners and textile engineers in the search for *ersatz* materials, resulting, for instance, in the Penel-Flipo factory hitting on the highly profitable *tapis-boulgomme*, a form of synthetic rubber which remained much in demand long after the Liberation. There was an equally ill-defined frontier between professional crime and operations that could be described as a form of resistance, especially in the supply of *faux papiers*. Despite the curfew and the extreme food shortages of the winter of 1943/4, Lille contained well-known pleasure spots where it was possible to eat extremely well and to enjoy agreeable female company. The Café Métropole, run by Freddie Beaufort, who had a finger in many pies and who was tried and acquitted after the Liberation, was the meeting place of many mysterious figures, among them the black-clothed Delrue, who figures so prominently in Lageat's book, *Robert des Halles*, and who, once on the run from Loos, eventually escaped to Paris, transferring from resistance to full-scale banditry. Lille, where most of the population was pitifully, and indeed visibly, undernourished by the time of the arrival of the British, was as much a capital of pleasure as Brussels, itself the capital of a European black market that extended from Poland to Brest. The statement that *on s'amusait bien à Lille pendant l'occupation*, though it provoked indignant protests at a recent colloquium organized by the *Revue du Nord*, was not denied by most of the participants. In the nature of things, frontier populations are seldom among the most virtuous, and in this part of France there was a long tradition of law-breaking.

But the principal appeal of Vichy – and one that took in so many patriotic Frenchmen, at least in 1940/1 – namely that the Marshal placed a screen, however fragile, between the civilian population and the German military authorities, would fall flat in an area under direct and complete military occupation. In Lille and elsewhere, even simple operations involving the French *gendarmerie* would always be carried out jointly with the *Feldgendarmerie*, emphasizing the fact of the enemy presence. Even more, *le Nouvel Ordre Européen* that had such an insistent appeal to the handful of Paris out-and-outers, would be shown up as a derisory, yet familiar, sham in departments that equated an onerous and often brutal German presence with an only too familiar *ordre européen ancien* (for, already, in 1914–18, the more theoretical of the German *occupants* were talking in terms of a new order for Mitteleuropa, of which French Flanders was apparently destined to be a part). No *Lillois*, no *Roubaisien*, no *Tourcennois* was likely to be deceived by such geopolitical appeals. To him, the New Order would look only too familiar – the curfew, passes required even to leave the town, white barriers outside German establishments, the obligation to get off the pavement if members of the armed forces were passing, massive deportations (only the initials of the *STO* were new, and the fact that young girls were not taken, much to the relief and even surprise of the *Lillois* and the inhabitants of the other towns of the Nord), billeting, requisitioning, the bitter winters of deprivation, the coal barges frozen in the canals, their contents providing momentary relief – a familiar combination of miseries and minor vexations harking back to the previous occupation and to the frightful winter of 1917/18. By his bark and his boot, General Niehof, the irascible garrison commander of Lille, seemed to the older *Lillois* to have taken his cue from his Bavarian predecessor. And, in both wars, Loos, the sinister and sad-sounding Loos (as if it represented indeed the loss of hope), spelt out summary execution, torture and interrogation, whether at the hands of the *Abwehr*, of the *Gestapo*, of the *Sûreté*, or of all three combined.

There was nothing novel about the German presence. To many it must have seemed as an endemic evil, recurring in a four-year cycle, roughly every twenty years. Van der Meersch, the author of *Invasion 14*, published in 1935, was at the time of his death in 1952 well on with its sequel, *Invasion 40*, a book in which I was myself to have some sort of emblematic part. Indeed, the Germans themselves seem to have been governed by precedent. Their Flemish policies, their annexationist ambitions, their plans for economic exploitation, even their clumsy attempts to promote the knowledge of German, in an area of France where English speakers were more numerous than anywhere else, by the provision of night schools at which the pupils would be provided with pastries and goodies, were all based on blueprints that had been drawn up, with minute care about detail, in 1913 or earlier, and that had been taken down from dusty shelves, for further use, in 1940. The Germans, it is true, had learnt *something*: the second occupation was less vexatious in terms of humiliation, the German soldiers being rather better behaved and better disciplined than their predecessors. But, otherwise, it was the mixture as before. So you could not fool a *chtimi* – 'un-boche est toujours un boche', even though friendly relations might often develop between individual soldiers and civilians. The result was that this was a much more clear-cut world than, let us say, the Dordogne of Lacombe Lucien, the Paris of Monsieur Klein, the Puy-de-Dôme of Laval, the Alpes-Maritimes of the *Milice*, the Allier of Pascal Jardin, the Haute-Garonne of Catalan anarchism, or, indeed, the Midi generally, where Vichy might draw on considerable local support, at least up till the summer of 1942. It is also true that the Northeast was more patriotic, and had always been so.

But patriotism came easily to a frontier region always the first to experience the fire of war and invasion. I can recall the pride of Georges Lefebvre when he reminded his pupils that his great-uncle had taken part in the defence of Lille, in 1793, in the ranks of the *garde nationale lilloise*, under attack from the enemy armies. In the Nord, there could be no *équivoque*, for there existed no choice. Vichy was a very long way away; it was almost impossible to travel even to Paris or to Rouen; above all, the Germans were everywhere. Both Vichy and Paris would seem irrelevant – even Carles must have seemed irrelevant, the representative of a distant and shadowy French government. There is nothing that more unites a community, contributing to its collective identity and thus to its apartness, than the double experience of occupation. It was an experience denied to much of the rest of France, at least up till November 1942. Vichy propaganda on the subject of Joan of Arc, meeting with some response elsewhere (in parts of Normandy) fell completely flat in the Nord, the inhabitants of which, even schoolboys, knew who the national enemy was. Even after November 1942, in what had been the Nonoccupied Zone, the German presence in the Massif Central and the South-west was unobtrusive. A recent study, published in *Cahiers d'histoire*, on the subject of the German troops stationed in and around Lyon, is a case in point. Most were young men in training, destined for the Russian Front. Few were ever *seen* in central Lyon, and the city was merely a temporary stage, on the way to a long journey east. It was only when the Germans started withdrawing from the Southwest, in the summer of 1944, that they often became vicious. It would be uncharitable and indecent to suggest that the inhabitants of the Nord, because they had suffered so much, in two wars, were in some ways more fortunate than their compatriots. But at least for them the moral position was much clearer.

In historical terms, ever since the 1790s, there has been much emphasis on what has been called, by several generations of historians, politicians (mostly southern) and travellers, *le problème du Midi*, however that may be defined. It has generally been a 'problem' largely of southern invention, arising out of a sense of deprivation and from hostility to Paris. Its most recent, and silliest, expression is *l'Occitanie*, wherever that may be. Any *Lillois* would have his own views on the subject: the South had always been a drain on the country; the *méridionaux* were empty braggarts and cowards, totally unreliable as soldiers, lazy and mendacious, lying about in the sun all day or playing *pétanque*, or sipping *pastis*; the territory was inhabited exclusively by eloquent and boastful *Tartarins*, while the northerner worked, scrubbed, whitened his front step and produced large families. I do not know whether General de Gaulle, certainly the most famous northerner, ever actually made the statement, so often attributed to him: *la France se termine à Lyon*. But it is one that could be echoed by many of his fellow *chtimis*. All right, if *boche du Nord* applied to people who were diligent, house-proud, clean to the point of fanaticism, then they were indeed *boches du Nord*, and proud of it. My purpose is to suggest that there is – or has been – *un problème du Nord*, derived from regional experience and a sense of apartness, and from a historical identity closely linked with that of Walloon Belgium. Despite a long Jacobin tradition, a new history of France, cognizant of regional stresses, might take the title of an English novel, *North and South*. Probably the *problème du Nord* has now been diluted into a great sense of identity with Brussels and the EEC, a system which has brought the Nord enormous advantages. But, in the past, it did exist in the form of a clutter of regional attitudes and prejudices of which I had direct experience, in 1944/45, in the course of a year spent in Roubaix (I was there too for VE Day). Both Lille and Roubaix have their own anthems, now appropriate mainly to football occasions (the former, *'Le Petit Quinquin'*, the latter the more obvious *'Roubaix, Roubaix'*), which were sung in unison on the trains that took the young *Roubaisiens* and *Roubaisiennes* off to forced labour in the Ardennes in the spring of 1915. What town can do better than have its own municipal anthem!

p.48 JUNE '41
p.64 Nov.'42
p.72 from 1943 on
see p.67

3

Paris Collaborationism:
French and Germans

*Le soldatenéme, dit-il . . . y a pas bon. Les Fridolins, ils sont
un peu trop fortiches pour moi . . .*[7]

*. . . Tout à l'heure, un Boche m'a demandé son chemin dans la
rue. Il voulait aller à l'Etoile. Je l'ai envoyé à la Bastille . . .*[8]

(Jean Dutourd, *Au Bon Beurre*)

*fei te pas de movesan on va iberleiben de-chir set letre,
orvor . . .*[9] *(Message addressed to his nineteen-year-old son in
the Southern Zone by a Polish Jew on his departure from
Drancy)*

(Henri Amouroux, *Les Passions et les haines*)

It would be tempting – and not necessarily inaccurate – to
describe an occupation regime in the crude and simple terms
of exploiters and exploited, and, certainly, from the autumn of
1942 and the spring of 1943, Franco-German relations, under
the pressure of increasing need, took on more and more that
simple and ancient relationship. But, especially at the start, in
the unbelievable (as much to the astonished victors as to the
shattered French) outcome of May/June 1940, the two-way

relationship was often much more complicated, more sophisticated, and, indeed, politer than that. There existed, on both sides, ties of friendship that had been created in the interwar years; and, finding themselves, almost overnight, in control of the complicated administration of a capital city – an event for which they had never planned (they had brought along an ageing, well-tried blueprint for a military administration of the Lille area), the Germans sought out in the first place those Frenchmen and Frenchwomen whom they already knew. A German railway engineer would seek out his opposite number, a German detective would have contacts in the *police judiciaire*, a German army medical officer would know some of the *pontifes* of Boucicaut, Bichat, Broussais and Lariboisière. Abetz, of course, had formed an enveloping pattern of relationships in the French literary world and in *le Tout-Paris*. One of the young university graduates who was all at once to find himself in charge of Paris publishing had written a thesis on a French literary theme and had spent several years as a *lecteur d'allemand* in the University of Toulouse. He embarked on his new task with a sense of personal excitement, for it offered him a unique opportunity to come into close personal contact – sometimes daily – with all the leading figures of the Parisian literary scene. To see him merely as a censor, the obedient instrument of the *Propaganda staffel*, would be to oversimplify a relationship that was much more personal and vital. He wanted to get to know as many novelists and poets as possible, and to publish as many of their works as he could. In both aims, he was extraordinarily successful; and at the end of an idyllic four-year stay in the French capital – a city that he loved – he could look back to a publishers' list of enormous distinction and variety. His concern throughout had not been to patronize as wide a range as possible of novels in order to illustrate the intelligence and moderation of the German cultural authorities – though the sheer variety of his list would have given much weight to such an interpretation – but to see into print the works of a host of authors whom he admired and liked.

Indeed, some of the well-educated young men in their late twenties and early thirties who all at once found themselves in positions of limitless authority in July 1940 were often sought out by French teenagers of both sexes, not because they were powerful and could exercise patronage, but because they were good-looking, fair and charming. Montherlant was not the only Frenchman to succumb to a sexual attraction for the well-groomed, blue-eyed victors. So many of these young Germans carried with them the mystery pertaining to foreigners, the physical representatives of a new race of heroes, and the fascination associated with total victory (and total humiliation). The French system had failed, so let us try to find out about the German system that had been crowned with such prestigious success. *Courir au-devant du vainqueur* is a reaction not necessarily as mean and as calculating as it sounds, and such admiration could be genuine, even if starry-eyed. And of course the recipients of such adulation were not just dumb instruments of Goebbels or Ley; they, too, were young and susceptible, and, as all would recall, Paris in the summer of 1940 was alluringly beautiful (so was Paris in the summer of 1944).

The collaborationists, technically traitors (and often punished as such) were not always the dupes, nor the servile instruments, of the Germans, even though they were bound to compete among themselves for German favour, because without the Germans, they would not have amounted to very much, would indeed have been nothing. But there were limits – depending on the individual – beyond which many could not be pushed. Paquis, for instance, emerges from his memoirs, written in Fresnes while he awaited execution, as quite a plucky little fellow, often involved in monumental rows with his

German superiors, as well as a disarming humourist. Men of such total and creeping servility as de Brinon or Benoist-Méchin were rare, even in ultracollaborationist ranks.

In fact, it was seldom a one-way relationship. The Germans, too, could be fooled (though their anger would be extremely dangerous). Above all, they too had their personal motivations and vested interests, especially in secure employment under the occupation regime. Those holding down temporary, or semi-permanent, jobs in delectable Paris were, of course, the object of intense jealousy and even hostility on the part of those who found themselves engaged in the dreadful war in the East. No one in Paris (or elsewhere in France) could feel entirely safe from the dreaded threat of a posting to the East. So they needed to exaggerate the importance of the various empires that they had created for themselves within the chaos of competing Paris administrations; and this meant inflating the importance of their French clients, who in this respect, especially from 1943 onwards, were in the process of becoming their associates, if not their masters. Abetz could no more dispense with Luchaire than Luchaire with Abetz; and one could point to a similar two-way relationship right down the scale of administrative hierarchies. The French had their respective patrons, but these had to convince Berlin (and Berlin spoke with a great many voices) that their protégés were worth patronizing and offered more than just the negative value of keeping someone else – less desirable – out. Only Sauckel and the *Gestapo* did not need to seek out French cooperation; but even the *Gestapo* would have been largely ineffective had it been deprived of the willing services of its spare rib, *le Gestapo français*.

Ultimately, all those who had succeeded in holding onto quite delightful posts in the French capital had to persuade increasingly hard-pressed higher authorities in Berlin that a French policy of some sort was worthwhile and that the French were worth wooing. Indeed, agreeable posts elsewhere had to be justified to superiors, posts in Dijon, Toulouse, Montauban, Bordeaux. The officer in charge of relations with the Bordeaux press told his friends among the journalists that nothing could have upset him more than to have to leave the city, especially if it were to go east; Lille was not much sought after, but even *it* was infinitely better than the Russian Front. At quite a humble level, in the case of Haefs – the limpetlike official who had attached himself to *Radio Paris*, following it, like a rejected suitor, from Paris to Nancy, thence to Belfort and Sigmaringen – could no doubt be reproduced over and over again. For Haefs, there *had* to be a *Radio Paris*, however useless it might be once it had set up tent in Germany, because it was the alibi that protected him from the Eastern Front.

Whatever directives came down from the various competing feudatories in Berlin – and there was a wide and constantly shifting variety of French (or anti-French) policies – at Paris level relations between *occupants* and *occupés* were obscured, twisted and complicated by all sorts of nuances of personal relationships, ranging from complete mutual trust to a jarring acrimony. Paquis always seems to have been difficult to handle, and he was by no means the only Paris collaborationist who had succeeded in persuading himself that he was a French patriot – what is more a Lorrainer (he was actually of lower-middle-class origin from the Vosges) – and that the Germans had some rather unpleasant national characteristics. For Paquis, one sometimes feels, the Germans were not really *worthy* of Hitler, and they fell short of the Nazi ideal. Céline was to end up lumping all Germans with the extensive ragbag of his other hate-figures. Ultimately, collaborationism would be subjected to a multiplicity of Franco-German likes and dislikes. Such and such a collaborationist would all at once fall out of favour; a few (Deloncle was one of them) were even liquidated when they became a nuisance. But such and such a protector might fall out of favour too, caught, along with his French protégés (and accomplices) with his hand in the till. As Delarue has shown in *Trafics et crimes sous l'Occupation*, collaborationism could spread downwards into some extremely murky areas involving *le milieu* and the bad boys from the Berlin criminal underworld. For, at the crudest level, collaboration could be a mutually profitable racket; indeed, from 1943 on, it became one increasingly so.

So the fascination exercised by the study of collaborationism on the historian (especially the Anglo-Saxon one) can be attributed partly to unfamiliarity with something outside the national experience, but, perhaps even more, to the sheer range of mutual personal situations involved in what was always a changeable, even fast-moving, process.

In most cases, collaboration represented a business relationship profitable to both parties. It could not be all take and no give. The German censor got French books published and French films financed. The reading public – bigger than ever since there was little else to do during the long nights of the curfew and many people read in bed – was satisfied with a particularly brilliant harvest; the film public was kept amused, and the Germans were provided with evening entertainment. French compositors – many of them former *CGT-istes* – set the type for the daily *Pariser Zeitung* with the same professional skill and the same indifference to content as they had, in peacetime, for the continental edition of the *Daily Mail*. The Germans took over most of the best hotels, while retaining their regular staff. It was presumably all the same for a chambermaid in the Crillon or a night porter in the George-V to cater for the needs of German tourists in uniform as to cater for those of American tourists in civilian clothes. At Chez Maxim's and at similar prestige restaurants it would be a matter of course for a white-coated waiter to go on waiting in white gloves, for what was a waiter to do, if not to wait? Indeed, in this respect, it would be important to take into account the binding element of habit and familiarity. Four years is a long time – long enough for the barman of Fouquet's to be able to greet his regular German customers by name and to serve them drinks without these being named. A recent book, *Paris in the Third Reich*, describes the genuine distress of the waiters and maids of one of the big hotels when their customers of four years' standing proceeded to pack up in the second half of August 1944. They had grown used to them and accustomed to meeting their unstated needs. People in the hotel, catering or restaurant business are cosmopolitan as much from habit as out of interest, and it is in the nature of their work to deal more with foreigners than with their own compatriots. The Germans seem to have been quite generous with tips, they were not given to quibbling over bills and they represented the ideal sort of customer in the hotel trade: the long-staying resident. Even the legendary newspaper lady at her *kiosque* who is supposed to have greeted her morning customer on something over 1,200 mornings (Sunday presumably excluded?), as she handed him the *Pariser Zeitung* with '*voici ta feuille, grand con*', was not expressing any deep-rooted hostility to the uniformed reader. There is something disarmingly familiar both about '*grand con*' and the *tutoiement*, even if it clearly did not get through to the thick-headed and rather obtuse *Feldwebel*. Equally, it is hard to spend four years working with a group of people without some sort of familiarity developing; this might take the form of mutual respect at a shared professional level, or of amusement, irritation, or sheer exasperation. In any case, unlike the forbidden areas of pavement, the barriers would be down and some form of dialogue would be possible.

Parisians had become so used to the physical public presence of the Germans that when, all at once, the helmeted sentries in

Richard Cobb

their boxes outside the Majestic were withdrawn – and this had
happened discreetly at night, so that the boxes were seen to be
empty in the morning – they simply could not believe their
eyes. Even the two nervous and heavily-armed sentries seen by
Guéhenno posted on the Pont-Neuf, holding their grenades
with one hand, their machine-pistols in the other, long after the
fall of the prefecture of police, were not immediately killed; it
was only after three hours that the two poor wretches who had
overstayed their welcome were quietly shot in the back by a
couple of civilians. The Germans had been there so long that
they had even succeeded in imposing on the daily awareness of
Parisians an alien topography over the familiar grid of streets
and boulevards and *métro* lines: *lazaret* this way, supply services
that way, the place de l'Opéra a veritable semaphore of boldly
lettered wooden pointers in red and black. Once the Germans
had gone, *sans trompette ni fanfare*, the signposts briefly stayed
up, pointing to destinations now meaningless and to institutions that were no longer there. There was a sort of shocked
pause as though of disbelief, before the message sank in and
people set about pulling them down and piling them onto a
bonfire. If, as some of my French friends have asserted, there
hung about the Germans a smell – a combination of leather
and after-shave – that was unique to them, well, then it was a
smell to which they had become fully accustomed and that
must have acquired a *droit de cité* almost as tenacious as the hot
breath of the *métro* or the odour of garlic that used to linger so
lovingly on the Orléans-Clignancourt line. No doubt it was a
smell that would be sorely missed by a certain number of Parisian women.

Collaboration is an endlessly elastic concept that is not easy
to define. Was anyone who worked, directly or indirectly, for
the Germans a collaborator? Was the driver of a *métro* train a
collaborator because in the first-class carriage somewhere well

74

behind his box, in the middle of the *rame*, there were German, as well as French, passengers, wedged fraternally like close-packed sardines? Was the driver of a *vélo-taxi* who hauled in the little wicker basket behind him two stout German officers a collaborator? One recent author at least, David Pryce-Jones, in the severity of his indictment of the Parisians – pretty well *all* the Parisians – would seem to suggest as much. He even manages to compare Paris unfavourably to Warsaw. It is certainly true that, as a result of their rising, the inhabitants of Warsaw managed to get their city largely razed to the ground. If Hitler had had his way, Paris would have been similarly reduced to rubble. The author in question seems to have regarded it as a sort of moral failing on the part of the Parisians that it wasn't. Few everyday people would be very likely to subscribe to a patriotism so demanding. *Occupants* and *occupés* at least agreed that life had to go on: an eminently sensible aim.

With this in view, collaboration often took the form of government and administration on a putting-out basis. The Germans gave the orders; the French carried them out. In return for a rather dubious semblance of sovereignty – more of an appearance than a reality – the *Gestapo* and the other police bodies delegated the exercise of repression to the French police, and, later, to the *Milice* (or, rather, they stood aside and left the *Milice* to get on with its own programme of torture and killing). Such an arrangement clearly suited the Germans, who, from the start, were desperately short of repressive personnel, even after Knochen and Oberg had set up shop in the avenue Foch and had expanded the various services of the *SD*: a total of ten thousand police of various affiliations, including the *Feldgendarmerie*, the main concern of which was military crime. The French, on the other hand, could offer a total force of a hundred thousand police (including the *gendarmerie*, but not including the *Milice*), ten thousand of whom were available in the Paris area (another author, Azéma, puts the figure as high as twenty thousand, on the basis of the total force of the *agents de la paix* who went on strike in the prefecture of police in August 1944). A formidable force, then, and, after 1942, with the formation of the *Sections Spéciales*, often an extremely zealous one, several Paris *commissaires de police* – Poinsot, David, Rigal, Rotée – earning notoriety in their eagerness to track down Communists and *résistants*. The Paris police as a whole were to receive a number of testimonies to their effectiveness as partners in collaboration and repression from Knochen and his colleagues. There were no doubt exceptions – many refer to individual *commissaires* who gave advance warnings of an impending *rafle* – but the general impression is that, despite the dismissal of Chiappe in 1936, the Paris police remained much as he had recruited it, and that those of higher rank were often politically motivated and had certainly not taken kindly to the experience of the Popular Front, even if individual *agents*, so many of them of peasant origin from the Haute-Saône and the Haute-Marne, had likewise the greatest antipathy for students and *lycéens*, of whatever political leanings. It was certainly a brutal and extremely effective force.

At the public level of collaborationism, the relationship seldom seems to have gone much beyond this everyday, businesslike partnership (though the partners were not equal). Senior and junior partners might dine together in the evenings (the Germans playing hosts in the vanquisheds' capital) or attend social functions that might – or might not – have a propaganda value (the test would be the presence or the absence of photographers and reporters from *Signal*). It seldom seems to have gone beyond such necessary administrative *politesses*. Even the French ultracollaborationists – the French nazis – stuck to their French wives or mistresses, and, in the last stages of the war, they travelled with them and their children to

Germany, transporting thither their often trivial and unedifying quarrels, jealousies and panics. The leading Germans kept
their wives in the Reich (supplying them with the luxury products of the rue de la Paix), or sought consolation among the
German womens' services on the spot. It was a relationship
in which both parties kept their distances and maintained a
certain reserve.

Collaborationism is a more public and political form of collaboration. The latter could also extend to a multitude of varying
personal relationships, ranging from the timid, tender plant of
love between individuals, a situation generally disastrous to
both parties concerned and subjected to the terrible fragility
imposed by a military situation in the rapidly changing conditions of war, to collusion between black marketeers (Joanovici,
'Monsieur Jo', though a Bessarabian Jew, thrived from such
underground transactions with the German supply services), or
the sporting rivalry between French and German torturers: rue
Lauriston versus avenue Foch. There were other, intermediate
levels; not all Franco-German idylls followed the tender path
of Tristan and Iseult or of *Hiroshima mon amour*. Many French
women latched onto the Germans for what they could get out of
them, whether in the form of presents, or the more elusive goal
of marriage (German serving soldiers were not allowed to marry
Frenchwomen nor those of other occupied countries, though,
presumably, at least up to 1943, they could marry Italians). In 1940
or 1941, a German husband might seem much the best hold on
the future; he was the man of the future, Germany was the
country of the future, and the passport to the Thousand Year
Reich would be a husband of that nationality. As it turned out,
such calculations were to prove short-term investments; by 1943,
the *côte* of the uniformed German male was already beginning
to plummet, and by the summer of 1944, innumerable similarly minded French girls – including a number of Marseille

prostitutes from the rue des Couteliers – had concluded that the GI was the man of the future. He was also much easier to marry. Wars always widen the areas of matrimonial tourism, and, after April 1945, a number of former French prisoners of war and labour deportees under the *STO* (Azéma puts the figure at about ten thousand, out of a total of one million and a quarter) were to elect to stay behind in a defeated Germany and to continue to cultivate thousands of hectares of rich Westphalian land, to run a hotel or a beer-house, or to tend with loving care vineyards in the Moselle or in Bavaria; this, too, could turn out to be a two-way process, with German husbands long since lost to sight and mind in the snow of the East.

In 1940 and 1941, at least, a German husband – or a German lover – would seem a most desirable catch for a *midinette*, an *arpète*, a cinema usherette or a *dactylo* from Belleville-Ménilmontant or the eastern suburbs. Even the *PCF* would make of natural inclination a political duty, for how better to fraternize? But a German husband being temporarily beyond administrative reach, one could at least make a less direct, more oblique, bid on the future by securing German children. By the middle of 1943, eighty thousand Frenchwomen – one would so much like to know of what classes and social origins, whether urban or rural, whether Parisian or provincial – had claimed children's benefits from the German military authorities and had requested German nationality for their offspring – and this only from the Occupied Zone; and Amouroux considers this figure to be only the tip of the iceberg. More banally, for the girl concerned with only short-term benefits, a German boyfriend could offer immediate and solid advantages not just to the working-class girl, but to the *lycéenne* from the XVIme and the VIIIme: *le prestige de l'étranger*, the hint of perversity and adventure, the wonderfully persuasive white dress uniform of a young *Luftwaffe* pilot, dinner in sumptuous surroundings, the best linen, starched napkins *en dindon*, fresh flowers on the table, heavy silver tableware, the obsequious deference of the waiters (one's own contemptible compatriots), the attentiveness and elaborate politeness of the officer in the uniform of the Master Race. This would add a delectable spice to the pleasure, the first step towards collaborationism, whether at a personal or at a public level, being a desire to opt out of one's own nationality and to cross the frontiers of an alien and adopted one.

One often senses that there is an element of rather childish provocation in such ostentatious forms of 'consorting with the enemy', a slap in the face to family and to compatriots – parlour games, *jeux interdits* indulged in by bored adolescents of the XVIme, games that could be quite agreeably combined with flirtations with the Resistance. Not a conscious *double jeu*, merely the excitement of trying out the temperature of the water at both ends of the pool: secret *résistante* in the afternoon, brassy *collaboratrice* by candle-light in the evening. A perverse game involving a double deception, nonetheless just a game, something not to be taken seriously. Also a claim to attention: 'Look at me. I've crossed the border. I've done the unspeakable. I've gone to the end of the journey.'

But, among grown-ups, such a proclamation of the latest version of an overgrown *épate-bourgeois* would become increasingly strident, aggressive and hysterical, as the situation of the Germans became more desperate and the sense of isolation and apartness from the national community increased, and as one after another line of retreat was closed behind them. It is so much easier – without being a great patriot or a committed *résistant* – to go along with a generally accepted national mood, however prudent, passive, lazy or plain cowardly, than thus to set foot on a foreign shore and proudly to display the pagan flags of the conqueror. There will always be a slightly mad, embittered minority within any national community – generally social misfits, academic or professional failures, people uneasy with a lower-middle-class background – only too eager to persuade themselves that the enemy begins at home. How Georges Darien, a rancorous *émigré de l'intérieur,* hated and despised the French! How he ranted on about their ugliness, their stunted physical appearance, their degeneracy, their racial contamination! The only difference was that Darien did not have a heroic *foreign* race to which to transfer his admiration; while despising all Latins and reserving his choicest scorn for Belgians, he did not idealize the north Europeans, though he had a sneaking regard for the English and a healthy fear of English judges and lawcourts.

Céline and Drieu harped on similar themes, while Rebatet – more than any of the others – describing himself as a French nazi, wanted desperately to be a German one. The Germans presumably treated him with amused contempt. For them it would have seemed like dressing up a monkey in German uniform.

Perhaps such attitudes represented a form of self-hatred. There was certainly a considerable element of this in the case of Drieu, though he was an intellectual who was prepared to try anything once – he had tinkered with surrealism, sipped briefly at the Marxist table, flirted with internationalism and pacifism, pondered, like his fellow trifler and narcissist, Malraux, on the Wisdom of the East, hovered between pederasty and lechery, between cruelty to women and delight in their (necessarily admiring) company. He prostrated himself before the German conquerors, then became disillusioned with them (which was something entirely predictable, for Drieu had never stuck to *anything,* picking up this or that toy only to throw it away in a tantrum). Even his collaborationism seems to have been tepid and rather half-hearted, not unlike that of the sad and ageing naughty boy, Cocteau (indeed, even in their forties and fifties Drieu, Cocteau and Brasillach remained utterly spoilt, rather *bored,* children, who had never grown up and never ceased to attitudinize, in public and in private); the only time that the sickly, effete Drieu actually went through with something, went to the end of the road, was when he committed suicide in April 1945, the logical conclusion of a life of frittered futility.

There is also no mistaking in such attitudes the expressions of misguided pride and ultimate arrogance, as if it should have been of some world-shaking importance as to *what* choice they should have made, *what* side they should have deigned to come down on (there was, of course, as much arrogance in the attitude of a Gide pointedly – and in print – electing to remain Above It All), as though the future of civilization were to rest on their agonized decisions. There is apparently no limit to the conceit – and to the humourlessness – of a French intellectual, ever ready to pontificate in public on this issue or that. Guéhenno refers – with disgust – to the *Manifesto of the French Intellectuals* of March 1942, in which a choice selection of the Elect took it upon themselves publicly to denounce – poor shades of Bertrand Barère – the crimes of Britain and of the British government. Guéhenno believes that they did it to order, so as to please the Germans. It is much likelier that they did it in order to get themselves into print. It is an interesting document, grouping Céline, Drieu and Brasillach with such literary hacks as Donnay, Ajalbert, Amiel and Fernandez, grateful no doubt to have conquered at least a *strapontin* in such an august literary academy.

Then, at least in the case of Drieu, Brasillach and Montherlant, there was the veritable obsession with what they regarded as the Decadence of the West (these people thought in capitals and in the points of the compass, as if they had been literary geopoliticians), an unconscious mirror-image perhaps, as all three were indeed decadent, and their form of collaborationism droops like a sickly flower out of Baudelaire's enervating

greenhouse. As the West is decadent, let us look further East –
but not too *far* East – to the virile Nazis: a dangerous geography
that could indeed direct the committed gaze even farther eastwards, this time towards the equally virile Soviets.

Such attitudes also represent a rather pathetic form of self-
deception (similar to Rebatet's fantasies when attempting to
will himself into the skin of a German). In his candid and often
humorous and observant account of the shrinking French
community in Sigmaringen and beyond to the shores of Lake
Constance, Paquis convinces us that, as this group becomes
more and more hopelessly committed to the consequences of
German defeat and disaster, in their personal attitudes, their
paltry disputes, their small acts of cowardice and deceit, their
evasions and their lies, or in the maintenance of a sort of desperate Parisian *gouaille*, they somehow become more, not less,
French, almost caricatures of themselves, each playing up his
or her provincial origins. The *méridionaux*, underneath the
Teutonic firs, become even more southern, and as they wander
through the pretty little German villages in their light-coloured
suits, white silk mufflers, loud ties and black-and-white shoes,
the *galéjades* pour out, and, with every move further away
from the Midi, the accents become increasingly *pointu*. The
Corsicans too seem set to revert to the peculiar mores of their
island, while the Parisian *a*'s lengthen. A similar self-caricature
can be observed among the companions of Tiffauges, the
French prisoners of war in their camp in faraway East Prussia
at the other end of Europe, in Tournier's novel *Le Roi des Aulnes*.

What could be more French than the way Christian de la
Maizière, when questioned as to how the members of the Division Charlemagne had described Hitler in conversations among
themselves, replied, without hesitation, as if it were the most
natural thing in the world: '*le Grand Jules, quoi!*' There was a
vague awareness of this ineradicable complicity as it were *entre*

Français, even among their enemies and executioners, when they treated the star prisoners of Fresnes with a degree of gentle pity, as fellow children who had somehow taken the wrong turn and had been unable to find their way back. Treason no doubt brings its own form of *frisson*; but the taste of treason must be very bitter when it is discovered that, however far one travels down that dangerous path (generally a lonely one, for, in Sigmaringen and beyond, there seems to have been little solidarity among fellow traitors, each driven more and more onto his own resources, couples scuttling furtively in different directions as time ran out), the Germans would never accept one as one of their own. The best they could do would be to offer such people diplomatic passports, false identities, considerable sums in Swiss francs, transport, a fighter plane, to enable them to get out *anywhere*. They were not even to be allowed the ultimate and saving grace of being permitted to participate in the purely national experience of total German collapse, as if their German masters wanted them out of the way so that they would not witness the death agony of the Third Reich. So they became unhappy, bewildered refugees in an indifferent Switzerland mainly concerned to pass them on, in a hostile Denmark, in a grudging Spain, till most at least crept back towards France, knocking on the door for readmission to a national community, to a national family that they had rejected, even if it meant the firing squad. At least the firing squad would be French. That at least seems to have been the message of the last, deeply moving pages of Paquis's memoirs. From the time when, with a sort of relief, he had been dumped on the French side of the border, at Bâle, by a Swiss taxi, till the date of his execution a year and one month later, Paquis had succeeded in coming to terms with himself and with his identity as a Frenchman and a *Vosgien*. One believes him when he asserts that he felt no hatred towards his political adversaries, and that, though they had fought on opposite sides, in what was, in late 1943 and in the bloody spring and summer of 1944, in the process of becoming a full-scale French civil war (a war prolonged judicially, or without even the semblance of justice, almost for another year, in the bitter vengeance of *l'Epuration*), they all remained *entre Français*, understanding one another as such. The vulgar and strident broadcaster of *Radio Paris*, heard every day from July 1940 to mid-August 1944 – few can have put more energy into collaboration, few can have worked harder in that dubious cause, *none* can have enjoyed himself so much; for Paquis, collaborationism had been a daily, perhaps even hourly, pleasure, a triumphant assertion of a talent and a personality not previously revealed (or only hinted at in his previous experience as a French speaker for *Radio Saragossa*), a reminder that national disaster can often be turned to individual advantage. The steady purveyor of hate acquired dignity, serenity, silence and a sense of peace in his last months in Fresnes, as he listened to the distant sound of the *métro, ligne de Sceaux*, a last link with a Paris that he would never see again. (Perhaps this was a merciful dispensation in its way, for how much crueller was the fate of those *résistants*, many of them Communists from the eastern and northeastern districts, noticed and heard by Guéhenno, who, in 1943, were driven from Fresnes right through Paris, almost from end to end, from the Porte d'Orléans to the Porte Maillot, in closed lorries, crammed together, and singing the whole way through the city that they could not even see, though, from the varying level of sounds, the more experienced Parisians among them were able to follow their tracks, before being shot at the Mont-Valérien?)

The terrible price of readmission to the bosom of *la famille française* would be the exemplary courage that most displayed, as a last gesture of complicity, a sort of desperate *politesse* when facing their executioners: Brasillach wearing a long, elegant red scarf, Paquis in his best suit, a bit frayed, but ironed, a plucky little chap at just over five feet, Bucard in the tatters of a uniform, Darnand, having written to de Gaulle – he got a reply – as from one soldier to another, thanking the soldiers of his firing squad, Bassompierre (whose brother had been killed on the other side, in the Resistance) cracking jokes, Paul Chack dignified in old age. The manner of their deaths was recorded at the time by their executioners, by the prison doctor, the chaplain, or the Protestant minister, as a sort of epitaph to lives that, for one reason or another, had taken a wrong turn. Only de Brinon seems to have failed in this ultimate and terrible test. Most met their end bravely, *à la française*, one or two puffing on a *gauloise* hanging on the lower lip, almost to the last breath.

At whatever level, whether timid, flirtatious or brassily calculated, run-of-the-mill technical and administrative, cultural or repressive, ideologically convinced or brutally cynical, collaboration and collaborationism would normally remain a temporary and largely accidental relationship, imposed by quite exceptional circumstances, for which there was no recent precedent, as well as by unique opportunities (for most collaborationists, whether Parisian or *Vichyssois*, 1940 was a sort of golden year that opened up undreamt of opportunities, eagerly seized on while the going was good), and confined within a time space of four years and one month – not a very large chunk out of an average life, though, however brief, a chunk that would generally have disastrous consequences for those lucky enough to have survived, even if time would generally erase the record of such unwise youthful choices. (Who would recall today, apart from two Anglo-Saxon historians concerned to put the record straight on the French origins of anti-Semitism and of anti-Semitic legislation, Maurice Duverger's youthful and wholehearted commitment to the violent politics of the PPF and to a legalized anti-Semitism?) For only a tiny minority of collaborationists had opted for the German variety of national socialism before 1940. Indeed, most could not have seen ahead to the fact that, in the circumstances of 1940, they would have chosen to become collaborationists. How could they have done so? Collaboration was not a profession bequeathed by father to son, at least in France; in Belgium, Flemish collaborationism spans two generations, even offering some of its leading protagonists the chance of a replay the second time around. In the previous war, there had been hardly any collaborators, at least in a political sense, and such as they were – like the small group of journalists of the *Gazette des Ardennes* – they were very small fry indeed, just seedy, paid-up traitors.

How could anyone, even in the summer of 1940, have foreseen that he or she would all at once embark on the even more perilous path of resistance? For no one could have foreseen the little spark of anger, the indignity of visible humiliation, that might push one over. Collaboration and resistance are both eminently personal stances that have no past, whether familial or historical, though it could no doubt be argued that some French Protestants would not have needed to be reminded of what *résister* meant in French historical terms. Only the lowest hacks of collaboration, *dénonciateurs* and *dénonciatrices*, could look back to past experience and to previous opportunities. It is true that a few special categories of people were likely to be excluded from the start from the tempting option of collaboration. Most Jews and gypsies, foreign refugees and Spanish republicans, not to mention enemy aliens, most of whom were interned (though there were one or two English collaborators operating in France during these years), were automatically placed outside the recruitment areas of collaboration, normally a privilege – of a sort – reserved for Frenchmen of non-Jewish descent (the fact that there did exist one or two Jewish collaborationists does not invalidate this general point). Such people, by virtue of their origins, were much more likely to enlist in the ranks of the Resistance, out of sheer desperation and as the only means of possible survival. There were a few black and creole collaborationists; and there was at least one English *vichyssois* (it is true that, for his services, Sisley Huddleston was rewarded with French naturalization, as a personal gift from Marshal Pétain).

No one – either French or German or anyone else (save one or two worried British observers of French morale during the 'phoney war') – could have foreseen the scale of the catastrophe of May/June 1940, though, once it came, there were many, from Pétain down – revealed as a very active, positive conspirator and defeatist, with lists already written and ready in his pocket, in the Prefecture of the Gironde – who sprang at the opportunity offered by such a totality of defeat. As Ory has pointed out, no one was born a collaborationist, it was not a virus in the blood and, though Louis Marin, Philippe Henriot, Emile Buré, and Henri de Kérillis came from similar backgrounds in interwar politics, they made totally different choices in 1940. No one could be *forced* into a situation of collaborationism, but for those already occupying positions of great power and responsibility the temptation must often have been very great. The greater the responsibility, the more insistent the appeal. It is a natural assumption among those used to authority and obedience to consider themselves indispensable.

Some *occupants* would return, quite unashamedly – for they had really enjoyed their time in France and considered themselves, therefore, as francophils – a few years later: former *Luftwaffe* personnel were much in evidence in the Tournon, a *café-tabac* opposite the Luxembourg, in the 1950s, this time as *real* tourists. A certain number of Frenchwomen presumably settled in Germany, once access to the French, British or American zones became easier for non-German civilians; for, while

serving German officers and soldiers were not allowed to marry
French girls, there would be nothing to prevent them from
doing so once they had returned to civilian life. But such individual instances of collaboration pushed to the extreme frontiers
of domestic privacy will generally elude us, just as much as it is
impossible to calculate how many – if any – German deserters
managed to remain undetected in their hiding-places in Paris or
elsewhere under the protection of their French female friends –
for a deserter cannot last more than a few days without the active
complicity of a woman, just as his most dangerous enemy is
another woman – before reemerging in the more favourable
conditions of the mid-fifties. (Unfortunately, the records of the
Feldgendarmerie and of German courts-martial are missing.) We
only know of those few who were caught and shot, like the poor
young man whose execution was witnessed by Ernst Jünger in
the woods round Fontenay-aux-Roses, the promenades for Sunday lovers and family walkers. (Military executioners seem to
favour Sunday walks, and Guéhenno, in a succession of Sunday
visits to La Fosse-aux-Loups, noted the gradual elimination, at
the level of a human heart, of first one tree, then two; perhaps
the shooting-grounds favoured the countryside south of Paris
because of its proximity to Fresnes?) A few *must* have got away,
to judge at least from the number of GI deserters, many of them
black, to be encountered living quite openly in the VIme
and doing their shopping, marché de Buci, with big black
cabas – the surest emblem of having crossed the nationality
barrier – accompanied by their French mistresses and their
Franco-American children. If Heinrich Böll is a reliable witness –
and there is no more convincing recorder of the dread fears of
poor German soldiers as they travelled on the long iron trains to
the horrors of the East, nor of the pathetic and hopeless attempts
briefly to discard the uniform of servitude, the livery of death,
by seeking refuge in the privacy and warmth of domestic peace

or in some little room inhabited by feminine tenderness – according to this German novelist, it had even been possible for a Russian prisoner of war to live in hiding with a German woman on the outskirts of a town in the Third Reich in the middle and at the end of the war, protected and surrounded by a whole network of attentive accomplices. It is a comforting story not totally improbable. For, even in the most totalitarian regimes, there subsist little chunks of undiscovered privacy, small, closed kingdoms of successful rejection of the iron demands of the military collectivity; this was true certainly in France, and even more so in the well-organized anarchy of Brussels – rue Haute, rue Blaes, a warren of steep streets, in les Marolles, where people simply disappeared, for months, even years. The *Feldgendarmerie* was not all that infallible, not all that efficient, remaining largely dependent on the unsolicited – but well-rewarded – help of *dénonciatrices*; and these would have little chance of effective survival in closed communities, well accustomed to the vigilant discipline of clandestinity and to living beyond the reach of the law and of a fixed identity.

Brussels – or those parts of it which lay on the steep slopes separating *la ville haute* from *la ville basse*, a sort of neutral frontier zone where, like the lion and the lamb, *occupants* and *occupés* might, literally, lie down together, or even reverse rôles, along with outward clothing – Brussels had a fixed place in the recent hierarchies of the New European Order as the capital of crime and of the black market and as the centre of a European trade in false identities, passports, military paybooks, ration cards, *laissez-passers* cut through with impressive diagonals in various national colours, police passes that, readily flashed would open the steel doors of the fortresses of torture and repression. The extraordinary resilience of the place may be judged by the fact, witnessed by myself with a sort of admiration in September 1944, that, within three days of the Liberation of the city, British army uniforms, leather jerkins, webbing and boots, brown books and paybooks, and even army-issue typewriters were quite openly on sale in the various flea markets off the Porte de Hal. Sten guns and other weapons would shortly follow. The providers of outfits so complete as to offer the full panoply of a British or a Canadian soldier from head to foot, plus accompanying haversacks and small arms, must be presumed to have themselves been transformed, in a matter of minutes, into equally convincing civilians, fully-equipped *Marolliens*, *de cap à pied*, incapable of speaking a single word of either French or Flemish, much less of the wonderfully hybrid *marollien* (though that would no doubt come in due course), their pockets bulging with a generous selection of real identities and of papers that were in fact not false. This ability to adjust, as it were overnight, to the needs and opportunities offered by an entirely new situation was the most striking testimony to the skills acquired by a population long trained in all the tricks of living below the level of the law, skills that ranged from those of engravers and of the manufacturers of impressive-looking rubber stamps, to those of pickpockets and of head-to-foot ten-minute (the time to transform a man and to send him out with all the appearances of a convincing civilian) tailors.

With the help of a devoted woman, a man could live in security in les Marolles, or, for that matter, in the quartier du Sentier, the Goutte-d'Or, the faubourg Montmartre, the Halles or Belleville-Ménilmontant in Paris. The German authorities were well aware of the existence of such relatively safe, almost impenetrable, enclaves in most large French cities (la Guille, la Croix-Rousse, les Terreaux, in Lyon; Martainville and Eau-de-Robec in Rouen; le Pollet in Dieppe) and it was with this in mind that, in 1943, they set about evacuating, at a few hours' notice, the ten thousand inhabitants of the Vieux Port in

Marseille, before systematically blowing up the whole quarter, street by street. How many German deserters were revealed in the course of this vast operation we are not told (it is not the sort of thing that any military authority would be likely to trumpet from the rooftops) but one suspects that they must have been numerous – perhaps as numerous and as varied as the enormous animal population thus driven from its ancient refuges: armies of huge rats swimming for safety across the harbour, cows, goats, chickens, geese, rabbits herded away with their owners in other parts of the city. And we know, from a more recent war, just how effective a hide-out *la Casbah* could be as it cascaded down innumerable steps, like the *montées* of Lyon, in the very centre of Algiers.

Of course, it would presumably be much more difficult – not to say impossible – in the countryside, where the presence of an unfamiliar, and therefore suspicious, figure would be signalled from farm to farm, ahead of the increasingly despairing progress of the man himself, as he plunged hopelessly further and further into the woodland, into gorse, heather and marshland, following no specific course, moving unwittingly in circles, anxious only to avoid highroads and the outskirts of towns, open country and the exposure of bare hills. In such conditions, a deserter might be indistinguishable from a tramp or a gypsy, from any man who walked and wandered without being able to give a clear account of his movements, and who wasn't a pedlar or a woodcutter, or even a poacher, all people acceptable to a rural community and, as such, liable to be covered, in an enveloping complicity, from scrutiny further up. Indeed, he would *look* like a tramp, having buried his uniform – his external passport to respectability and recognition, enabling him to shelter within the at least identifiable communities of *occupants* and *occupés* and giving him the relatively harmless, because by now perfectly familiar, even banal trade name of *soldat allemand* (in the countryside, a more formal society, people neglected, or were ignorant of, collective terms of insult). And what farmer, what farmer's wife, would be prepared to take the terrible risk of taking in a uniform, or any part of it? He would have to clothe himself from such threadbare, ill-fitting and varied resources as were available: the shapeless coat and the bleached hat of a scarecrow, or some article of clothing stolen surreptitiously from a washing line or taken from a riverbank while the swimmer, luxuriating immobile on his back in the silvery water, looked up at the still perfection of a summer sky or at the scurrying clouds driven fast by the west wind. It would be unlikely in the extreme that he would be able to equip himself from head to foot in one single go, giving him the full and convincing walking-out gear of a recognizable civilian. There would be something missing, or he might keep his very identifiable *Wehrmacht* underwear or thick socks. Footwear would be the greatest problem, for people do not readily throw out shoes or boots while they still have a little life in them. And so the detailed description of the weird, tattered figure, in browns and blacks – *l'homme des bois* – would walk well ahead of him, causing prudent fear, the closing of bolts and the drawing of shutters: a tall man with straw-coloured hair and very blue eyes, a scraggy yellowish beard, talking gibberish, and expressing himself in gestures to indicate hunger, thirst, the desperate need to sleep.

We encounter just such a man wandering in the woods in the neighbourhood of the Breton town of Saint-Brieuc, in March 1944, in the first volume of Louis Guilloux's *Carnets*. He arrives at a farm in a pitiable condition; the farmer, just in from the fields, pulls up the bottoms of the man's trousers (he knows the drill, then – this is not the first time that he has encountered such a wanderer) and *there* is the giveaway sign: a pair of long, soft-leather boots. He has not succeeded in demobilizing his feet and legs; his upper half might pass as civilian, but he still walks, however wearily, as a soldier of the German army. He indicates by gesture that he would like to exchange his boots for a pair of *sabots* – the one thing that might enable him to *prendre la couleur du paysage* and allow him to prolong for a few more days or even weeks his perilous existence as a deserter (what chance has he got to survive from March to the relative safety of August?). He has already been refused *sabots* in half a dozen farms, and it will be the same in a dozen more. For the man on the run, the feet are the weak spot: he cannot walk barefoot in March, so he is stuck with his unmistakable boots – which, in popular memory, long after the departure of the *occupants*, are the very symbol of the strutting, stamping conqueror.

Give him a bowl of soup and a *pichet de cidre*, says the farmer, then send him on his way. The farmer, the *patron*, then returns to the fields. When he comes back, he is vexed to find that the man is still there. Well, let him just this once sleep in the hay, give him coffee in the morning and then send him on his way. The next morning, after the farmer has gone, the man persuades the womenfolk to let him help unload a cart of manure. He is trying to gain time. This the farmer has foreseen; he sends back one of his farm boys with the message: *patron* says *promenade*, accompanied by the unmistakable international gesture of dismissal; the poor man understands. He shakes hands elaborately with the wife and the daughters, kisses the children, sets off. But, still within sight, he turns back; more handshakes, more kisses for the children, then sets off again, without looking back. Later someone says that they have met the man further along and that he was crying.

And that is the last that we hear of the poor German deserter. There does not seem much hope for him, and one wonders how much more walking he will have to do before reaching the end of the road, the almost inevitable firing squad.

Guilloux, as delicate and discreet as he is compassionate, does not put the dots on the *i*'s; he refrains from mentioning the firing squad, leaving his reader desperately hoping that somehow the shambling and increasingly mad-looking figure may somehow survive in the Breton woods for another five months, when the Liberation would free him at least from the threat of death and when defeat would be victory for him, as well as for the French. Five months is a terribly long time, and when Guilloux leaves him – or, rather when the man simply walks out of the novelist's wonderfully evocative account of the occupation years in and around the small Breton town – all the odds seem to be against him. If only there could be a happy ending. Perhaps, after a few more days, he will encounter a compassionate and lonely woman – her husband a prisoner in Germany – who will take him in, feed him, and hide him in an attic. Such things have happened. But the countryside, even the depths of the *plat pays*, is like a public thoroughfare, lined with many eyes, all watchful and retentive. If the deserter is a townsman, there is very little hope for him as he stumbles on through bracken and undergrowth, moving in circles. Only a large city could offer an even chance for the deserter from the *Wehrmacht*.

Escape, then, could occasionally exist, in the realities of brick and stone, attic and cellar, courtyard and *impasse*. But thoughts of escape, the *illusion* of escape, of getting away from it all, of making a complete break, found their most persuasive refuges in those palaces of make-believe: *les salles obscures*. When considering the enormous success of the cinema during the Occupation – in Paris, audiences reached their highest figures in this century – one cannot make too much of *la nuit factice*, the comforting, enveloping night of the Rex, Normandie, Lord-Byron, Alhambra, in contrast to the stark blackout, the alarming night of the streets after curfew. *La nuit factice* is blue, silver and velvet, rather than black; it is warm, almost maternal; it is punctuated with brilliant light – a night of blue and silver, even a perfumed night. Robert Lageat and his female partner, *la môme Andréa*, are dressed in brilliant colours as they perform on the high wire – the most German film fantasies drip in rich technicolour (*Agfacolor*). *La nuit fantastique* is a very escape from the night. The *grandes salles* are warm, with the warmth of many bodies crowded together. French and German. This is perhaps the *only* terrain in which the *barrières blanches* are removed, the frontiers that, in real life, constantly emphasize the separation between *occupants* and *occupés*, an intermingling of ploying, exploratory hands, knees, feet, possible without the flags of national identification going up: here French and Germans can meet without being seen – or seen only briefly during the intervals (*chocolat glacé Esquimau*), their encounter, however brief and flickering, not being scrutinized.

It was a fantasy, an escape, a sense of liberty that might have as much attraction to the German soldier as to the French civilian. *L'Eternel Retour*, *Les Visiteurs du soir*, *Les Enfants du paradis* all offered as much a temporary escape – among the battlements and halls of medieval castles inhabited by dwarfs, reeking in magic, and in the presence of an engaging (Belgian) devil, or among the streets, noisy theatres and *bains chinois* of the *boulevard du Crime* – from the gnawing fear of what lay to the East (and reachable, from the Gare de l'Est and the Gare du Nord, by night train, even, for the high-ranking officer, by sleeper) as from the daily humiliations of occupation: privation, cold, loneliness, worry. Indeed, as a shared experience, and one shared perhaps several nights a week, it represented a disguised, yet potent, form of collaboration. Such films were seen – and appreciated – by French and German audiences, who responded to them at the same time (*Ooo!*) in similar fashion. But, more important, this was an experience from which the Anglo-Saxon (and Soviet) audiences were excluded, just as their reading public was excluded from an awareness of *L'Etranger* and similar works, so that there remained a cultural gap and a sentimental backlog of four years to be made up in 1944.

This, of course, applied both ways. The French could no doubt catch up on *Mrs. Miniver* after the Liberation; much more important was to be the colossal impact of *Citizen Kane* and of the Soviet films shown at the Cinéma du Panthéon. By the physical nature of occupation, *leisure* at least, especially in the collective form of welcome immersion in *les salles obscures*, was a type of *conversation à deux*, a conversation that, in an unknown but no doubt significant number of instances, resulted in actual verbal exchanges, and the first groping steps towards a hurried and unobserved intimacy.

Of course, the Germans could see films free in their own *Soldatenheime* (the best cinemas had been taken over for the *Wehrmacht*); yet one can be sure that many would prefer to attend the *grandes salles* individually, not perhaps in a conscious effort to commune with French civilians (though the foreign female presence would be a draw) as to escape, for an hour or two, from the constant collective promiscuity imposed by uniform. The *Soldatenheim* – like the *foyer du soldat* – was a trap, the purpose of which was to hold the individual soldier within the safer collectivity of nationality and of regimental or corps loyalty during the always potentially dangerous hours of leisure. In Lyon, the Germans seem to have managed to isolate their military personnel, many of them young recruits, from the civilian population altogether. But Paris, as a leave centre, as a reward for the active soldier, was a different matter. Capitals are dangerous places for military discipline and cohesion. Immersion in a *salle obscure* might be only the first step on an escape route that could end in desertion, or even, if he was caught, the firing squad. More often, it represented a brief step into fantasy and illusion. And fantasy and illusion were never more brilliantly exploited, in works of genius, of great subtlety, and in a strange language of hints and allusion, of *double-entendre*, than in the films of the German-controlled film consortium, La Continental, in 1942 and 1943.

After such a brief excursion, not entirely fanciful, I hope, into the vast palaces of dreams of the *grands boulevards* and the Champs-Elysées, it is time to return to more mundane matters, such as the various motivations that might be at the origins of commitment to one form or another of collaborationism. Among the French, one could at once distinguish between the tenacious careerists and adventurers eager to push themselves forward to meet the more menial needs of the occupying power, the immensely relieved and timorous souls for whom June 1940 spelt out the welcome message – something that seemed to make even total defeat worthwhile, namely that France was now out of the war – and the convinced idealists, however confused, flawed, or odious the causes of their commitment (anti-Semitism, antiparliamentarianism, elitism, the cult of leadership, corporatism, anglophobia, anti-Communism after 1941, and antifeminism). Those in the first category often seem to have been genuinely surprised by the degree of hostility they generally inspired among their less fortunate, less pushing, or more honourable compatriots. There had been a job going, and they had done that job. What could have been more natural? They were the sort of people who would have queued up to serve *any* occupier; indeed, Paquis suggests that quite a few, in *Radio Paris*, may have served the Americans after having served the Germans; for, as he and his friends were hastily packing their bags, prior to departure in German lorries to Châlons-sur-Marne and Nancy, he had had time to notice one or two familiar figures lurking outside the building in the Champs-Elysées, ready to move back in 'under new management'. Such people were not necessarily pro-German; it just happened that it was the Germans who had turned up. The Italians or the Russians would no doubt have met as ready a response; indeed, the latter possessed a far more effective potential fifth column than anything that had been available to the Germans before 1940, at a time when the adherents of the German Institute could be counted on one's fingers. (Attendance at German classes began to increase rapidly only at the *rentrée* of 1940, when the German Institute and Berlitz – an eagerly collaborationist institution from 1940 to 1944, when it switched massively to the teaching of English – both enormously expanded their facilities for the teaching of German.) The Soviets could count, at any time, on the disinterested devotion of a highly skilled army of potential – and no doubt dreadfully frustrated – collaborationists, longing to be employed and denied such an opportunity, though a number seem to have had little difficulty, at least in the summer of 1940, in switching to service with the Germans, who, in their anxiety to get Paris back to work, found them useful when seeking the cooperation of the old unions.

Careerist collaborationists of this type were prone to argue that if *they* had not volunteered for the job, someone else would have. By taking it on, they had protected their more timorous compatriots (and, sometimes, just to be on the safe side, they may even have done just that, laying in store for themselves testimonials on an uncertain future).

A related group of collaborationists would consist of those who, far from volunteering for new jobs, had merely gone on doing the jobs that they had had before the defeat. M. Langeron remained prefect of police, until he was removed in 1941. André Tulard remained at the *fichier central*, the pride of his life and the most elaborate system of identification then in existence. It was so much easier to *hold on* and to persuade oneself that this was the proper course of action, than to make a complete break and plunge into the unknown, family and financial interests apart. Also the resignation of a high-ranking official would be certain to be taken as an anti-German gesture that could have dangerous consequences for the protester and his family.

Some professions would be more exposed to the temptations of collaborationism than others, if only because they operated within an unusually brief time span and were subject to a sort of daily death and daily renewal. This would be especially the case for journalists and for those in related activities, such as caricaturists. A journalist who does not get out his daily column is no longer a journalist, he ceases to exist, falls into an unbearable and unremunerative obscurity. A novelist, a historian, a poet can afford the luxury of a temporary silence, an internal retreat, while waiting for better times (though, as we have seen, very few novelists and poets were prepared for such acts of self-immolation, and, throughout the Occupation – as before and after – Gide continued to indulge his taste for elaborate self-examination and to look at himself in the mirror of vanity, as if this were in some way to expel the shadow of the occupier). Déat – one feels – eagerly offered himself to the cause of ultracollaborationism, not just because he admired the Germans, wanted the New European Order to succeed, and looked to the Germans to satisfy his twenty-year-old thirst for supreme power as *chef* (or *Chef*), but also because he could not bear to cease hearing the sound of his own voice and reading his daily thoughts in print. Déat's greatest contribution to collaboration was not in the rôle of *chef*, a rôle so constantly denied him, but in the production of some thousands of editorials. From October 1940, when *L'Oeuvre* reappeared, *avec trompette et fanfare*, till late August 1944, when it disappeared, with an imperceptible whimper, rue Louis-le-Grand, Déat never missed a single issue. It is a colossal achievement and a suitable tribute to the man's limitless vanity. One wonders whether he gave much thought to his readers and to what they made of his tirelessly insistent message; one knows that he did not *have* very many readers. (At its height, in 1940/1, when its apparently pacifist appeal to those who had not wished to 'die for Danzig' was likely to be the most insistent, the paper reached a ceiling circulation of about 130,000 – as compared, in 1943, to the 300,000 copies of *Je suis partout*. But then Déat, with plenty of German money behind him – and all collaborationist journalists were also themselves extremely well paid – could afford to look beyond the circulation graph; he had never been interested in such mundane matters.) *L'Oeuvre* kept afloat not so much because of his editorials, but because the paper continued saying the same things. Déat was engaged in a daily dialogue with himself: *il s'écoute parler, il s'écoute écrire*.

There is a similar element of narcissism in most of the Paris journalists of these years (as there was in Gide, Drieu, Giono, Montherlant, and Brasillach), though none can have totted up quite so many articles as the indefatigable Déat. There was also between them a similar lack of talent and a common nastiness as they turned out their turgid output of hate – the capacity to hate collectively and continuously is perhaps the defining characteristic of the fascist, and it was no mere literary exercise, Déat looking forward with delectation to a France covered in concentration camps and to the crisp orchestra of the execution squads, while Brasillach lovingly evoked the advent of a French civil war longed for since the early thirties – or denounced one another for being weak on collaborationism. As Guéhenno observes, the full-blooded traitors denounced the demitraitors as not being the real thing; treason, too, it appeared, could be cut to several sizes. It was still a competitive world as between mediocre and mediocre, rancour and rancour, hate and hate, conceit and conceit. Perhaps the most surprising thing about these French nazis and fascists, all contestants for the leadership of their own particular brand of *parti unique*, is that they should have been such obsessive individualists.

It must have been the same with broadcasters, announcers, and caricaturists. Henriot, who was better heard than seen – he was strikingly ugly, with enormous protruding ears that gave him a batlike appearance, and eyes that seemed to fall out, in the intensity of their fanaticism (Trouillé has a memorable passage on the subject of Henriot's sepia photograph displayed all over Vichy following his assassination, and showing him in the black uniform of the *Milice*) – had a warm, velvet, caressing voice, giving no doubt a false impression of sincerity, as if he really cared about what he said. Even his London listeners had to admit that he was an extremely effective speaker. But he must have been his own most enthusiastic listener, and it is doubtful if he could have got through the day if he had not had his evening performance to look forward to, as its culmination and its reward. Here was a man who lived – and indeed died – for 9.15 P.M. As Guéhenno observes, with his usual acuteness (not unmixed with compassion), the circumstances of Henriot's death covered the man in a shroud too big for him. He was murdered because he had talked too much, an outsize conclusion to the life of a compulsive chatterbox (his conceit was offered an ironical posthumous tribute when his recorded voice was broadcast every night till the final departure of *Radio Paris* in August 1944, rather as if the voice had outlived its owner and had acquired a momentum of its own). To have expected Henriot to be silent would have been as pointless as to have expected Sacha Guitry to give up listening to the sound of his own voice. Moâ, too, could be heard, from the stage, pretty well every night of the Occupation, the summer closures excepted, as he talked to himself out loud, in the presence

Richard Cobb

of an ever appreciative Franco-German audience. Sacha's immense conceit could be accommodated *à toute sauce*. After the Liberation, he was punished according to his deserts: not shot, or anything drastic like that; merely reduced to silence, at least in public (he presumably continued to perform in front of his many mirrors in the privacy of his sumptuous apartment). When unable to bear it any longer, he decided to break the public silence imposed upon him by giving a performance at the casino of Charbonnières, outside Lyon; this was too much for the leaders of the Lyon Resistance, who kidnapped him and, having removed his trousers, made him kneel down in front of the *Monument de la Résistance*, on the corner of the place Bellecour and the rue de la République.

Paquis would not have amounted to very much if deprived of his microphone, a far more important part of his standard equipment as a French fascist than the small revolver he wore in an elegant leather holster attached to a wide belt in bright yellow pigskin – part of the walking-out uniform of all the Paris collaborationists (even Déat had one, a huge affair), presumably as the visible assertion of their eventual participation in the longed for French civil war. For whom else were they going to kill other than their fellow French? Paquis had to admit, later, that he had never in fact shot anyone – nor indeed had most of the other leather-belted brethren, which must have been very disappointing for them. Like other collaborationists, Paquis had found his opportunity in the Spanish Civil War, as a regular speaker on the French programme of *Radio-Saragossa*, a circumstance that gave the remainder of his life the public dimension that made him in a small way memorable. This was a new departure. For, in his memoirs, there is a touching reference to the joyful clatter of the print-room, to the old, appetizing, reassuring smell of printer's ink, as a reminder of younger days and early *barrésien* enthusiasms when a young journalist in Nancy. Paquis is revealed to be as much a compulsive journalist as a compulsive broadcaster. And, stopping for a night or two in Nancy, on his way to exile, he cannot refrain from a nostalgic visit to the offices of the old *Républicain de l'Est*, just to get his fingers stained on *le marbre* and to choose between *elzévir*, or *didot*, or another form of type. Paquis was as much an *enfant du marbre* as Lageat was of the sweaty gymnasium or boxing ring. Journalism and its familiar instruments represented for him a way of life and the reassurance of continuity. Even in the midst of the collapse of all his political aspirations, the clatter and the smells drew him back to the naïve hopes and enthusiasms of a young, right-wing, confused provincial journalist. In a modest way, Paquis was a poet, not a very good poet, but still one aware of the immense attraction of continuity in its simplest form: the *daily* paper, the *daily* broadcast, a short-term prospect that would in fact eventually be denied the consolation of continuity. In prison, he managed to transform himself from the man who had worked so diligently through the night for the morrow, from the broadcaster who had screamed and shouted for the immediate present, into a wiser, humbler person able to take stock of his whole life and to come to terms with a future that was rapidly running out. His execution seems rather a big price to have to pay for a combination of conceit and habit. As Simenon would no doubt have said or written, he should have stayed in Nancy: Spain, then Paris had been the undoing of this provincial.

When one glances at the collaborationist press, one is confronted with the old, familiar caricatures of prewar days. *Albion* is still long-toothed, bespectacled and scraggy, but Hitler has disappeared. Jean Effel still signs his drawings with a flower or a butterfly, Pol Fer Jac remains faithful to his powdery line. The caricaturists have not changed; it is the butt of their drawings that has changed, Churchill replacing Ciano, Roosevelt (again, like *Albion*, very toothy) replacing Mussolini (an inestimable loss). The caricaturists were mostly luckier than the journalists, most surviving to depict the long, gangling de Gaulle embracing the Eiffel Tower, or Edith Piaf singing a song of love and praise to '*Mon Légionnaire*' (a Pétain in a white *képi*), or Pétain himself dozing in an armchair, with a cat on his lap and Germanic fir trees glimpsed through the long double window: *Travail, Famille, Patrie*. What could a caricaturist do other than to draw? Perhaps the indulgence shown towards them, in contrast to the severity shown to journalists, is a recognition of the fact that they were little more than *amuseurs publics*, and that laughter at whoever's expense, far from being treasonable, represented a small article of consolation at a time when most pleasant articles were in desperately short supply. Who would remember the contents of their caricatures, even on the morrow? Who would recall the bestial traits inflicted on a bloodsucking Churchill? Who would linger on the Semitic features of an emblematic Jew? These artists of pen and pencil could presumably be forgiven because they had provoked a moment of laughter in a time of weariness, dreariness, fear and sorrow. Anyhow, they got away with it.

Relief at escape from the war was often the first step towards a more positive participation in collaboration. The Germans, who treated their own pacifists as traitors, had been quite happy to encourage French ones before the war and during the months of the 'phoney war', and, even after June 1940, they saw in them potential allies. This offered the basis for a bargain that was mutually satisfying. German victory had brought an immediate return to peace (though no peace treaty was ever to be signed; but, so long as Germany had not conquered the world, such a peace would still be fragile, so that, for many French pacifists, the success of the New European Order became identified with the assurance of a general peace; it was

no accident that the most anglophobe among the collaborationists should have been drawn from the ranks of the pacifist
left.) Relief at the conclusion of hostilities, even if one is on the
losing side, is a perfectly understandable response, especially
after a campaign which, though destructive – at least in the
Northeast, for it had left the Massif Central and the Midi quite
unscathed, as if in preparation for Vichy – had at least been
mercifully short (just what all sides had hoped for in August
1914). Such a response was more understandable in individual
and in family terms (and families are so often the alibi for what,
at best, could be described as prudence, at worst, as cowardice),
at least in the summer of 1940 – *l'heure du choix*, when so many
choices were made – than the concern, on the part of a professional minority and of a handful of bold and eccentric aristocrats,
to set about rebuilding a clandestine military organization to
ensure for France a place in the future, whatever the future
might contain. Few people, in France at least, would have had
much thought for the future in the shattering circumstances of
1940, such were the enormous and immediate exigencies of a
totally dislocated present. There is no doubt that Pétain exactly
hit the national mood when he made a national virtue of a
visceral form of cowardice that had already been dramatically
displayed at the time of the middle-class panic of August/Sep-
tember 1938, when shivers of fear had run through the stifling
Paris boulevards, a fear orchestrated by the incessant laments
of the newspaper sellers, '*édition spéciale, édition spéciale,*' twice
or thrice daily, rising to a shrill climax in the torrid evenings
and in the stuffy nights of foreboding and listening that had
preceded the immense physical relief brought by the impact of
Munich. How can one ever forget the sheer joy of that moment,
the realization that one had been granted a reprieve of a few
weeks, perhaps even of a few months (few, in that moment of
delight, could have counted on a whole year) if one had lived

through the crisis, as I had, in Paris? The stress on a return to family life, on the everlasting virtues of domesticity and on 'business as usual' was more than a brilliant propaganda coup: it showed an acute understanding of what was, for a few weeks at least – and vital weeks during which many irreversible decisions were taken and many risky options were closed – the mood of the nation. Guéhenno is no doubt right when he insists that the particular ignominy of Pétain was to have elevated cringing cowardice into an expression of patriotism. But one suspects that this austere republican was making too great demands on the majority of his less exalted, more selfish fellow countrymen. The Breton writer must have been one of a very rare breed of Frenchmen to have evoked, in the summer of 1940, the imagery of the embattled Republic of the Year Two. In a situation in which, in places like Clermont-Ferrand, people were exclaiming with enormous and mean relief, *'Bah! ils ne prendront pas le Massif'*, M. Homais and M. Prudhomme would have been more appropriate emblems than Saint-Just and Carnot. Pétain was an elderly Homais in a peaked cap surrounded by oak leaves. His invitation to seek refuge in the bosom of the family and to sit it out at home would be to most middle-class people a more comforting programme than blood, sweat and tears. And not just to middle-class people. Dutourd's Poissonard family, sitting in their van, place des Quinconces, in Bordeaux, were quick to realize that the right thing to do, indeed the best way of responding to the Marshal's patriotic appeal, was to scrounge some petrol from somewhere and get back on the road to Paris and open up their *crémerie*. The *SNCF*, with the help of both Vichy and the Germans, responded to the natural instinct of Parisians of all conditions to get back to Paris and resume work as soon as possible by laying on scores of extra trains each day, throughout July and August, to bring the work force back to the capital.

What is more, up to 1943 at least, the Vichy leaders could point to the fact that, while the young men of the belligerent powers were dying in their tens of thousands, the youth of France enjoyed the unique privilege – and one denied even to the more active neutrals such as the Swiss and the Swedes – of living at home, albeit in some discomfort, and of struggling through the old familiar educational track of *baccalauréat*, *licence* and *agrégation*. Guéhenno notes, with some surprise, that the *rentrée* of October 1940 was much like any other *rentrée*, and that his pupils appeared amorphous and apolitical, apparently indifferent to the fact of national humiliation, and concerned about forthcoming exams, prizes and positions in class. Perhaps he was expecting too much of them, for there is nothing very surprising about such a mundane and unheroic reaction. If this were the situation in a prestigious Left Bank *lycée*, how much more so would it be in a school in a quiet provincial town. Emmanuel Le Roy Ladurie, recalling his time at St. Joseph, a Catholic school in Caen, could remember little enough of the crisis of 1940. Term had started as usual, the food had been perhaps a little worse than usual, the prayers and edifying readings had been the same as usual, public events had scarcely penetrated the thick walls of the *internat*, members of his family had gone on the pilgrimage to la Délivrande as usual, the Flemish boys in his school had been rather more uppish than usual, regarding themselves as true Aryans, and therefore associated with the might of German arms.

Until the STO began to threaten the entrenched safety of their male children, middle-class parents could not fail to feel grateful to a regime that had enabled their sons to remain at home, well protected from the perils of war. It could, of course, be pointed out that perhaps even greater numbers of Frenchmen – still nearly a million by 1944, that is, more than half those taken in 1940 – were to remain as prisoners of war in

Germany, but most of these belonged to different age groups, and though their continued absence might cause both grief and hardship, it might be presumed that these too were relatively safe (safer, anyhow, than those caught by the *STO*, nearly half of whom – about 35,000 – were killed in German cities); at least they were out of the war.

Such an appeal would be more likely to recruit to the less extravagant forms of *maréchalisme*, as well as to a prudent *attentisme* that would endeavour to keep all options open and to wait for outside events. But, as we have seen, ultracollaborationism drew heavily on the ranks of former pacifist movements, especially among the generation that had had direct experience of the trenches in the First World War. One of the many ironies concerning commitment to collaborationism – at least in ideological terms – was that, in a matter of a year (from June 1941 precisely) so many of those who had started off from a violent and emotional rejection of war should have themselves started carrying weapons in public (whether for use or not) and should have begun displaying themselves in various *uniformes de fantaisie* – leather belts and pouches, bulging riding breeches, leather leggings – not to mention a facial expression that represented an unsubtle combination of cretinism and hate, as if they had been ready there and then to run off to the nearest front or, preferably, to do a bit of killing at home, within convenient walking distance. It is true that, to judge from the photographs, they do not look very convincing soldiers – they are too self-conscious – but they are at least *trying* to look martial.

In short, there were almost as many approaches to collaborationism as there were collaborationists, and most such approaches were easy, almost painless, at least for those with little imagination, less dignity and few moral scruples. The Germans had come to stay, and it was not much use trying not to *see* them, to close one's shutters on their victory parades and to pretend that they were not there, though no doubt a great many Parisians, especially those of middle-class and professional origins, were to adopt this rather negative form of internal resistance, a closing in on themselves, and a deliberate retreat from public life and society. This was a line of retreat also available, in less intellectual and more agreeable forms, to men of the lower middle and working classes, to those proverbial and permanent *attentistes*, to those embattled individualists, *les pêcheurs à la ligne*. Henri Michel tells us that the basement of the Bazar de l'Hôtel de Ville, specializing in the full range of fishing tackle, had never been so busy as during the occupation years, fishing being the only leisure activity still available to male civilians as a result of the confiscation of all fire-arms. On 11th August 1941, Guéhenno takes the first *métro* of the day, at 5.30 in the morning, in order to be well up in the queue outside one of the German military offices. At each successive station there get on fully-equipped fishermen – their rods, their little tins of worms, their landing nets, and, most significant of all, their folding canvas chairs – not to mention their slender, modest hopes of a catch. More and more they come, cluttering up with their voluminous gear the already crowded carriages. Then, as if in response to a common word of command, at Châtelet they all get out, rushing to take up their positions for the day on a well-lined riverside. Their brief presence seems to have reassured Guéhenno, as a reminder of happier times, perhaps also as an indication of the right form of priorities. Certainly, nothing could have been more disturbing, nor more provocative, to any Germans travelling at this early hour than the sight of this small, but determined army of what Queneau has called *les fanatiques de la gaule*. And let us be sure that their precious rods were for *use*, that they were not being carried as a coded reminder of the name of the 'general over the water'.

These were no doubt the most convinced of all those who had decided to withdraw into the apparently unassailable fortress of quiet and harmless leisure, their eyes on their red-and-white floats as they bobbed up and down in the scintillating silvery water of an August Seine.

Communist militants and their supporters, on the other hand, displayed their usual discipline and obedience to party orders, related to them from Brussels via 'Clément' (the Slovak Eugen Fried), the *Komintern* agent attached to the exiled Duclos, by positively seeking out the German soldiers, offering them drinks, sitting with them on café terraces in Belleville-Ménilmontant or in the XIIme. After June 1941, they would display a similar alacrity to follow the new party line by assassinating individual German soldiers, in the street, in the *métro*, or on café terraces. (They would not be the same soldiers as those who had been the object of their previous blandishments, as most members of the Paris garrison were rapidly moved on to more pressing sectors. But what of that? Such soldiers were not living individuals, to be fraternized with, or to be shot in the back; they were symbols in whatever 'class struggle' was currently on.) It was, however, a switch so radical that some militants – a minority – found themselves unable to make it, a sudden personal revolt that might account for the frequent individual conversions from *PCF* to *PPF* after the summer of 1941.

Unlike those professional people who retreated back into private life, collaborationists could continue to enjoy public life and collective forms of leisure and entertainment, often on a scale and at a level of luxury that had previously been denied them. In Paris at least, collaborationism was a vehicle of rapid, often sensational, social promotion, making of a hack journalist from Nancy, such as Paquis, a national figure, fêted by *le Tout-Paris*, titillated by his sheer vulgarity. Here was the nearest thing to a genuine *prolétaire*, for he sweated copiously, wore an assortment of pens and pencils in the top pocket of his double-breasted suit, and spoke with an accent that would reasonably pass as *faubourien* – indeed, in the course of time, Paquis managed to perfect his long Parisian *a*'s, as well as a *parigot* slang and cheekiness that could be accepted, at least in such social circles, as the genuine article, though a true connoisseur like Lageat would not have been taken in. In this respect, collaborationism had an appeal that could be described as pre-*poujadiste*, long before Poujade had ever been heard of outside Saint-Céré (Lot): the wiping-off of old social scores and the gratification of social acceptance of a sort. At the German Institute and at Abetz's parties at the embassy, rue de Lille, like could meet like, communing in a common vulgarity, as German and French eyed one another, somewhat uneasily, as similar newcomers to rather gawkily assumed social graces. Neither would pocket the sandwiches, in order to take them away and eat them at home; that much they had learnt. Both would make a rush, pushing and shoving, towards the copious buffet. In the winter of 1941, moved by curiosity, and because he had nothing else to do that particular evening, Guéhenno attended what claimed to be a mass meeting of the *RNP*. The masses were not there; but, looking over the ranks of shop assistants and bank clerks, *ratés* and semiintellectuals who had responded to the appeal (there was to be a buffet, too, afterwards), he sums up this rather seedy army of frayed fanatics in suits shining at the seats and at the elbows and stained under the armpits, in the marvellously evocative phrase, '*de petits bourgeois à manches de lustrine*'. How often have we encountered, in the 1950s, just such eager but uneasy provincials, fresh to the capital, but *à la conquête de Paris*, and wearing, like overgrown *lycéens*, their long, black, shiny ink-sleeves, like tellers or cashiers in a bank, in order to protect their tight jackets from the venerable dust of centuries, in the *salle du public* of the Archives nationales! After a few months, or perhaps a year, the ink-sleeves would be quietly abandoned; someone had had a word in the ear of the wearer. I can recall, in particular, a young historian from Lyon – or rather from Villeurbanne – who had ink-sleeves longer than any I had ever seen before: they came right up to his shoulders and appeared to be attached from behind. But, quite soon, the ink-sleeves were abandoned, along with his Villeurbanne wife. He then married into the *haute-bourgeoisie parisienne*, soon abandoning the *PCF*, of which he had been a militant, for the more fashionable *PSU*. This was ten years on from the seedy brigades of the *RNP*. Now such provincials or suburbanites were more likely to be recruited into the equally rancid and rancorous ranks of the *PCF*.

But there was also, from the start, a high price to pay. Easy *in* – or relatively so – not so easy *out*. Very soon – and because, in Paris, they were working so close to the Germans – collaborationists would begin to find themselves prisoners of their institutions, their papers, their political groups, their well-provided canteens and shops, their regular invitations to the German Institute and to the embassy – both on the Left Bank, like the bookshop, *Rive Gauche*. This was nicknamed by Sorbonne students *Rive Gauche du Rhin*, a location that lent to collaboration something of both the hysteria of prewar right-wing *monômes* and the poor dottiness of the ineffable Ferdinand Lop (the permanent presidential candidate of the boulevard Saint-Michel). They would find themselves prisoners, too, of their outwardly polite, but dangerous, uniformed friends in the various technical, propaganda and cultural services (the military high command tended to avoid all contacts with Frenchmen, whose cooperation, in the purely military sphere, they did not need). At the same time, rippling waves of isolation would gradually envelop them, as many of their former friends, and even relatives, began unobtrusively to shun them.

Of course, if there undoubtedly existed a common social appeal from the rancorous to the rancorous across the national barriers, by no means all candidates to one form or other of collaborationism gained admittance to what still remained a fairly wide open club. Guéhenno, though a good observer, even a sympathetic one when commenting on the loneliness and bewilderment of the individual German soldier, lost and wandering purposelessly amid the stony-eyed Parisian crowd, even noting the signs of wear and tear on uniforms no longer impeccable, displays his middle-class prejudices when dismissing with such marked contempt the ink-sleeved outsiders of the thin ranks of the always seedy *RNP*, third-class collaborationists and even conscious of the fact. These were the collaborationists who had *not* made it, who were not needed, who often could not even find anyone to collaborate with, and so who were irrelevant. The Germans did not keep absolutely open house, the *Maison Collaboration* was not a Salvation Army hostel, and the *occupants*, as well as displaying a ready hospitality when it suited them, knew how to make themselves unapproachable and elusive. Collaborationism was something of a maze, and, even at the top Vichy level, a politician such as Flandin would have to be scrapped, because, in a matter of months, he had not succeeded in making contact with any Germans of importance. The Germans knew when to make themselves coy.

So, at a much humbler level, the German masters would certainly not be likely to be appreciative when reminded of their *own* ink-sleeves, of their *own* suburban or small-town origins (it would have been like reminding Heydrich that he had been dishonourably discharged from the officer corps of the German navy). They would reach out only to collaborationists who, while sharing a sense of rancour and a feeling of renewal, of having been born again (part of the process of becoming a nazi, whether German or French) had long since discarded, with shame, the *manches de lustrine*, whose suits were not shiny, whose trousers were not baggy, whose socks were not holed and odorous, and whose overcoats were not stitched and frayed. Collaborationism had to be seen to be successful; it would not be allowed to walk about in the visible tatters of failure. Short hair, a stern, unflinching eye – one can see Déat and others in eye practice – a straight back, as collaborationist and senior partner marched resolutely away from the nagging memory of past humiliation and towards the radiant future of the New European Order and its well-clipped lawns and gigantic vistas. How many would-be collaborationists fell at the initial hurdle? It is something that we will never know, for they are not likely to tell us of their ill-deserved luck.

Paquis's pathetic memoirs, perhaps more than any other collaborationist work (for it was written in the shadow of death) make one understand how, within these rather narrow circles, tempers so easily flared, quarrels became so bitter and so prolonged, rivalries became so personal, so intense and so unforgiving. It was not just that this often admirably suited the Germans' book, for the Germans, while encouraging collaboration, were as much concerned to keep the collaborationists at one another's throats (they may even have been amused at the spectacle). It was also that the collaborationists, as time went on, were thrown more and more on one another's company, their wives and their families, willy-nilly, being drawn in behind the invisible *enceintes* guarding a besieged, despised, privileged and increasingly shunned minority. How to get *out*, when there was nowhere to go, when all doors were closed? The only thing was to go on to the end of the line, wherever that might be. By the summer of 1944, the leading Paris collaborationists were reduced to clinging to such desperate straws as the German secret weapon, or the imminence of a counterattack that would drive the Allies back, into the sea. In their heart of hearts, they must have realized that it was all up, a realization, that, far from endearing them to one another, would only fan the flames of acrimony and mutual accusation. Some, not unnaturally, took to drink – there was always plenty of that in Sigmaringen and in the southern redoubt – in efforts to prolong a shrinking present and to seek the heavy deadness of snoring slumber. They drank individually, and in corners, hiding their drink supplies, as others might hide hoards of petrol, obtained from drunken German soldiers. Much of what Paquis has to say about his colleagues during the last, sultry days in an August Paris – all those desperate telephone calls, late at night, across the silent, waiting city, from flat to flat, so many appeals for reassurance – or in the course of their chaotic journey from the East of France to South Germany and their stay there, is both unedifying and comical. There was not much left of solidarity even in the common experience of collaborationism, or in the shared knowledge of the common fate that was liable to await them back in France, at the time of the final, undignified *sauve-qui-peut*. The luckiest were those who moved with the most discretion, at the dead of night, while their normally watchful colleagues slept, who did not tell anyone, lest others be tempted to join them, for larger numbers would make them more conspicuous. Marcel and Hélène Déat set out alone, well wrapped up and in strong boots, to undertake a personal crossing of the Dolomites. Others managed, improbably, to obtain Spanish passports which might enable them to reach at least temporary safety in neutral Switzerland (which displayed little neutrality when confronted with the ex-collaborationists). Poor Paquis – not important enough, now reduced once more to his original stature as a hack journalist and a small-time propagandist – was unceremoniously chucked out of the German fighter plane that would have brought him to safety, to make way for Abel Bonnard's brother. He was not even surprised at this outcome, for he had never been much more than a third-class collaborationist, an executant, not a chief, a follower, not a leader, a voice that relayed the orders, hopes and fears of others. Paquis, one can see, was as expendable as all the fourth-class collaborationists who had not even been collaborationists at all, the so-called *horizontales*, who had merely gone to bed with German soldiers (many of them they had no doubt put out of action, for months at least) and who were to have their heads shaved.

Paquis at least had few illusions. But what of all those would-be leaders? *Déat*, a bizarre mixture of half-baked intellectual, of failed politician, lacking in even the most elementary human touch, a typical victim of *la philo*, and a peasant unable to shake off the traces of an earthy Auvergnat accent, Déat who, for twenty years, with a dog-like persistence, had sought only one thing: *power*, not to accomplish anything in particular, but just for its own sake, to satisfy his own inexhaustible vanity, who wanted to be a *chef*, or rather *le Chef*, under any conditions – if it were the only path to the throne, under German patronage – and who did not even vaguely look like a leader, a squat, hunched, weedy little man hiding behind his pipe. Why should the Germans have picked on a Déat as national regenerator? What had he to offer them, apart from his daily article in *L'Oeuvre* and his consistent hatred of Vichy, because Vichy would not even make him a minister (it did, in the end, but only in March 1944)? Déat was a *fantaisiste* who seems to have believed in his own destiny.

And what could the Germans have made of the indolent, effete and unpredictable Drieu, yet another candidate for leadership, a self-appointed *apprenti-chef* by virtue of the elevation of his bourgeois conceit and his hatred of ordinary human-kind? Drieu, too, was a *fantaisiste*, an ageing adolescent, thinking up new games, greedy for new toys. What had a Bucard to offer, save the scourings of the Paris streets? Darnand, in many ways a natural leader, was bought off by being transformed into a brutally effective policeman, at the head of *la Milice*. Indeed, in the French context, collaborationism represented the grave of most ambitions to leadership, which, deprived of all reality, was little more than an *exercice de style*, a litany on the word *chef*, a boy scout vocabulary that had taken a wrong turn and that, though farcical, had begun to take itself seriously. Could one even take a *franc-garde* seriously? However ridiculous the title, it would have been as well to have done so, for young men in black uniform and wearing the gamma sign shoulder-flash were both heavily armed and trigger-happy and took *themselves* decidedly seriously.

In any case, the Germans had no *use* for French leaders as long as Laval and Henriot were available. It was indicative that, after Henriot's assassination, the dead man was replaced by his ghost voice, repeating, from beyond the tomb, recorded renderings of his previous broadcasts, night after night, punctually at 9.15 P.M. (What, Guéhenno wonders, did his wife and children make of the prolongation of a public voice? Did they listen to the dead man?) Doriot alone might have met some of their requirements, but it was only at the last stages of the agony of the Third Reich that they were prepared to grant him any effective power. And then *le Chef* (mourned by Paquis and a handful of gunmen) was killed as the result of an attack from the air. At best, the French could be allowed to be *chefs de gare*.

Collaborationism, then, had been a working partnership, between unequal partners, in a temporary relationship in which neither party could do without the other and in which neither party ever had complete trust in the other. Despite a few shared interests – a German victory and so a German future, above all – and even a few shared prejudices and beliefs (anti-Semitism, anti-Communism) it had never been a particularly happy relationship. The Germans needed their own chosen French collaborationists in order to demonstrate their own importance to their superiors in Berlin, many of whom had increasing doubts about the need for maintaining permanent bodies in Paris in the first place, particularly after 1943, when the rôle assigned to France, apart from being the most promising potential source of labour supply for war production, was to offer the principal training ground for young recruits to the *Wehrmacht* and for the re-formation of units that had been decimated in the East. A body that engaged the services of forty civilians must seem to have more value than one that had only twenty on its payroll. Military bureaucracies, particularly those on the fringes of armies – technical and supply services, transport, lines of communication – have their own inimitable ways of perpetuating themselves and of arguing, from more 'strength' to yet more 'strength', an argument familiar to those who have experienced the potency of the British military concept of *On Strength*. Given a certain number under his orders, the person in charge could claim promotion from lieutenant colonel to full colonel so that, in 1943/44, colonels and their equivalents in *SS* ranks were thicker than ever on the ground *sur la place de Paris*.

And so, in their turn, the French would be likely to be drawn to the big battalions, rather than to what could be merely peripheral or ephemeral organizations. The Armistice Commission, which lasted out the whole period of occupation, was clearly a good investment for all parties concerned even after the withdrawal from it of the Italians. On the other hand, people like Paquis must have always felt insecure, propaganda being a mercurial substance subject to very sudden shifts in emphasis. The Germans might lose interest in it altogether, if they were no longer to care what the French thought, and Dr. Goebbels would take a great deal of convincing that French opinion was really a matter of importance. It still had been in 1942, when some German leaders had still been considering a French option. But by 1943, all that the Germans wanted of the French was *labour*; and force and threats, rather than persuasion, seemed the most effective means of ensuring a steady stream of French workers to the Reich. Indeed, the very pressure of the *STO* undermined the diplomatic and cultural efforts of Abetz, Epting and Grimm. The wonder is that the propaganda network managed to survive at all. The fact that it did is an eloquent illustration of the incoherence of Nazi administration at the very top. One sometimes suspects that Berlin simply did not *know* the current state of play in Paris and that certain bodies survived simply because people in Berlin had forgotten about them or did not know that they still existed. One can well appreciate why the German officials in Paris – like French conscripts before them, or *STO* conscripts at the time – should have regarded the Gare de l'Est with such alarm; for it was not only the point of departure (almost certainly on a single ticket) of the much dreaded posting to the East; it was also – and quite as alarmingly – the point of arrival of important officials sent to enquire into the various organizations that had proliferated in the French capital since the summer of 1940, and likely to ask a number of highly inconvenient questions. Of course, no doubt some of these unwelcome visitors could be softened up with a dinner Chez Maxim's or at the Tour d'Argent, but there was always the danger of an inflexibly puritanical visitation. Mercifully for those with a vested interest in staying put, puritans seem to have been in short supply in the higher *échelons* of the Nazi hierarchy. Indeed, as the years went by, Goering, in his steady pursuit of loot, employed an expanding army of German agents and French go-betweens to scour out the Paris art market and set aside the treasures hidden away in the cellars of the Louvre and the Petit-Palais. And so Goering became the most reliable protector of the Paris *bandes amarantes*, whom he expected to entertain him according to his own lavish standards.

So, in their turn, the more calculating French *collabos* would seek employment in what was, at any time between 1940 and 1944, a going concern, though with even heavier demands put upon it from 1942 onwards; a *police* organization: the prefecture of police and its multifarious services, the *Sûreté*, the *police municipale*, and the limb out of that enormous body, the *PQJ*, the *Section Spéciale*, and even the rather reassuring *gendarmerie*. The prefecture worked in daily cooperation with the whole gamut of German police and intelligence agencies and repressive bodies. The *police municipale* carried out arrests at the behest of the German authorities and put deportees on the death trains that left from Drancy. The *gendarmerie* worked in close links with the *Feldgendarmerie* (they were indeed in exactly the same line of business) and the French *Gestapo*, as its name implied, was the most effective arm of Knochen and the avenue Foch. The Germans, with a total repressive force of only ten thousand available to them in the whole of France, were wholly dependent on the vast body of French police: a hundred thousand – Amouroux, as we have seen, has even put it at double that figure – with ten thousand alone available in the Paris area. In this respect, the magnificent machine of French repression enabled the Germans, from the start, to cut down on their own police requirements, making the maximum number of members of the *Feldgendarmerie* available for service in the East. As things turned out – with the notable exception of the *Gestapo français*, whose members were to go on trial and to be executed – collaborationism in police organizations would ensure both survival and subsequent security of tenure, partly thanks to the carefully staged police mutiny of August 1944 that gave the *police municipale* a semispurious testimonial as *résistants*. They had certainly waited till the very last moment to resist! The result was that there was scarcely a *commissaire de police* in Paris who was replaced at the Liberation. There was nothing new or exceptional about this; it had happened in 1789, in 1794, in 1814 and again in 1815, in 1830, in 1848, the only partial break occurring in 1871. Nineteen forty and 1944 both represented the truly remarkable continuity of the Paris police force to which the Germans owed such an enormous debt. Much the same happened in Lyon, and no doubt everywhere else.

The ultimate form of collaborationism was service in German uniform, on the Eastern Front. This involved only a handful of collaborators, a few hundred at the most: *doriotistes*, *miliciens*, and a very thin scattering of *déatistes*. It was a form of collaboration in which the Germans, even in 1944/45, showed only a reluctant and grudging interest; and most such volunteers, once having forced their way onto German military awareness, were assigned to second-line functions rather than to combat duties, though, at the very end, disparate elements of the Division Charlemagne were fighting alongside fourteen- and fifteen-year-old *Hitlerjugend* in the tunnels of the Berlin *U-Bahn*.

Collaborationism of this extreme kind, as well as previous enrolment in the uniformed ranks of the *PPF*, the *RNP*, the *Milice* and the *francistes*, was confined to males, these various bodies not possessing women's sections. So it is difficult to quantify *feminine* collaborationism and to assess the impact of feminine participation in collaborationist activities. Let us exclude, once and for all, the prostitutes, who were merely doing their job as before. Let us also exclude the nonprofessional *horizontales*, who lay down for a variety of motives, few of them ideological. Let us exclude the 80,000 mothers who claimed German nationality for their offspring. It is hard to place the wives and the daughters of the leading collaborators; they may, or they may not, have shared the commitment of their husbands or their parents; certainly most stuck to their husbands in Sigmaringen – I do not know of any who sought a divorce, either in 1944 or later. Corinne Luchaire shared the views of her father. Later, some of the widows of those executed would be concerned to vindicate their memory and to keep the guttering flame of collaborationism burning. There were women actresses and singers who delighted German audiences during these years; and social collaborationism was able to enrol some of the big names of the feminine branch of *le Tout-Paris* with the suggestion that dishonour was as much the motto of the faubourg Saint-Germain as its opposite (though the women of the provincial nobility often gave the lead to early adherence to the cause of *honneur et patrie*); perhaps such *duchesses*, *marquises* and *vicomtesses* thought that, but for their presence, the social round would simply grind to a halt. They were, after all, almost professional *hôtesses*, and monocled German officers were agreeable and enthusiastic guests. Perhaps the least that could be said of such ladies is that they were utterly selfish and were lacking in imagination. Their eager participation in such junketings gave a veneer of social respectability to collaboration, a point that was eagerly exploited by the photographers from *Signal*, quick with their *flashes* to reveal the gleam of elegant shoulders and the scintillation of jewelry.

Numerically, the most important element in feminine collaboration would be supplied by the secretarial personnel employed by the various German organizations in Paris. Secretaries were extremely well paid – double the wages offered in the civilian sectors – and they also had access to German canteens where they could purchase goods not obtainable in ordinary shops. They might also have ready access to the favours of good-looking or high-ranking German officers. The attraction of such employment may be gauged from the steady increase in the number of students – nearly all of them women – enrolled for courses in spoken and written German at the German Institute and Berlitz, between 1940 and 1943 (when numbers began to decline). Michel points out that one-fifth of those – 20,000 in all – brought to trial in the Département de la Seine after the Liberation were women, no doubt most of them secretaries, typists and interpreters in German organizations.

delotion

But, undoubtedly, much the greatest service rendered by women to the German and French repressive authorities was in the ancient form of delation. There was an uninterrupted flow – Sundays included, for there was still a Sunday post – from July 1940 to late August 1944 (individuals were still being denounced by name at the time of the Liberation, though some of the letters must have gone astray or must have fallen into the wrong hands) of both anonymous and signed letters addressed to the Germans, to the prefecture, to the *PQJ*, or to the rue Lauriston, the work of the dark battalions of yellow-faced *dénonciatrices*, the bile and slime of times of disaster; the work, too, however, of women of substance, wreaking vengeance on some neighbour who had gossiped about them, had hinted that they had been showing undue favours to members of the German forces, or who had insulted them in food queues. (Guilloux reports hearing from his window in November 1943 an early-morning dispute between two large women. 'Oui, vous êtes une sale femme', etc. The other one, picking up a brick: 'Foutez-moi le camp, ou je vous jette la brique à la gueule. Sale Boche!' 'Ah! Boche! Vous avez dit "Boche"! C'est bon! Je vais vous dénoncer.' What amuses Guilloux, as he puts on his clothes, is that the two women, in the course of their row, should have employed the gestures of small children.) Probably more of these letters were signed than were anonymous, Amouroux making the important point that it was only a signed letter that would bring the financial reward due to a successful denunciation of a *gaulliste*, a Communist militant, or an Allied agent. Greed was certainly as great a motivation as jealousy and the desire for revenge. Many Jews, *gaullistes*, *insoumis*, and *résistants* were detected by these means, the *PQJ* regularly informed by a network of *concierges* spread right across the city (though, as Guéhenno reminds us, there were also patriotic *concierges* who covered up for their *locataires*, like the aged Madame Etienne, who, having opened the door four times in the course of the night by the *cordon* next to her bed, died early in the morning of cold, having expressed her sorrow at not living long enough to see Paris free again). What prompts such literature it is hard to say, though the promise of a reward, often considerable, jealousy and rancour seem to have been steady stimulants; and it is reasonable to suppose that most such *corbeaux* were not young. Perhaps such compulsive *dénonciatrices* should not even be qualified as collaborationists, for many of them were merely doing what they had always done, and what they would go on doing in the equally favourable circumstances of *l'Epuration*.

In his *Journal*, Guéhenno returns several times to the phenomenon of homosexual collaborationism. Sometimes this took a purely literary form, in the enthusiastic evocation of the blond and muscular beauty of young German manhood, as echoed in Montherlant. It is possible that pederasts, like other social outcasts, may have sought in collaboration a more secure status for their own minority interests, if one envisages collaboration as a gigantic new deal in which the picture cards go to those previously deprived. They may also have been drawn to a period during which youth movements pullulated and shorts – no doubt in imitation of the leather model – got shorter. A few seem to have been stimulated by the sheer enormity of the defeat. Certainly Peyrefitte set the tone in *Les Amitiés particulières*, published in 1943 (it was at once forbidden in Vichy!); and Peyrefitte also had solid personal grievances against a Third Republic that had expelled him from the *Carrière* (he was reinstated by Vichy, in rather an open-handed gesture in view of their prohibition of his book). Guéhenno remains intrigued by the problem, but is unable to find an explanation for what he believes to have been such a massive and enthusiastic adherence of this rather closed community to the collective pulls of collaborationism. Perhaps it represented the possibility of an escape from moral isolation. Whether it ever took the more practical form of collaboration across the national borders, whether there rose up and lay down a small army of *horizontaux* we do not know; it is something that must be confined, for ever, to the *secrets de l'oreiller*. But a regime – or rather, regimes – that shortened shorts and exposed bare knees (while lengthening skirts) was bound to raise secret hopes, even if these were not openly expressed. The *culte du chef* could also contain homosexual undertones, though both Degrelle and Doriot were pretty far removed from Jean Marais, being, on the contrary, sweaty, earthy men with a strong appeal to women. Perhaps homosexuals will always welcome some dramatic turn in national fortunes or misfortunes as an opportunity to move in and secure the best jobs.

To conclude, as far as the sexes and the ages are concerned: Collaborationism tended to be masculine and adult, because men possessed the technical skills that were likely to be of value to the Germans, and because women, adolescents and children did not. There were no women railway engineers and very few women in the police, there were no *miliciennes* nor any fascist *amazones*, there were more waiters than waitresses, *chauffeuses de taxi* were extremely rare (a profession that began to emerge in the 1950s and that has considerably expanded since), men drove the *métro*, women clipped the tickets at the barriers (but not those of the Germans, who did not have any tickets and who travelled free), and women were not even subjected to the operations of the *Relève*, nor, later, to those of the *STO*. Collaborationism was a striking case of the inequalities of opportunity. Within its generous, expansive confines, women could only be assigned to secondary or subterranean rôles: typists, telephonists, secretaries, chambermaids. There were no women publishers or printers; even the most famous woman journalist, Geneviève Tabouis, had left France for New York in July 1940. Most of the *ultra*-collaborationists, if not active antifeminists, tended to *despise* women, seeing them as incompatible recruits to the politics of 'virility'. As we shall see, the language of ultracollaborationism was an aggressively – not to say, stupidly – masculine one. The crusade to the East was a journey for men only, an opportunity to reassert their masculinity and to prove to the German masters that Frenchmen were men indeed. What the Germans made of all this posturing and claptrap we do not know: probably not very much. Certainly, most were not indifferent to the feminine allures of *la doulce France*; and in their now ageing memories, it is this feminine aspect that they would be most likely to recall of the golden years in Paris.

In this section, I have attempted to illustrate or to suggest some of the complexities of collaborationism as envisaged in personal, as much as in organizational, terms in the form of both a dialogue and a cohabitation between Germans and French of both sexes. In this respect, a vast, anonymous city like Paris is likely to be particularly uninformative to the historian, just as it must have so often presented a blank and stony face to the military tourist. To recapture something of the familiarity, the everydayness, even the sheer banality – the Anglo-Saxon historian would be inclined to overemphasize the dramatic quality of the enemy presence – of day-to-day relations between French and Germans, a provincial terrain would be likely to offer a more intimate picture of life, as shared, in common awareness of one another, and indeed of the simple need to keep things going, by German soldiers and French civilians.

The first volume of the *Carnets* of the Breton novelist, Louis Guilloux, describing the occupation years in his native Saint-Brieuc, succeeds both in giving human proportions and even faces to individual German soldiers, and in reducing their presence in the town, on the beach or in the surrounding countryside, to something so familiar as to be taken as a matter of course, unaccompanied by expressions of anger, indignation or surprise. Indeed, for Guilloux, an attentive and delighted observer of the changing colours and sounds of dusk and nightfall from his window overlooking the bay, the coast, the sea and the scattered houses of the semirural suburbs, the Germans have become, by November 1943, part of the landscape. As he watches the darkening of sea, sky and hills as they blend into a single black, he recaptures the peaceful sounds of a still winter evening: two neighbours talking in a nearby garden – he cannot pick out the words, just a murmur of masculine voices – a man hammering in a wooden stave, groups of young people joking and whistling as they hurry along the boulevard to reach home ahead of the curfew, from the centre of the town the sound of a group of Germans singing in clipped rhythm, and, close by, the shrill cry of a seabird and the song of a starling. It is an utterly peaceful scene, holding no trace of menace. And it is much the same, though in brighter, more vivid colours, in June/July 1944: the happy voices of young people, the snatch of a sentence in German to the accompaniment of the heavy tread on the quiet boulevard of two pairs of long army boots, soft voices in gardens, the shouts of children at play, and, very close by, the sound of a cricket. Far away, on the horizon, there are occasional dull flashes, the only suggestion of the slaughter taking place, by night as well as by day, in the long Normandy peninsula.

We can observe so much through the eyes of the local novelist. The French policeman, as he passes the *Feldgendarmerie*, raises his hand in familiar greeting to the *Feldgendarme* standing smoking on the step, the collar of his jacket unbuttoned. Guilloux is at the station, watching three busloads of madwomen being entrained, the population of the lunatic asylums being evacuated from the coastal areas: a *Feldgendarme* standing near him says something to him in bad French, accompanying the phrase with the gesture of using a syringe: '*Chez nous*, this is what we'd do.' Guilloux walks in, without knocking, to the house of his friend, Léopold. A young German officer is having a French lesson: 'Winner takes all,' he says, 'we will win this War even if we have to go on for fifty years.' Léopold disagrees; then they resume the French lesson. One of the officers at the *Kommandantur* is known to be more accommodating than the others. 'Let us hope that he doesn't get posted away.' Emil, a fifty-year-old bald man from Kiel, the chief gaoler at the prison, is very good about visits: 'Yes, let them come after hours, but keep quiet about it.' A red-haired woman in her forties who keeps a *bar-restaurant* has a German lover; she is good about providing information about what the Germans are likely to be up to next, enabling those who should get out to do so in time. In July 1944, Guilloux goes to the beach; it is crowded with swimmers. Of those in the water, it is hard to distinguish between French and Germans, though some of the latter stand out as being much darker than the blue-eyed local Bretons. The children know that some members of the garrison are a good touch for a packet of sweets.

In all his tranquil chronicle – almost a *pastorale* – of these years, there is hardly a word of anger; and, when there is, it is addressed to individual French men or women. So, like the author, we soon learn to take the German presence for granted. And even their final departure appears quite undramatic. Most of the shooting and looting occur after they have gone. His account, maintained throughout in a low key, and taken up primarily by family matters – concern for his mother's health, long walks, visits to friends, plots for the next novel, the visual awareness of the changing seasons – is a wonderful antidote to any temptation to see French and Germans merely as mutually hostile groups. Its sheer banality is as reassuring as it is convincing. But then, of course, Saint-Brieuc, a community of manageable size, offers a more all-embracing observatory than Paris, and Guilloux, in his home town, has the sharp eye of the miniaturist.

Such a dialogue and such a cohabitation are forms of sociability that must be of particular interest to the social historian and to the historian of privacy and of everyday life, in that it is almost unprecedented – particularly over such a length of time – and in that, being unprecedented and so quite unfamiliar, it had to construct its own rules as it went along, and secrete its own temptations and its own specific forms of repulsion. It is a dark frontier area of history which the historian can explore only very tentatively, through suggestion and allusion, and with considerable reliance both on imagination and on supposition: 'it must have been so' or 'so'. It is also an area of human relationships dominated by accident; individuals might slip, almost unconsciously, into collaboration, just as others might slip, step by tentative step, into resistance. The narrow balance of choice is very well put by Balavoine, a character in Marcel Aymé's short story, *'La Bonne Peinture'*. 'Je suis la déveine en personne,' he complains, after the Liberation.

Quand je me suis donné à l'Europe, j'avais pas encore d'idée politique. On m'offrait deux places: ou garde du corps ou livreur de produits de beauté . . . Dans le personnel de chez Fantin, on était à la résistance . . . Si j'avais choisi livreur . . . je serais dans le tricolore avec un condé officiel, bien payé, bien bouffer, les dactylos de la République et fumer des américaines . . .[10]

A humble man's dream of attainable bliss on three counts, and with only the whisky left out: *whisky, cigarettes, et petites pépées,* as in the popular song of the mid-1950s. He had made the wrong choice, partly because being bodyguard to a leading collaborator had seemed rather more prestigious – and had been no doubt much better paid – than being a commercial traveller in beauty products. How was the poor man to have known? How could he have read into the future? In 1942, to a simpleton like Balavoine, the future would have seemed to reside in a certain conception of Europe, something much bigger than France, more powerful than the familiar *Hexagone*, and how much grander than peddling cosmetics, in a couple of fibre suitcases, from door to door. If only the two offers had not come up together! But there it was; and, having made the wrong choice, he had been awarded – at the very least – *l'indignité nationale,* the loss of his civic rights – not that he would have much missed them – and, worse, the virtual impossibility of landing a new job. A very thin wall, indeed, on the other side of which lay at least one decoration, probably the red ribbon, a *carte de résistant,* a job in a ministry, and, as he says, government typists galore,

Chesterfields, Camels and Lucky Strikes. Balavoine, poor fellow, is a character in fiction, but the results of a mistaken choice could be illustrated, again and again, in the personal case histories of *le menu fretin* of collaborationism. In the ambience of 1944/45, little mercy would be shown towards those who, faced with two contrasting offers, had gone for the wrong one.

A somewhat similar case is quoted, sympathetically, by Jean Galtier-Boissière, in his post-Liberation journal. It is that of an anarchist schoolmaster and militant pacifist, Maurice Wullens, one of those craggy, homespun, bearded rural cranks so often thrown up on the more innocent shores of French – or British – pacifism: a Tolstoyan beard, china-blue eyes, reddish eyebrows and a pleated blue peasant smock. Wullens had been severely wounded during the First World War. As he lay bleeding on the ground, he had been confronted by a German soldier who, instead of finishing him off with a bayonet, had carefully dressed his wounds and checked the flow of blood, thereby, as Wullens saw it, saving his life twice over. He had concluded from this act of humanity that the Germans were decent and kindly people, and had devoted the interwar years to pacifist propaganda in a little-read journal called *Les Humbles*. Defeat and occupation did nothing to alter his views – he was still back with his merciful German of 1916, however archaic he might have become in a Reich dominated by Nazi fanatics – and he continued to preach the purest doctrine of pacifism and to remain faithful to his extreme left-wing commitment. Wullens, one feels, was one of those obstinate, rather tiresome village prophets, a Tolstoyan autodidact who would not easily consent to remaining out of print, would, on the contrary, insist on selling his pottery and his rustic wares, his herbs, health foods and patent medicines, hand-woven garments and rope-soled *espadrilles*, however little suited to altered circumstances. For him silence would seem like treason, like letting down his handful of eager disciples, as well as deeply wounding to a man long convinced of his own utter rightness, one of those tenacious individuals who could always be relied upon to get his timing completely wrong, and to go on witnessing at a time when just common sense and prudence would have called for silence. Wullens, then, almost innocently – had they not offered him print, and did it matter where the truth appeared, so long as it appeared? – ended up in the company of the extreme right – a transformation to which militant pacifists fell easy victims. To the consternation of his friends and followers, Wullens ultimately wrote articles for *Je suis partout*. Luckily, after the Liberation, the bearded and smocked seer had – prudent for once – returned to the obscurity of the rural existence he should never have abandoned, settling in his native village in French Flanders, where he died, almost unnoticed, in January 1946.

Galtier-Boissière is both touched to learn of the death of this village innocent and relieved to hear that he had escaped the retribution which would have overtaken him had he remained in Paris. Few of those who had been unwise enough to have contributed to *Je suis partout* can have got off so lightly. Yet we can see that it was right that poor, simple Wullens should have got off. Galtier-Boissière, like Guéhenno and Louis Guilloux, is an unusually generous observer, well able to distinguish between those who went into collaboration with their eyes open and for what they could get out of it, and those, like Wullens, who merely lost their way in a world of cruel choices and wandered, almost unconsciously, into dangerous company and dangerous publications. He expresses a similar sympathy for the far more unfortunate Gérin, literary critic of *L'Oeuvre*, given a savage sentence, and for Francis Delaisi, released from Fresnes with one of his arms paralysed. And, at the same time, he observes bitterly, in the course of the trial of Jean Luchaire, that, out of the hundreds of people who had obtained favours from this all-powerful, venal, but generous collaborationist, only seven had been prepared to come forward and witness in his favour at the high court.

Understanding and mercy were not at a premium in 1944–46, and there were few people prepared to admit, publicly at least, that one might have stumbled, almost by accident, into some mild, relatively innocuous and even eccentric form of collaborationism, as one might have stumbled, equally fortuitously, into an equally eccentric form of resistance. Both sides had their mild loonies, their sillies, their jokers and their bores. The ex-serviceman in *Au Bon Beurre* is more pathetic than wicked, and he is above all an intolerable bore, a heavy-footed *casse-pied*; but resistance *casse-pieds* were even worse. Just as the *PCF* militant killer has his perfect counterpart in the *SS* officer or NCO with an exemplary Nazi background, so, as between minor collaborationist and minor *résistant*, there remains a largely uncharted common ground of silliness and naïveté.

Most Parisians had only peripheral contacts with the Germans: serving them at table, cutting their hair (they were assiduous customers for a short-back-and-sides), hauling them along in a basket behind a bicycle, selling them a paper, showing them the way, waiting for them to relinquish a rowing-boat or a *pédalo* on one of the lakes in the Bois de Boulogne, taking their bets at the *PMU* in Longchamp or Vincennes, enticing them into expensive night spots and clip joints. They represented a presence that came to be accepted almost as a matter of course, almost as part of the physical landscape, something to which they could readily become accustomed – as one might to a thundershower or a gale or a terrible winter – and would regard with the same sort of blind indifference as present-day Parisians might vaguely register the presence of the garish Dutch, German, Scandinavian, Belgian, Spanish, Italian and Jugoslav buses parked behind Notre-Dame, or a be-flagged, fibreglass-topped pseudo-*bateau-mouche* passing under a bridge.

Guéhenno, more observant than most, constantly anxious to take the moral temperature of the *occupant*, if only to detect some tiny chink of weakness and uncertainty, of doubt and unease, detects the loneliness and lack of assurance of individual German soldiers lost in the unseeing indifference of the native crowd and denied even the small favour of a living glance, recognition at least of his *presence*; and his watchful yet sympathetic appraisal can take in the shininess and the thinning material of a uniform worn for too long and showing as many signs of war-weariness as the elderly soldier or the bewildered peasant boy it contains. He can remark on the ridiculousness of the toy pistol – it is in fact a real one, but designed more for display than for actual use – in its holster and the elaborate dagger in its sheath, both worn at the hip. (Is the pistol, he asks himself, supposed to intimidate the defeated? He thinks, on the contrary, that it is more likely to amuse them.) The Germans, in his eyes, are as much comical as bewildered and embarrassed, as if apologizing for their presence (what *are* they doing in this foreign city when they could be at home?). He is amused at the stiff gestures of the *Feldgendarmerie* as they direct the rare traffic as if impelled by an interior clockwork mechanism, he finds the exaggerated salute, accompanied by a resounding stamp of boots, grotesque and unnatural. The military bands that play on Sundays in the Luxembourg and the Tuileries have instruments that are topped by clusters of tiny brass bells that remind him of the sentimental rusticity of Bavaria or Austria (or, indeed, of a Swiss Sunday village band). He has an eye too for the vulgarity of the tall, stiff caps of German officers, less impressive than cheaply ostentatious, as well as for the thick, close-shaven necks bulging over tight-fitting, strangling collars, as if there were some military merit in such acute discomfort.

Every Wednesday, as he waits for his office to open, in a western district, he looks out for a tired, frayed old soldier who smokes a squiggly porcelain pipe and whose only friend is an equally tired and run-down old horse who nestles his pink nose up against him: weary and faithful companions of so many journeys across Europe, in victory and in defeat, first this way, then that, eastwards and westwards, the ancient couple of peace and war, a reminder, too, that the shining, metallic, ultramodern *Wehrmacht* of the proud summer of 1940 dragged along behind it, in unprestigious and obscure supply services, the semirustic baggage trains of medieval, eighteenth and nineteenth-century armies that were the refuge of the old and the broken-down. (Guéhenno notes the presence, in this transport company, of a dwarf, his long overcoat dragging along the pavement among the horse droppings; he notes, too, that the old man and his animal friend avoid the dwarf.) Later, after the Liberation, he would find himself missing the regular early-morning presence of the old man and the old horse, as they waited in patient resignation for whatever they were waiting for, before slowly moving off – twin reminders of Wednesday, of a series of Wednesdays, and thus admitted – all unknowingly – to the intimacies of the personal calendar of a compassionate and observant Frenchman. (Had the old man, puffing on his pipe and lost in his dialogue with his chevaline companion, ever noticed *him*, as he sat waiting on a street bench? As likely that he hadn't, his eyes far removed from the realities of Paris, taking in the memory of some black-and-white village or the flat northern plains.)

Guéhenno has also spotted the *luckiest* German serviceman in Paris, the perfect and accomplished *embusqué*, a young blond

Nordic god who has got the best job in the bitter war, as he polishes the brilliantly shining brasswork of the immaculate boat, *La Lutèce*, requisitioned by the Germans for the last two and a half years, then lazily stretches his long limbs in the brilliant spring sun of the quays between the Pont-Neuf and the Pont-des-Arts. Does the young man, he wonders, have a single thought for the terrible slaughter of the East, as he proceeds methodically and unhurriedly to scrub down the immaculate deck, his muscles rippling under the striped vest of the *Kriegsmarine*, a reminder, too, that Paris is a port, if in this happy instance, a *port de plaisance* (barge traffic had almost totally disappeared during these occupation years, as a consequence of the cutting off of northeast France and Belgium). The young Adonis must have had a powerful protector, perhaps a naval officer.

Guéhenno, like his friend Paulhan, knows how to walk through the occupied city to a purpose in order to distinguish between the familiar and the unfamiliar, the reassuring and the alarming (the appearance of a yellow poster in the corridors of the *métro*, shiny and menacing), and so he has an eye too for the desolate little groups of field-grey soldiers – *les hommes verts* – as they wander through the sordid, seedy, sweaty, run-down topography of a declining *Luna-Park*: a shadow of its former self, its dirty, deforming mirrors throwing back the grotesque reflexions – pulled out or squashed down – of the bored, purposeless occupiers, the rendezvous too of very low-class prostitutes and of a few *zazous* engaged in smashing plates, a *Luna-Park* of despair and desolation, far removed from the noisy attractions of *Pierrot mon ami*. What a place to come to! – as sad, as used up, as the broad deserts of the *portes de Paris*, and the heartless yellow-brick blocks of the *HBM*. Is this the way to spend a precious, exiguous leave, so much looked forward to?

He can gauge the loneliness and despair of the single soldier, the solitary conqueror, separated from his group, as he wanders aimlessly along the heartless wide streets (the wider, the more heartless) of the foreign city, so uninviting, so uncommunicative, his thoughts on home or on the dread East; and he feels pity for the fellow – rather shabby by now, and no longer strutting – due for inevitable slaughter, putting it off, gaining time just hitting the boulevards, nowhere to go, just *walking*, as if sheer fatigue would deaden fear. He has even spotted, in a *pissotière* opposite the *lycée Henri-IV*, in neat Gothic capitals, the chalked words: *Heimat, Süsse Heimat*, the *cri du coeur* of some homesick soldier with his fly undone.

But Guéhenno is a man of exceptional imagination and generosity, capable of seeing the German soldier as an *individual* – like the bewildered, well-meaning Hans Pfeiffer, a *paysan de Paris* indeed, hankering for his Brandenburg village, who makes an intermittent, grinning appearance in *Au Bon Beurre* – a poor, increasingly shabby and shiny creature, caught up in a struggle quite out of proportion to his modest needs and timid hopes, his personal *Lebensraum* contained in a few frayed family photographs in his wallet, taken in his village on a background of steep-roofed black-and-white houses and vast, dark wooden barns. A constricted vision of world conquest – and not as a *symbol* to be stalked and hunted down like a beast, *à chacun son boche*, by a *PCF* killer squad of three (the killer, a second gun, and a scout). They set out on their human hunt by train, with all the equipment, acquired in the basement of the BHV, of a camping holiday (tent, groundsheet, *duvets, butagaz*) and for them such carefully rehearsed and organized assassination outings offer an interesting and exciting replacement to *les congés payés* a few years before: a breath of fresh air, camping out in the woods or in an urban garden belonging to a reliable militant couple – their children are also in the know – and at the end of the trip a nameless dead *boche*, preferably an officer – go for the uniform, do not bother to look at the face (it will be done from behind, in any case). Then back to Belleville-Ménilmontant, Saint-Denis, Ivry, Montreuil, or Noisy-le-Sec. *Bonne chasse.*

Guéhenno, as acute an observer as a novelist like Marcel Aymé, was also becoming aware, by the beginning of 1943, of the increasing parallelism in the outward appearances presented by both *occupants* and *occupés*, as if imitating one another as a result of an imposed familiarity, their clothing, civilian and military, showing common signs of wear and tear, as if they had become yoked together, for better or for worse – in 1943, it would seem to both unwilling partners that it was for worse – as they travelled on the same downward slope, equally exposed to the same relentless cold, a silent reminder of the priorities to the East. It seemed as if shabbiness were now crying out to shabbiness in a fraternity of shivering discomfort and frayed elegance. There was Martin, the veteran of the Dardanelles in *La Traversée de Paris* carrying his two immense suitcases on the eight-mile walk from the rue Poliveau to the rue Caulaincourt, a bulky man with a huge black moustache, just contained in a splitting brown overcoat, shiny with age, but still bearing traces of elegance, likewise hinted at in the immense gold horseshoe pin through his tie, and wearing a homburg hat, greasy with use, with its bold turn-up – giving the general impression of an *inspecteur de police*. Or there was the elderly seamstress in her threadbare, wafer-thin overcoat, once woollen. These are the unconscious counterparts of the *Gefreiter*, his uniform worn down to the seams, his trousers shining at the seat, his long boots cracked and unpolished, the heels revealing their uneven nails. All three have travelled a long way by then towards a shared cynicism and a common concern to keep the cold at bay, increasingly indifferent to the likely course of public events, their thoughts taken up exclusively with private worries. Could there then be signs of mutual recognition between Martin and his companion – stealthy walkers in the arctic night – and the silent group of German soldiers encountered cycling past the Porte Saint-Martin in the direction of the Hôtel Majestic? Members of a common army of shabbiness, a fraternity of *ci-devants*: the Germans still showing traces of the elegance and brassy freshness of the glittering army of 1940, Martin, the seamstress and their like carrying around on their bodies the frayed tatters of the double-breasted fashions of *l'année Expo*, the lost hopes and illusions of 1937. Both were living outside and beyond their allotted time: yet another instance of the Time Machine having gone wrong. But the French were dragging even further behind than the Germans, as they shivered in the thinning wardrobes of Stavisky, the 6 *février* and the *Front Populaire*. By 1944, however, they would be more or less neck-and-neck in the shared inelegance of vestimentary weariness. But, a year later, the civilian population of the ruined Reich would be well ahead, their nakedness covered in the ragged decencies of the débris of the *Wehrmacht*, a whole people, children, women and old men, clothed in *camouflage*: a brilliant jungle green, sand-coloured yellow, and splodges of deep black, two-legged lizards, regiments of upright crocodiles.

Few Parisians can have taken in so much, have read so deeply in the humbly complaining language of a tired clothing, have detected such secret signals linking soldier to civilian, but merely seeing *through* the grey-green figures as if they had been transparencies, as if they had not been *there*. Guéhenno's vision and Aymé's alert eye for detail take in not just the creases and the stains (dark stains), the traces of clumsy stitching, the pitiful thinness of the material, itself *ersatz*, but go beneath and beyond to the wallet, the family photographs in the top pocket of the tight jacket, the long army-issue underwear, to the naked man underneath.

There was, however, another sign of military decline that the philosopher and the novelist fail to mention: the increasing proportion of German soldiers wearing metal-framed spectacles. Henri Michel refers to a requisition order made by the authorities of the Majestic for 100,000 pairs of tortoiseshell frames, 80,000 pairs of metal ones and 200,000 lenses of various categories. Given the origin of the order, this can hardly have been to provide for the civilian market. By 1943, the German army was becoming short-sighted as well as shabby.

As few Parisians would seek them out, try to use them, attempt to work with them (more would work *for* them, whether voluntarily or not: Michel has the figure of 590,000 Parisians working for the *occupant* by 1944, 171,000 in Germany, the remaining 420,000 in the Paris area), as would take potshots at them, spit in their faces, shout insults at them (which they did not understand) or turn their backs on them. Despite the strident litany, *A chacun son boche!* – that hymn of hate tapped out again and again by the underground *L'Humanité* – there were relatively few takers. The militant killers had names (some of which, most inappropriately, were later given to Paris streets or *métro* stations), they were exceptional individuals, almost copybook militants, and, in the sheer perfection of their fanatical commitment, they were the direct counterpart of their *SS* opposite numbers, whom – across the gulf of political Manichaeanism – they so very much resembled, both in terms of common ruthlessness and cruelty and often in shared social origins. Take, for instance, Pierre Georges (alias Frédo, Albert, *capitaine* Henri, Camille, Patrie, and, in his final persona, Colonel Fabien), whose life is that of an unswervingly exemplary militant, born into militancy and dying a hero in de Lattre's First Army, with everything in between exactly in line and as it should be: born in January 1919 to a Communist family (or one soon to be, that is, in 1920); at ten already in charge of a small group of *Pionniers* in Villeneuve-Saint-Georges, a *commune* of fairly strict orthodoxy (though it did also produce the unorthodox and individualist René Fallet); at seventeen, a volunteer in the International Brigade in Spain, then back in France with severe wounds and the rank of lieutenant in the Republican army, in 1938; in 1939 working in an airplane factory in La Courneuve. Interned in December 1939, he escapes from prison during the chaos of *l'Exode*, enrolling shortly after, with Ferdinand Vigne, in a *PCF* killer squad in Marseille; then he is in charge of a clandestine printing press in the suburbs of the same city. Soon after, he is sent to Corsica, with the task of reestablishing contacts with the local cells. Next he is to be found in charge of the undercover *Jeunesses Communistes* in Lyon. Spotted by the Vichy police, he returns to Paris one step ahead of arrest, in June 1941, to become the leader of the local *Jeunesses Communistes* and an officer in its military wing, the *Bataillons de la Jeunesse*. It is this implacable and dedicated militant who heads the murder squad and who fires the shot that kills the unfortunate midshipman Moser, 21st August 1941, *métro* Barbès.

But Georges and his contemporary, Brustlein, born in 1919 in the XIIme and the leader of the murder squad sent to Nantes, are – mercifully perhaps – individuals quite exceptional in their ruthlessness and fanaticism, figures indeed out of a *PCF* primer, capable at the most of inspiring by their example a few dozen young men and even more fanatical young women. They were not leaders of a whole army of faceless fanatics. We even hear of a case when a member of a Communist killer squad, his revolver at the ready, failed to pull the trigger on a German officer as he came down the steps of the Madeleine. He was presumably excluded from the party. Even *PCF* militants can occasionally lapse into human emotions. There is evidence that Cachin, from the Santé, wrote a letter to the German military authorities in order publicly to disassociate himself from individual acts of murder; and this 'lapse' – if it were one – was brought up again in an article published in *Le Populaire* in 1951. Some party militants, when ordered to undertake a particularly dangerous mission in 1943 or 1944, simply lay low and failed to carry it out. One such, it was widely held, was a very eminent party historian. The *PCF*, after the Liberation, thought better about making a public example of a man so important. But he had to earn his passage back to the bosom of the party by a particularly zealous display of orthodoxy over the next few years. A great many Communists during these difficult years were primarily concerned with survival in a world in which everything was stacked against them. They were indeed members of what already called itself – with an eye to the future – *le parti des fusillés* – but they did not always see why *they* should be one of these elect. So the call, *à chacun son boche* generally went unheard, not out of any concern for the Germans, but out of simple prudence. The Germans were dangerous game, best left alone. Indeed, even the killer squads were to display rather more zeal for removing from the scene ex-militants, some once on the *bureau central*, who had gone over to the *PPF* taking with them some of the best-kept secrets of the party's activities during the period 1939–41, than with random murders of probably harmless German officers who did not possess any such inconvenient knowledge. Even within the ranks of the politically committed, there was room for *attentisme*, for sitting it out, for simply ignoring the Germans, and keeping well out of their way, if one were one day to enter the Communist heaven and enjoy the future *lendemains qui chantent*.

For most of the Germans – not those lucky ones who had secured a permanent posting to Paris, but all those soldiers and NCOs rewarded with a brief stay in the city as part of a leave (and one of the functions of Paris – as of Brussels – was as a leave centre, both for the Germans and for their successors) – it would have been much the same. They would be isolated by language (how few would have known more than a few scraps of French – enough perhaps to ask the way, with a finger on their street plan, to some utterly unpronounceable locality, totally resistant to the Teutonic tongue: Rueil-Malmaison, Barbès-Rochechouart). Often bewildered by the *métro* system (for some of these peasants were very stupid), they would first of all have gone on a shopping spree, using their inflated marks or their army purchasing coupons to sweep up knickknacks, miniature Eiffel Towers and other *articles de Paris*, scent, silk stockings, groceries, alcohol, carrying to the transport office of the Gare de l'Est enormous parcels to be sent to their families, customs-free. Then – their families thus provided for – they would have done their dutiful round of the sights, have taken hosts of snaps of each other against easily recognizable backgrounds: Tour Eiffel, Notre-Dame, Arc de Triomphe, Moulin de la Galette, Carousel, Sacré-Coeur, Opéra (Hitler's favourite too), Invalides, moving around in shoals, only vaguely aware of Parisians, in the almost unseeing way in which tourists regard natives, perhaps even thinking, with some envy, how lucky they were, for *they* did not have the Eastern Front awaiting them at the end of their brief period of leave. But, perhaps they would recover a more acute eyesight at the sight of a tight skirt, a small, shapely, undulating bottom, or firm legs well set off by high-heeled *cothurnes*.

(Later, a visit to one of forty-odd licensed brothels could look after that aspect of military tourism, though, as we shall see, some soldiers struck off on their own, rue Berger, rue d'Aboukir, rue Saint-Denis, to take a dip in unlicensed French flesh, perhaps in an effort to 'get away from it all', or as a rather pathetic groping for female companionship, the ladies of the licensed premises no doubt operating with suitable military expeditiveness, precision and unfeelingness. This initiative was an act of military indiscipline and often the first step towards a furtive visit to a *pharmacie*: one can imagine the wretched soldier going from *pharmacie* to *pharmacie* in order to find one that did not employ any female assistants, and then waiting in the shadows till the place was empty, before throwing himself, in broken French, and with the help of gestures in the general direction of below the *Gott Mit Uns* belt, on the mercy and discretion of the white-coated chemist. Members of that body must have acquired a unique sum of knowledge on the subject of such undisciplined sex. But such lone flyers, escapers from the herd, were no doubt rare. Most would have played safe. And it *would* be safe, in every sense. As Henri Michel observes, rather wrily, *'Boule de suif'* does not seem to have been a source of inspiration to the *professionnelles* of the first half of the 1940s, though he does quote instances of *résistants* having been given refuge in brothels during the hours of curfew, having missed the last *métro*.)

Tourists, travelling in groups and staying at special hotels (all on the Right Bank, most boulevard Haussmann, avenue Wagram, République, none on the Left Bank), whether in uniform or not, are insulated from the inhabitants of the cities to which they are brief visitors, and they follow a fixed circuit that is unlikely to take them behind the scenes, into courtyards and *impasses* (Dutourd's only German soldier, Hans Pfeiffer, who somehow found his way to *Au Bon Beurre*, in a quiet street off les Ternes, showed quite unusual initiative, or he may have been lured there by the enterprising Mlle. Léonie). There is no *intimacy* in their standardized circuits, nor any *memory* in the prestigious buildings that line them. The Louvre, the Invalides, the Opéra, can swallow, in common indifference, a Hitler or the anonymous hordes of military tourists in different uniforms. Of the German soldiers, all that would survive of their brief encounters with Paris would be the group snapshots of themselves, an arm round the waist of a fellow soldier, against the background of a monument as artificial and as totally unfeeling as one of those painted-in backcloths used in military photographs of the First World War: a French soldier sitting in the painted-in cockpit of a Farman, a German soldier grinning from a painted zeppelin little more than his own size. The final irony would be that so many of these photographs would be likely to survive their owners and their momentary photographic companions, amidst scattered pieces of the human rubbish, strands of clothing and ammunition, in the snows of the East or on the hot, dusty plains of the Puszta, very many miles from the Parvis Notre-Dame, and without ever having been proudly displayed to family and friends back home. Like so much else about life in wartime, there is something cruelly unfeeling about such carefully organized tourism, in well-drilled and numbered groups, a brief respite, a halt on the road to death. They had merely passed through, gaped, and moved on, to make way for others. What would stay the most vivid in their minds for what remained of their lives was to have slept two or three nights in clean, crisp sheets, before being returned once more to the filth and the bugs of the East. There is something hideously cruel about those unfeeling sheets, constantly washed and laundered for the use of the next batch of temporary tourists. The sheets, like the busy chambermaids, who, in a few deft and determined gestures, shook them out, spread them, and tucked them in, or who changed them and threw them in untidy bundles onto the floor, also had no memory. But Otto von Stülpnagel, who spent so much time walking about, taking in the window displays, staring at the tasteful contrivance of Yvonne de Brémond d'Ars, opposite the closed British embassy, *would* be remembered, for he was *not* a tourist; he was a resident – indeed the number one resident.

The intimacies that, rarely, lay beyond the well-mapped itineraries of the guided tour, in the secret places of the city, in the anarchy of what was left of the *Zone* will elude us: maids' bedrooms at the top of tall apartment blocks, the hut in a piece of wasteland, the abandoned garage, the former dormitory of railway workers among the sidings, unobtrusive in the confused maps of marshalling yards, *any* place, in fact, beyond the double searching eyes of the prefecture and the German military police, the soldier's dream of a quiet corner and a place in which to hide, beyond the reach of nocturnal checks on papers, a haven in which to sit it out, under female protection, so seldom – yet sometimes – attained. The stumbling dialogue, in ponderous, halting Franco-German will also elude us. 'Mademizelle Léoni, si fus plait, je peux foir?' 'Krieg. La Guerre. Triste.' 'Cherard, fus êtes un garzon remargable, vous feriez ricoler un mort!' – the new, timid *langue de l'oreiller* we cannot perceive. From the French side of the bed, there would be greater facility, thanks to the German Institute and Berlitz (the latter as ever on the make: 939 doing German, 2,470 doing English, in 1939; 625 doing English, 7,920 doing German in November 1941 – an eloquent vote of confidence in the future of collaboration and of the belief in a long occupation, and lack of confidence in an Allied victory, though the figures for German courses must have started to go down in 1943). The German must have shown some sign of improvement in the course of four years; and, if 'M. Anse', also known as 'M'sieu Féfé', the peaceable German soldier in *Au Bon Beurre*, acquired only a very tentative and rudimentary French, his teacher in bedroom arts, Léonie, had presumably achieved a good working knowledge of German, before following one of her military lovers to Germany in the summer of 1944. We cannot perceive such consoling intimacies directly, though they may be recreated in works of fiction, such as Dutourd's celebrated novel, one of the most convincing accounts of daily life in occupied Paris, at the level of a peaceful, provincial street in the quartier des Ternes. Such is the case of Mlle. Léonie and the naïve, bucolic Hans Pfeiffer, who was fortunate enough to stay on in Paris the full four years – he was thirty-eight – as a *Gefreiter* in a Flak detachment, shooting ineffectively at Allied planes from a rooftop in the avenue d'Orléans, and simply waiting for the war to end, heading for *Au Bon Beurre* and civilian company (and Léonie) as soon as he was off duty, staying on after the German withdrawal in August 1944, to be captured by a squad of self-appointed FFI – one hopes that they did not treat the unwarlike Brandenburger too roughly. There must have been, one hopes at least, quite a number of such unwilling and untidy soldiers – his uniform worn thin and greasy, his long boots unpolished, though he was buttoned up all the way down the front, in the approved manner – as the candid, sentimental 'M. Anse'.

Both Jean Dutourd and Marcel Aymé managed to introduce us to the realities and the irritations of the Occupation witnessed in miniature: from within the manageable, enclosed, and, even in these terrible times, reassuring world of neighbourhood: Julie and Charles-Hubert Poissonard, *crémiers*, and their customers; or from Aymé's favourite observation post on the steep rue Caulaincourt, on the upper slopes of the faubourg Montmartre – Simenon's world, but against a period background, in which shattering outside events, great battles, huge advances and retreats, are muted and reduced to a scale strictly unheroic.

Such literature is the best that we can hope for. For we are interlopers, gatecrashers at a party to which we were not invited, we were not *there*; the Germans and the French – and, perhaps, at one time, some Italians (though there is no record of them, so that, in Paris at least, they must have been rarely sighted, familiar figures though they would have been in Nice, Gap, Sisteron, Digne, Briançon, Manosque, Valence) – *were* there.

We are eager eavesdroppers after the event, when that particular play is over and the leading characters are dispersed and sent about their business; and so we can only capture impressions at second or third hand, or through the printed evocation, in a nostalgic novel or in a journal such as that of Guéhenno or of Galtier-Boissière. Here is the memory of endless winters that are always bitter and in which the biting wind is always from the north and the east, making the *grands boulevards*, the *quais*, the *Sébasto*, the *Boulmich* and *métro* Glacière (boulevard du Port-Royal) agonizing chasms, rendering the crossroads Strasbourg-Saint-Denis, that house of two of the most inhospitable of the four winds, so cold that the prostitutes are driven to huddle behind the heavy blackout curtains of the cafés on the corner of the boulevard Bonne-Nouvelle and the rue Saint-Denis. As the years pass, *les années noires* will seem less black, and more bizarre, an upside-down world containing mysterious intermediary zones of half-shades and semicollaboration and semiresistance, in which many go about in disguise, in which black marketeers announced their activities in their shiny black macs, in which the *Gestapo français* wear grey *chapeaux taupés*, like prewar Marseille gangsters (some were), in which a certain café in the Place Blanche will make available, for a considerable sum, a full set of papers. They are less black too because we know that it will all work out in the end – the allusive vocabulary, half-coded, wry, cynical, a language of hints and city inventiveness (it must have been much the same with the Berliners), revolving insistently around such well-worn themes of hardship and privation, the harking back to the believed splendours of *avant la guerre*, the new insults that drew on the constant preoccupation with provisioning and rationing, with queueing, hoping and waiting, with the thread-bare protection of overcoats, with shoes that let in the snow and the wet, with persistent chilblains on feet and hands, with the lack of soap and the prevalence of skin diseases. These were years during which the prevailing and timid light attempted to escape through thick blued filters: *les années bleues*, an anaemic and unsightly, ungenerous blue that even covered the vast glass roofs of the termini, giving the rare and patient passengers, awaiting ancient pre-1914 carriages (all the modern ones having been taken for the needs of German military transport) the impression of walking in the dim, opaque light of a deep ocean bed.

War and occupation will bring new sounds and create new silences. Many, recalling the occupation years, in Paris or in Lyon, will remember the *silence* and the *stillness* of the long winter nights under curfew, broken occasionally by the dull tramp of a German foot patrol – the *agents cyclistes* (the *hirondelles* as they were known to Parisians, in their long blue capes) and the German bicycle patrols, pedalling silently through the dark streets, could not be heard, which made them potentially all the more dangerous to the illicit nightwalker, fearful of the moonlight and constantly endeavouring to remain in the shadows. An inhabitant of Lyon, who had lived for many years near the quays of the Rhône, not far from the pont de la Boucle, would identify the occupation years with the fact that, all at once, he could actually hear the fast-flowing, greenish river, a dull, steady murmur, its waters heading southwards over the shallow sandbanks and the deep, swirling central bed, an eerie, powerful sound, drowned in peacetime by the constant noise of the traffic and the roar of the night lorries.

In Paris, the night hours would also bring, to the light sleeper, to the man or woman reading in bed – and this was a

Richard Cobb

time for reading in bed; indeed people had never done so much reading in bed – the realization that the city was not just shared out between French and Germans, whether in cohabitation or in confrontation, and that there was a third element of population to be reckoned with which, like the night patrols of the *hirondelles*, favoured the still watches of the small hours. This other army of occupation, far from coming from the East, had always been there down below, and now, driven by privation, started coming up from the sewers, moving into the cellars and the ground floors of offices and houses, fighting, biting and screaming over the disputed contents of dustbins, running, in tight, well-ordered patrols, ten abreast, those ranks behind keeping close up, at great speed, and with a dire sense of purpose, through the dark streets and along the wide, black boulevards. This time, not members of an invading army, but *old* inhabitants, previously content to remain below ground, but now laying claim to a chosen terrain on the surface, as if the time had come to assert their ancient rights and to take the place over. They, like the *occupants*, were in uniform: dark black, russet, several shades of brown, but they were well-coated against the cold. And even more effectively than the *occupants*, because they were much more intimately acquainted with the layout of the city, its quays and riverbanks, canals and markets, its narrow streets, courtyards and *impasses* – a network that they had been scouring since the time of Villon – they patrolled the frozen streets from end to end. Nothing would escape the little gimlet eyes of *these* urgent fast-moving watchers. Henri Michel, Delarue and many other observers comment on the sudden, impudent, almost open presence of these swift-footed soldiers, the ancient advance guards of disasters, plagues, floods, famines, thickest in the area of the central markets and near the black river – armies of enormous, long-whiskered, dark-coated, red-eyed *rats*, a match indeed for the

Germans and all their sophisticated weapons of hygiene: the familiar *gaspards* that lurk, in brown hordes and as obscure moving shadows, around the sinister and filthy *commissariat* of the rue des Prouvaires, well-known figures quartier des Halles, in the remembered childhood recollections of Robert Lageat, familiar enough even to be awarded a collective first name.

But, thanks to the silence of the night and the absence of a population of nightwalkers and revellers that emboldened these inhabitants of the nether regions of the city, it was only during *these* years that their presence above ground could actually be heard, as, with piercing screams and squeaks, and amidst the dull crash of heavy dustbin lids, they fought indiscriminately for what both *occupants* and *occupés* had rejected (presumably the fur-coated, low-slung invaders concentrated most heavily outside *Soldatenheime* and hotels and restaurants reserved for the Germans, as a sort of high-pitched, squeaky tribute from one invader to another).

Later, at the time of the floods of February 1952, standing on the platform of the *métro* Solférino late at night, I noticed first a thin, slow trickle of brownish water coming between the lines, from the direction of Chambre des Députés and the river – the water, then, was actually running up a slight incline – closely followed, first by one – the leader was an enormous beast in brown and black – then by ten, then by fifty, scuttling in Indian file, as they too rushed uphill to safety, just ahead of the brackish floodwaters. I had seen the advance guard, the shock troops, of a second occupation, this time only of the VIIme and the VIme, that lasted only a few weeks before the *'occupants'* once more withdrew from the cellars of the rue de Seine and the rue Mazarine, to return to their own quarters lower down. One could appreciate the enormity of *La Peste*, the rats of Oran dying with their pink feet in the air, in the streets, heralding the death of the human inhabitants of the port. And one could

Richard Cobb

appreciate the prophetic note in Pierre Gascar's short story, 'Gaston', in *Les Bêtes*. Gaston, a rat the size of a mastiff, was the scout of an army of invaders about to come up from below ground and take over.

The Occupation brought other, less sinister, dislocations to the animal world of Paris. While many of the more exotic inhabitants of the Jardin des Plantes died of cold, a few of the wolves escaped, enjoying a few hours of joyful freedom, and spreading carnage among the chicken, rabbit and hamster population of the shops on the quai de la Mégisserie. French police and German *Feldgendarmerie* patrolled with the wolves' cousins, Alsatian dogs, some responding to words of command barked in German, others to words of command barked in French (but none coming to heel in both languages) but equally zealous in the service of order and repression. (The result of this language difficulty – and one beyond even the resources of the ever-greedy Berlitz – was that the guard-dogs placed to protect the parcels offices of the main Paris stations had to be withdrawn after they had attacked individual German soldiers coming to check in food parcels who had been unable to communicate with the monolingual beasts. After their withdrawal, on orders from the Majestic, thefts of food parcels sent from the countryside to Parisian families who were fortunate enough still to have relatives there – Henri Michel makes the point that the occupation years witnessed a massive rediscovery of previously neglected country cousins, aunts and uncles – or awaiting despatch to the Reich, increased to quite catastrophic proportions.)

Apart from the Alsatians, whether responding to French or to German words of command, the canine population of Paris declined dramatically, indeed so dramatically that, when I first returned to Paris in October 1944, I had the agreeable – and unfortunately rare – experience of walking, in complete safety,

in a dog-free city. Even wars and occupations bring *some* peripheral benefits. What is more, cats, like *les gaspards*, had managed
to survive, though, unlike the rats and like their owners, most
had visibly lost weight. Living in the southern suburbs, in an
area of market gardening and rabbit breeding, the writer Léau-
taud, totally indifferent to the humiliation of France, and rather
amused and intrigued by the arrival of the Germans, spent a
great deal of time during these years seeking out titbits for his
numerous cats. Another case of getting one's priorities right.

In his recent book, *Paris-Montpellier PC-PSU, 1945–1963*, the
historian Emmanuel Le Roy Ladurie, recalling his wartime
experiences as a boarder at a Catholic school, Saint-Joseph,
in Caen, refers to the pro-German element among his fellow
schoolboys, the sons of local farmers of Flemish origin whose
parents had settled in Lower Normandy after the First World
War. One of these Flemish boys had the enviable gift of being
able to address a German military horse, regularly tethered
just outside the main entrance of the school and employed by
the local garrison, in *German*, bringing an appreciative response
from the animal. The boy's prestige among his contemporaries
was, of course, enormously enhanced by a skill so unusual. As
the Germans requisitioned huge numbers of French horses for
army transport, there must have arisen some difficulties in the
transmission of simple orders from man to beast.

Another negative aspect of early occupation, another
absence, was to strike many Parisians who had remained in
the city, or who had returned to it, in June 1940: the parks and
the gardens seemed strangely silent, though the nature of the
silence was not at once apparent. Then it would occur to the
listener that what was missing was the song of birds. Following
the destruction of the huge petrol dumps on the Seine Estuary,
Paris had been enveloped in an oily black cloud which had
wiped out most of the bird population. Other birds had flown

away towards healthier skies. (Much later in the war, in fact right at the end of it, we hear of a similar migration of storks, rooks and blackbirds from the polluted skies of Berlin, as they flew westwards, the storks in regular formations and in vast numbers, away from the doomed city, soon followed by as many ducks, both a little ahead of the advancing Soviet troops.) But, by the late summer of 1940, the familiar *moineaux de Paris* were back in their usual haunts, while the Germans liked to have themselves photographed feeding the pigeons outside Notre-Dame or the Sacré-Coeur, or on the upper walks of the Tuileries. It was one easy form of fraternization and domestication. Throughout the Occupation, the bird market continued to be held on Sundays, quai aux Fleurs (just as the stamp markets, the stamps displayed on iron park benches, continued to be held, on Thursdays, under the trees off the Rond-Point, bringing together, in shared and equally engrossed enthusiasm, uniformed and civilian philatelists, a *terrain d'entente* that was no doubt to be the first stage in a certain amount of verbal exchanges, borrowings of magnifying glasses and tweezers leading even to friendships – Thursday friendships that might extend to other days of the week – between *occupants* and *occupés*). Some tiny, brilliantly flashing exotic birds – from Indonesia, South America, the West Indies or Africa – were no longer to be had, depriving Paris of its brief weekly joy in tropical colours, even on Sundays in November, but there seems to have been no shortage of canaries. It would indeed be hard to imagine a *loge de concierge* without the little yellow bird in its cage.

Les gaspards and their fellow animals have caused me to digress. Let us return, then, to the semicoded language of the four-year span – long enough indeed greatly to enrich popular vocabulary. We know the meaning of *fumer sa décade* (there is a surrealist quality about the action of thus smoking *time*, a quality of which Marcel Aymé is well aware and which he exploits so imaginatively in his fantasy on 'La Carte du Temps' – March 43rd, April 34th, and so on), no mere fantasy in fact, when applied to a period of some 1,500 days – 1,531, to be exact, dating from Saturday 15th July to 19th August 1944 – when Paris lived under German time, one hour ahead of the proscribed French time (no doubt in accordance with German railway timetables for the whole of occupied Europe) so that one of the first acts of the provisional government was to put the clocks back one hour, with the result that Paris was no longer *à l'heure allemande*. *Fumer du belge* and *manger ses tickets* are self-explanatory, the former, even familiar. The adjective *national* lingered on into post-Liberation years (as, indeed, it did in Italy, where it designated the execrable *nazionali*, possibly the worst cigarettes ever produced) to qualify anything that was of poor quality, was not what it claimed to be (*le café national* had not the remotest connection with the coffee bean), or was simply unsmokable, undrinkable, uneatable, unwearable. A variant on *national*, as designating something of Orwellian seediness, both in English and in French, would be *municipal* : 'municipal restaurant', *restaurant municipal*, communing in equally execrable food.

Chleuh, fridolin, verts-de-gris, doryphore, souris grise, bande amarante lingered on, like forgotten clothing left in a drawer, devoid of its human contents, some months after the departure of those to whom the words applied, but they were mere shadows of themselves, deprived of virulence and hate or of sneaking regard and even hesitant friendliness (*les Fritz, les frisous*), and their use had lost the risky savour that the actual presence of the *occupants* had lent them, for there was always the possibility that the overhearer might understand.

I did not need to read Guéhenno to recall the snivelling

vocabulary of cloying hypocrisy and sackcloth-and-ashes *mea culpa, mea culpa*, retribution and atonement poured out nasally from *Radio Vichy*, as if the station had been taken over by battalions of French Uriah Heeps, trained in high-frequency seminary-voice control, whining and shrill clerics speaking as if they had pains in their tummies. Vichy, a clerical regime, admonished its erring and incorrigible *administrés* in clerical tones of high-pitched lament.

But one could be only retrospectively at home with the sloppy, woolly language of *Etat Français* propaganda and so-called thought – more admonishments, delivered in querulous tones, and as if not counting on getting through to the so insist-ently admonished: *penser proprement français (propre, proprement*, as we shall see in the next section, were key words in the vocabulary of a regime that, while making a cult of cleanli-ness, could not offer much-needed soap to the to-be-cleaned-up, though, in this phrase, the adverb has of course a more abstract sense), *reprise de conscience de l'essentiel autochtone, les confluences spirituelles*. Vichy, in its muddy thinking, was very keen on things that ran together, to form a sort of *maréchaliste* mish-mash, in a common communion with the elderly redeemer. But *Confluences* was also to be the title given to a literary review published in Lyon with vague Resistance connotations, but with similar imprecision: indeed, again, a running together of this and that, as if to evoke the topography of the Second City, as the timid Saône runs into the impetuous Rhône, just beyond the tip of Perrache, at La Mulatière. *Confluences* has at least the negative advantage of meaning anything or nothing, so that it would be unlikely to offend or exclude any particular group. In the sparse bookshops of the spa (censorship was far more severe in Vichy than in Paris, especially in defence of the New Moral Order) one would be confronted with such titles as *Présence de Péguy* (the presence of the dead poet seemed especially to thrive in that of the occupier), *Immanence de Nietzsche* (or of Kierkegaard), *Pour une ethnie française*, and, of course, *Vers* this or that (*Vers l'Europe Nouvelle*, *Vers l'Ordre Nouveau*, *Vers la paix universelle*), pointing, in whatever direction (towards Vichy, Berlin, Rome, Madrid, Lisbon, Quebec, Berchtesgaden, or Mercier's *L'An Deux Mille*), but *always* in a dishonourable one, and happily, as it nearly always turned out, to a terminus never reached and to a future as elusive as that of the Thousand Year Reich. Wherever it got, or failed to get, it was always a 'towards-ing' that would be likely to leave many corpses along its relentless and futile path. Perhaps it did not very much matter about the final destination: the journey was the thing. And both Vichy and Paris, using such contrasting language about most things (though communing in a common humourlessness – a sense of humour would hardly be able to accommodate either ultracollaborationism or the idiotically *gaga* language of Vichy), laid great stress on the word *movement*. Movement is action, and action is the liberating force.

The Prefect Trouillé was to describe the ambience of the Vichy régime in his diary for March 1944: 'la fausse dévotion au Maréchal, le conformisme tricolore des marchands de berlinguots', a fair enough description of a system born of hypocrisy and surviving anaemically on doubletalk. Vichy had so little to offer in the present: less and less each month, especially to young people, though the word *youth* was constantly in its mouth, as it was – but a very different, crueller, more vicious youth – in that of the Paris group, and it made increasingly pitiable efforts to lay a tentative hand on a choice of golden future times (resembling, in this respect, the litanies of the *PCF* on the subject of the 'singing tomorrows'), just as, for an octogenarian marshal of France, time was running out.

But, in Vichy, if not so much in Paris, there was as much looking back, to a hazy past, as looking forward to an equally hazy future, in an effort, again, to rediscover this or that – the same muddiness and confused groping: *roots* (a word even more in favour in Vichy than in Paris, for the *pétainistes* were much given to a vocabulary of trees, of which there were many in the Southern Zone), an expurgated past, a distant time when people had *known* where they were going (as if such a time had ever existed!). In the winter of 1940, announcing his new list, the Paris publisher Bernard Grasset launched a new series of books under the somewhat Proustian title – though Proust would have been firmly rejected at this stage, his works being placed on the first *liste Otto* – of *A la recherche de la France*, as if France too had disappeared down a side road in the course of *l'Exode*, an evocation of times past that might take one safely back to Saint-Louis, or better still, to Charlemagne, or *le bon roi Henri* (he and Sully also got onto the Vichy banknotes, under the inspiring motto: *Labourage et pâturage sont les deux mamelles de la France*), but, more profitably, to Napoleon's European Order. Grasset's series was to start at a time when the existing France, a truncated France that had shed well over half its out-lying territories, at least as seen from Paris, was just beginning to settle down, gingerly and without too much immediate pain, to the fact of German occupation. And the Germans were hardly likely to object to such distant soul-searchings, to such flights into a semimythical past that might help to disguise the realities of a stark and humiliating present. The occupation years were years of make-believe, representing the careful reconstruction of an idealized rural past and of rugged rustic virtues that bore no relationship to the cruelties of agricultural life in the seventeenth and eighteenth centuries: no room in such stained-glass-window history for the bitter memory of dearth and famine, cold, poverty, dirt and disease. *A la recherche de . . .* might lead anywhere but towards the truth. Picture-book, folksy history: *Comment naît, vit, et meurt un paysan bas-normand*, a book illustrated with woodcuts in black and white depicting *la veillée*, published in Caen in 1943, which I bought in Bayeux in the following year, tells us nothing at all about any of the three processes. Such an obsession with a carefully sanitized past would result merely in the proliferation, on breast pockets or on handbags, of the coats of arms of the old provinces: the fleur de lys of Flanders and the Ile-de-France, the three leopards of Normandy, the rampant lion of the Lyonnais, the red cross of Languedoc, the black and white lozenges of Brittany, the rearing bear of Franche-Comté, and under whatever mystical beasts and emblematic flowers or trees marched Aunis et Saintonge, Maine, Anjou, Poitou, Aquitaine, Guyenne, Gascony, Dauphiné, Savoy, and the rest of them. In short, history reduced to its most inane and harmless form: heraldry and genealogy, history for boy scouts and girl guides, a *fuite en arrière* into myth and fantasy that could accommodate Joan of Arc – but not Jehanne la Lorraine – Bayard, du Guesclin, Bernadette, Lammenais, Dupanloup, history with the sting taken out, a harmless *bestiaire*.

Vichy, a dishonourable, equivocal, and ludicrous régime, was likewise profuse in its evocations of the *emblems* of nationhood – one had to cling on to such few baubles as had been left one, toys to keep potentially naughty children quiet. The flag was always being raised or lowered, carried in procession, dipped, its golden-tasselled fringes kissed; Vichy was at least rich in woodlands that would supply tall flagstaffs, so it was a *régime drapeautique* (and one that even secreted, at one time, the abortive *légion tricolore*). And being a régime born of defeat, indeed owing everything *to* defeat, it tended to march at a fast pace behind *la clique*, to '*Sambre-et-Meuse*' or '*les Allobroges*'. The Marshal, in particular, was tireless in his references to *de chez nous, de France, de nos provinces*. *De simples poules de chez nous*, as if there were something specifically French about chickens, and, indeed, about all animals born in what remained of l'*Hexagone* (*de belles vaches de chez nous, de petits chien-chiens de chez nous, de braves chevaux de chez nous, de petits poulains de chez nous, des vipères de chez nous*). In the Marshal's baby talk, the French become *des Français de France*; a little boy cannot stand alone – he is *un petit garçon de France*. And, rather in the manner of those bizarre juxtapositions that used to be favoured in the names of hotels (Hôtel de Romorantin et de l'Univers, Hôtel de Vercingétorix et des Jeunes Cyclistes), in his always ineffable conversations with admiring delegations come to offer him presents (*de beaux produits de chez nous, des fruits de la bonne terre de France*) he strings along combinations that have an absurdity specifically *vichyssois*. The Poissonards and their two awful children are preceded, Hôtel du Parc, by a delegation of electricians, who sing to the Marshal a song of their own composition vaunting the triumphs of '*La Fée électricité*' (*Electricité de France*); the Marshal comments sagaciously: 'c'est une très belle chanson. J'aime beaucoup la musique et l'électricité.'

Vichy is not only dishonourable, it is inane, obsessive, desperately provincial, and exceedingly boring. One can appreciate the eagerness with which successive Vichy ministers took the Thursday government *autorail* for Paris, under one pretext or another – that is, if they could obtain German permission to visit the former capital. Vichy was no place for an intelligent man to linger in. Even its topography could seem slightly dotty. Wags (brief visitors from Paris) would point out that the Ministry of Colonies had set up in L'Hôtel d'Angleterre; Trouillé noted, with a mixture of amusement and alarm, that Darnand and his gunmen had taken over le Thermal. The navy ministry was situated in the Helder, its new inhabitants setting about scrubbing the wooden floors as if they had been decks of a man-of-war. Darlan himself lived, most appropriately, 1 avenue des Cygnes. (The inventory of the contents of his Vichy abode, drawn up by a local *huissier*, in November 1942 – *inventaire avant décès*, as Amouroux calls it, in questionable taste – makes astonishing reading: 11 suits, 12 pairs of socks, 27 white shirts, 1 admiral's cap, 2 *bérets basques*, 25 ties, 55 pipes, 16 boxes of cigars, 37 packets of cigarettes, 1 black vase *'TFP et francisque'* – Vichy's own *kitsch* – 1 round tray *Maréchal* [ibid.], 1 plaster bust of the admiral, 1 tricolor flash *'Base aérienne de Pau 27 août 1942'*, 16 sheets, 79 pillow-cases, 51 serviettes, 1 set of embroidered naval table mats [red and blue with anchor], 6 kilograms of coffee, 630 cakes of soap [a suitable tribute to cleanliness], 500 litres of wine in barrels, 100 litres bottled and 225 Hermitage red, 54 Hermitage white [from the Marshal's estate], 12 Château-Chinon, 48 Beaujolais, 40 Roussette, 28 Pouilly Fuissé '38, 106 Champagne, 12 White Label, 16 Johnny Walker.) Collaboration, naval style, certainly removed all the usual problems of shortage.

The hammered-out slogans and the unlovely clichés of the clandestine Communist propaganda prefigure much of the dreary newspeak of the Zhdanov era; yet they could be lethal at a time when *we* could not actually hear them or read them: *les valets du nazisme, la camarilla de l'Hôtel du Parc, Pour un Noël de combat* (for two or more could play at the *Pour* ... game, though only those hidden figures who guided the hands of the *PCF* killer squads could have thus called for a Christmas celebration in the form of exemplary individual murders, as if *A chacun son boche* was the ideal gift to be placed in the *sabot* waiting in the fireplace; and, of course, the party could not neglect Christmas, for, like Stalin, it loved children, and middle-class Communists tended to spoil theirs). The clandestine *L'Humanité* was always on about *les boches*, as if to make up for its total silence on the subject of those of that nationality throughout the period from June 1940 to June 1941, when *l'impérialisme britannique* had been the principal target. The aim now was *l' écrasement du fascisme assassin et barbare* (two adjectives rather than one being a rule of Communist clichés); after 1941 it would favour, as for the killer teams, threes. *Que le sang boche coule, coule, coule* (that litany of incitement to murder, the message of hate tapped out again and again, designed to penetrate the thickest and most unreceptive of militant skulls, a child's primer, an *alphabétaire* of assassination, a message shrieked out in the sort of *martèlement* later favoured, when spokesman for the party, by Auguste Lecoeur, the stark brutality of whose adjurations was accentuated by his ungraceful northern accent). *Que le sang boche coule, coule, coule*, was no empty formula, as we have seen. And *any* German in uniform would do. This was not a coded, or semicoded message, such as that described by Le Roy Ladurie, generally to announce a change of line and followed by a denunciation of those who had failed to see it coming: *Nous vous le disons bien tranquillement* (which would then bring in the following, alarming phrase: *le camarade un tel n'a pas raison*). Outside France, in the 'Popular Democracies,' the adverb *tranquillement* would take on a particularly sinister premonitory connotation, as if one were to lower one's voice before delivering the death sentence.

Le Roy Ladurie is always informative on the evolution of *PCF* allusions and of what he rightly describes as 'verbal terrorism:' à la Robespierre: *flic d'Occident* (Slánsky), *vipérine, termites, laquais*, the dismissal of a whole sector of humanity, ready for the dustbin of history: *les débris des anciennes classes exploiteuses*. The awful pseudofrankness of Courtade: *Croyez-moi*, introduces another death sentence: *c'étaient des traîtres*. Nothing much has changed since then, and the old verbal terrorism was recently seen and heard to be even more effective if strung out and hammered out in nine contemptuously shouted syllables, *Monsieur-Valéry-Giscard-d'Estaing*, or in the lethal politeness of *Le Prince Poniatowski*. It is the voice of Fouquier-Tinville, of several generations of public prosecutors, designating the enemies of the Republic. It is also the voice of Céline and Paquis, of *Je suis partout* and *Au pilori*. The language of the *PCF* echoes, almost to the syllable, the language of hate and incitement to murder of Paris collaborationism. Linguistically, nothing could have been easier than for a *PCF* militant to transform himself into a *PPF* militant: just a matter of hate speaking to hate.

We have not actually heard the self-congratulatory language of the black market, as it unconsciously harks back to the usage of the Franco-Prussian War and of a much older, but shorter occupation, only dimly remembered, and by the 1940s experienced only by people in their eighties and nineties: *c'est autant de pris aux Allemands* (it would have been, in 1870/71: *autant de pris aux Pruscots*), or *encore une bouteille que les chleuhs n'auront pas*, the enjoyable verbal commentary on a meal both vast and rare, and all the more delicious because quite beyond the means of the vast majority of Parisians, lending to gluttony a joyful alibi of patriotism (even if the statement can only be accurate in fact, for what went down went down). Save in the form of *J3* (for a teenager) the surrealist language of rationing – another *alphabétaire* less insistent, less strident than the Communist appeals for blood to flow – of *carte D* and *carte W*, is lost to us, as are so many of the bureaucratic formulae of a period during which the technocrats were allowed a free range in their attacks on the purity, clarity and brevity of the French language, and in their persistent efforts to trip up the poor, wretched *administré* (more administered than ever) in the byzantine trip wires of *Le Journal Officiel* and *Le Bulletin Municipal* (*contingentement, semelles compensées*).

Nor have we ever encountered, much less had to eat or to drink, such dreadful concoctions as started to appear in grocers' shops and *crémeries* in 1941/42 as *le Malto fruit, le Miel de*

Guinée, la Springaline, la Datima, unwelcome newcomers, crooks in fact shoving their way into the familiar, respectable, but diminishing ranks of the old prewar veterans, *Banania,* with its wide-grinning Senegalese, a grocery gollywog, *Eléxa, Meunier,* the copious Dutch lady of *Van Houten,* the friendly *La Vache qui Rit.* The tunnels of the *métro* still flickered with the little Dubonnet man as, in a series of jerks, he raised, savoured, and emptied his glass; but, during a period when every other day was, officially at least, a *jour sans,* his continuing presence and obvious and active enjoyment in raising his arm were something of an affront. However, he survived, thus linking, for people like myself, the Third to the Fourth Republic, as if erasing the years between, that homely little man, a *résistant malgré lui.* The Dubonnet cat came out the other end of the Occupation too. So did the *cothurnes,* products of the Occupation that were still clop-clopping on Paris pavements months after the Liberation. I have seen and touched – easy to tear – suits and jackets made of *la fibrane,* but *le complet Pétain* eludes me, though I imagine it to be double-breasted, electric blue with a narrow white stripe, and designed to show off to advantage *le ruban rouge* and the *francisque.* I have, of course, never encountered a *porteur de francisque,* though I could not help noticing buttonholes in lapels that looked all at once unoccupied (like their owners). But very soon there were plenty of new *rosettes,* ribbons and metal objects to put in old buttonholes.

There were some newcomers that were to be (most unwelcome) heralds of the future, *préfets régionaux* (Vichy had discovered – or rediscovered – *les régions*) notably among them. *La drôlette, l'Occupance, la Préfectance, faire viandox, le blaquaoute,* 'l'homme n'était pas rare; il voulait du linge' (as placed in the mouth of one of Aymé's rue Caulaincourt prostitutes) are more in line with the traditional skills of Parisian slang, but *la*

Carlingue presumably disappeared with the departure of the institution to which it briefly applied. The semimilitary *contre-pêtreries* – a form of humour much favoured by *Le Canard enchaîné* before and after the war – would find new subjects for their bizarre, inverted skills, while being reduced to a clandestine and purely verbal existence: 'Il faut dire, "Métropolitain"; . . . il ne faut pas dire, "Pétain mollit trop."' I have no doubt that there were plenty of others, delicate spring flowers thriving briefly in the shade, but soon killed off, like *la Carlingue*, with the loss of their terms of reference.

But there was *one* area of spoken (and even sung) French in which *les Français de Londres* (*gaullistes* or independents, or even their English friends) enjoyed an advantage over those whom Vichy propaganda so persistently and belabouredly referred to as *les Français de France*, even to the extent of contributing directly to the new vocabulary in current use under the Occupation: 'Radio Paris ment / Radio Paris ment / Radio Paris est allemand', soon to be hummed by errand boys and in the *métro*, perhaps the best-known jingle of the whole four years. Even the expression *prendre Londres* was given a new meaning by those who, at 9.15 or so in the evening listened to 'Les Français parlent aux Français'.

The language of love, and that – closely related to it – of pregnancy, both intimate, and the latter easily descending into a sort of litanic baby talk, managed to resist the pressures of hard times, constant ill-temper, discomfort, fear, uncertainty, and rumour, thus providing the happy reassurance of continuity, and illustrating the ancient theme of the survival of private worlds and private values even in the midst of public calamities and national humiliation. Léon, a refugee from Paris with resistance inclinations, and Madeleine, a native *Lyonnaise*, are seen walking hand in hand through the dark streets of the Second City – rue Désirée, rue Romarin, rue Terraille, rue

Bouteille – or crossing, over and over again, le pont Morand, or walking blindly along the quays of the two rivers. Léon has a rendezvous with a fellow *résistant* on the pont de la Boucle, after which he returns home to the attic in the quartier des Terreaux, whereupon the very pregnant Madeleine addresses him: 'C'est mon Lélé? Comment vas-tu, chou-chou? Tu sais, le petit fan-fan a bougé trois fois dans mon ven-ventre aujourd'hui . . . Il y a du nan-nan à manger. Tu vas faire miam-miam. Des blettes au su-sucre pour Lélé, des blettes tout-à-fait tsouin-tsouin, vi, vi, vi, vi . . . Les Anglais ont envoyé un gros zin-zin sur Villeurbannette, chic, chic, chic. Lélé va me faire un bis pour fêter ça . . .' A feminine and effective manner of putting war and occupation in their proper place and of reducing a high explosive bomb to the childlike *zin-zin*. A language, too, that would not make a stranger of the temporarily absent Englishman, excluded from so much else.

Indeed, we have never seen anything like such an experience. The study of the endlessly varying relationships between *occupants* and *occupés* lies outside our national awareness and our national memory. We may attempt to envisage it in such measurable terms as economic exploitation – what the French, when it had been their turn to be *occupants*, in Belgium and elsewhere, had crudely and candidly called *extraction* – pillage, deportation, extortion, repression and resistance; but its *physical* reality continues to escape our perceptions. It remains a blank page (though it may one day be filled as a result of events that are not entirely unpredictable, though one hopes that in fact they will never occur) in our national history, but one that I have endeavoured to sketch in mainly by an effort of imagination, by drawing on literary sources such as the novels and short stories of Dutourd and Aymé, both of whom had a quite remarkable gift for rendering direct speech in a manner so utterly convincing, and often so refreshingly crude, that one can actually hear the speakers, as if one had been with the other travellers in the train from Paris to Chalon, or with the fourteen friends who met so regularly in a queue, rue Caulaincourt, during the 1939–73 war (Aymé's characters are pessimists, as well they might be in 1943).

Here, for instance, from Dutourd, is an entirely convincing *collabo*, a poor creature all the same, wearing (of course) a *béret basque*: '. . . Je vois, Monsieur, que vous lisez *Mène Camphre*. Beau livre. Et intéressant . . . Non, Monsieur, la France ne mérite pas le Maréchal . . . Et la jeunesse! . . .' And he moves on to the subject of the *occupants*: '. . . Leur attitude, leur discipline, leur correction forcent le respect. Un jeune soldat de la *Vermate* s'est levé dans le métro pour céder sa place à une vieille dame. Je l'ai vu, de mes yeux vu.' It *must* have been just like that. And in shop conversations in which rumour plays an enormous part (as always in time of war) one is equally convinced by the *gaulliste* Madame Lécuyer, another character in Dutourd: 'On m'a dit qu'un officier boche, à Noisy-le-Sec, la semaine dernière s'est tiré une balle dans la tête après avoir embrassé trois petits Français dans la rue . . . Hier, dans le métro, un soldat m'a offert sa place. Il essayait de se faire pardonner d'être là . . .' It is the beautiful precision of Noisy-le-Sec that gains one's admiration. And here is a plumber, in one of Aymé's queues, lamenting the golden pre-Occupation period, when he got through his daily 6 litres of *gros rouge*:

. . . Qu'on nous donne du vin, j'en peux plus . . . J'étais solide comme le Pont-Neuf, jamais un jour de maladie . . . Comme le Pont-Neuf, oui, je me portais. Le Pont-Neuf, bon Dieu . . . Assez c'est bien, mais trop c'est trop. Le Pont-Neuf . . . Si c'est pas révoltant. Le Pont-Neuf . . . Un litre par semaine. Un litre. Non, *un* litre . . . J'en peux plus . . .[11]

Richard Cobb

Aymé is reporting verbatim conversations heard in food queues, always the most sensitive and representative form of assembly.

Another approach to the problem posed by such a chasm has been to ask so many of my French friends what it was like and how it felt at a time when 'it' was only just round the corner, when my friend Maurice was still driving around in a *camionnette* somehow acquired from the *Vermate*, and while a few scattered objects – a dagger in its sheath, a *Gott Mit Uns* belt, a cap-badge, the jaunty cap itself, a couple of regimental buttons – lay abandoned in drawers in bedside tables, perhaps not to be discovered for months or years. It was a time, too, when the extended stomachs of very pregnant Frenchwomen still contained yet unborn Franco-German babies – a very visible hangover from a previous period of history that seemed to be making an effort to prolong itself, and a matter, too, of unfortunate timing (the public calendar running faster than the unalterable and leisurely private one) – it was a time also when the *smell* of the recently departed *occupant* lingered in odd corners, cupboards and wardrobes, as well as, more potently, in barracks. There the white walls were still adorned with the pornographic strip cartoons, the dreams of womanless lustful soldiers (a member of the women's services of the German army, a *souris grise*, her grey skirt pulled up from behind, being penetrated standing up, on a station platform, by a private soldier, belted but unbuttoned, in field grey, his cap at an angle over his ample nose) combined with sentimental poems in Gothic script, and pictures, of the German Forest, of a village with steep red roofs and medieval protruberances, of the holly and the firs of Christmas – the curiously juxtaposed work of once present military artists, the combination of lust and sentimentality, on the ample wall space of the dormitories and eating places of the *Caserne des Grenadiers* in Malines.

In the next chapter, we consider another, less personal, more traceable, aspect of occupation and collaboration: that of a reassuring, but partly fictitious, continuity, set up to disguise the more alarming reality of discontinuity and rupture.

4

Paris Collaborationism: Continuity and Discontinuity

. . . Le bonhomme a une culotte courte dont sortent des cuisses maigres et des jambes verdâtres de vieux monsieur. Ses genoux polis, émergeant de gros bas de laine, ont quelque-chose de faible et de fatigué qui ne va pas avec l'aspect martial du reste . . .[12]

. . . Une musique défilait, jouant les Allobroges de la façon la plus martiale. Derrière la clique, des civils coiffés de bérets, bardés de croix et surmontés d'un drapeau tricolore large comme une voile de brigantine, marchaient au pas. Les badauds se découvrirent . . .[13]

(Jean Dutourd, *Au Bon Beurre*)

In his study, *Les Collaborateurs*, the French historian Pascal Ory makes a very valuable point on the need on the part of the *occupants*, but recently installed and still in the process of setting up house for what looked like a long, comfortable and enjoyable stay, to reassure their perhaps unwilling, certainly surprised and bewildered hosts, the *occupés*, through a sense of continuity, however artificial and deliberately misleading that sense may have been. The main thing was to convince middle-of-the-road opinion – the timorous, the peaceable, the unadventurous, those always concerned above all to keep out of trouble and to avert their gaze from those who might be in trouble – that, for all essentials, life was much the same as it had been, and that all the old, reassuring landmarks were still in place.

It was a clever gambit, for instance, to have ensured that the *Nouvelle Revue Française* should continue to appear, under its familiar red, black and white cover, with contributions by most of the big names of the Paris literary scene, with the same publisher, and under the editorship of Drieu la Rochelle, who, in thus supplying the appearance of continuity and lending his celebrated name to a prestigious publication, rendered the Germans a signal service. It was even more imaginative to have revived the very fashionable *Comoedia*, the favourite review of *le Tout-Paris*, after an eclipse of six years. Not just back to 1939, but back to 1936, but a 1936 that contained no alarming hint of the *Front Populaire*. The implication of the reappearance of *Comoedia*, also in its familiar cover, this time a glossy yellow, in the autumn of 1940 was that social life and entertainment, perhaps momentarily disturbed by the 'phoney war', would be resumed on a peacetime scale, even on a more ambitious scale than in peacetime.

Equally, *L'Oeuvre*, from its letterpress, looks exactly like the pre-1939 newspaper, it still bears the name of its founder, Gustave Théry, and its editor, Jean Piot, though the contents are now rather different, and the famous column on the third page, a daily exercise in the use of the French conditional ('le Maréchal Goering *serait* sur le point de donner sa démission', '. . . Dans une réunion de gauleiters, Hitler *aurait* déclaré . . .', '. . . L'Allemagne *serait* sur le point de manquer des matières premières les plus essentielles à son effort . . .') of the supposedly well-informed Geneviève Tabouis, had gone. The conditional was in any case little suited to a situation when there could be no doubt about the present and little doubt about the immediate future, and when the immediate and shattering past belonged to a *passé défini*. The guessing game was over, *la pythonisse* was momentarily out of business. *L'Oeuvre* was still sufficiently like the prewar daily to have much the same appeal to a largely anticlerical, pacifist and rather naggingly disrespectful readership consisting largely of schoolteachers; and the groups, so often identical, were to be among the earliest and most enthusiastic adherents to the various brands of Parisian collaboration. *L'Oeuvre* continued to bang away at its traditional *têtes de turc* – generals, *képis à feuilles de chêne, académiciens à bicornes*, priests with shovel hats, cigar-smoking capitalists – in the equally familiar column of Georges de la Fouchardière; and to these could now be added the more clerical exponents of the New Moral Order emanating, in waves of unction, from Vichy. The paper even gained a certain number of new recruits from among the more pacifist ranks of the *Canard enchaîné*. At the same time, a very different clientèle could find reassurance in the reappearance, in its familiar dowdiness, of *L'Illustration*. Had the underground leadership of the French Communist party had its way, another clientèle might have had its needs supplied with the official reappearance of *L'Humanité*. The Germans had been approached, in August 1940, with that in mind. But, after some hesitation, they quietly shelved the proposal.

It is not just a matter of convincing people that life in defeat and dishonour is not dramatically different from life before defeat and dishonour; it is also a matter of disguising the more brutal facts of occupation and exploitation, repression, and lack of liberty. Thus there is a double face to occupation, perhaps even more in Paris than in Vichy: the ultracollaborationists preach the New Order, and, with abject eagerness and cruel joy, scream for vengeance, both on the personnel of the previous régime and on specifically designated groups such as Jews and Freemasons. But old, familiar institutions survive, the calendar of *la rentrée*, rather to the disappointment of Guéhenno, is much as it had always been, at least in Paris, where continuity matters most, and where no schools had been destroyed or requisitioned by the Germans. No stations, no boulevards, no streets are renamed, though one or two statues do disappear, the school term starts on time, the old textbooks are still in use, even though certain pupils gradually fall out, in the discreet, almost painless manner described a bit later, and in the context of Lyon, by Georgette Elgey, in her schoolgirl diary, *La Fenêtre Ouverte*. Perhaps the hysteria of Céline's style is stepped up a little bit; but the general tone of hate, spite, abjection, and, above all, palpable lack of talent links the press of collaboration with that of the prewar extreme right. The only difference is that calls for vengeance against named individuals may now be more than a mere literary exercise in nastiness.

Perhaps, indeed, things are very much as they had always been for a great many ordinary people, and defeat, its face once recognized, its magnitude taken in, might even be an object of relief. Certainly it would seem, once the dust had settled on those two terrible summer months of 1940, that the world had not come to an end, and that, indeed, the physical environment, especially that of Paris, had remained intact and recognizable. It was no doubt a bit of a shock at first to take in the sudden presence of German soldiers on the café terraces; but these could no doubt be assimilated, and so dismissed, as a new breed of tourists – in uniform, it is true, but with cameras slung over their shoulders, and certainly fair game for the Pigalle touts and for the vendors of dirty postcards. By all accounts, the new military tourists behaved quite well, did not smash the place up, did not commit the sort of excesses that had often brought the BEF a bad name in the towns of the Northeast.

By September, more and more people were starting to reappear in the occupied capital. The editors and the staff of the dailies were the first on the road back north, followed, soon, by most of the leading Paris publishers, drawn back as much by habit as by the belief that, barring a cataclysm far worse than a total military collapse and an unprecedented national humiliation, books simply could not be published from provincial towns (and, indeed, through the Vichy period, very few were). The police, on the orders of M. Langeron, had never left, had stayed put, in order to make contact with the German military authorities. Theatres and cinemas were quick to reopen – nightclubs probably never closed – ready to serve the needs of the new uniformed tourists.

It was with a sentiment of profound relief, of homecoming, that more and more Parisians followed, so that, by the autumn, once the bits and pieces had been collected and reassembled in familiar patterns, people could once more settle down to family life and the family routine, not just in the Vichy zone, but also in the Paris region. If Jacques Chardonne, from the safety of the Charente, could welcome German victory and the rapidity of national collapse with the rather abject phrase: 'Barbezieux n'a pas voulu la guerre' (what town *had* in fact welcomed the outbreak of war in 1939 in France, or, indeed, in Britain?), it was a sentiment that could be expressed, with even more conviction, in Paris, thus preserved intact for the future of European civilization. One would simply have to manage without the absent prisoners of war; indeed, it was a patriotic duty to manage without them, so that things could get back to normal. Parisians seem to have adjusted themselves without too much difficulty to carrying on short-handed. Perhaps it was as much a matter of difference of location as of basic selfishness. East Prussia, Pomerania, Mecklenburg were a very long way from Paris, and though those in these distant *stalags* might find their thoughts returning to the familiar movement and bustle of *la rentrée* and to the light of early October in the Ile-de-France, those on the spot could hardly place themselves even in imagination in an alien topography of fir, silver birch, scattered lakes, marshland and sand. From such personal accounts as have survived, what seems to have been the greatest preoccupation of the prisoners was the growing conviction that, back in Paris, they were becoming forgotten, that life was going on without them, and that their places had been taken even in bed.

Such a sentiment of relief, both physical and moral, derived both from the resumption of normal family life by the imperative calendar of the French educational system, and from the discovery that outwardly Paris had not changed, was indeed intact, resulted in a sense of apparent continuity and was something that the Germans had every reason to encourage, and that any intelligent *occupants* in similar circumstances would encourage. Let Paris run itself. The prefect of police was in place, the *agents* had never left, the *pompiers* and the *boueux* were back, the restaurants had reopened, just as if *la rentrée de* 40 had been like any other *rentrée*, and both Parisians and Germans could now settle down to all the familiar pleasures and excitements of October, no doubt even with the oyster stalls back in place. It was in September/October that Montherlant published his hymn of praise to the virile German army, to the virile young German *tankistes*. Let France prostrate herself to her proud conqueror, let Paris be the first to be raped by the travellers from the East.

And thus one can readily appreciate that one of the broader, gently sloping channels leading first to the mental acceptance of defeat and humiliation, of the *fait accompli*, then to semicollaboration, and eventually to full-scale collaboration, might start off from a prewar position of pacifism, of opposition to certain types of weapons. But another channel might spring from indifference to public issues and from a desperate attachment to privacy. Most people want to be reassured, and will indeed cling to reassurance all the more desperately in the face of apparent disaster. The first requirement of any *occupant* is to supply that reassurance; no matter what is to come later, or even what is the price to be paid from now onwards, in the form of crippling indemnities, there is always plenty of time for the revelation of such unpleasantnesses. Meanwhile, what a tremendous relief to be invited, politely and firmly, to carry on as before, under the wonderfully welcome programme of 'business as usual'! One could hardly have hoped for anything better.

Hence the posters of the correct German soldiers lifting up little French children. The setting up of an occupation regime is a matter that goes on behind temporary screens, rather like those on a building site. Even later, the torture places and the killing sites are discreetly placed; they do not advertise themselves with brass plates or in neon lights, lurking, on the contrary, behind meaningless initials sprouting in a thick foliage of Ks, Ws and Zs. No doubt, during these years, most people would have tended to avoid the avenue Foch or the rue Lauriston, or, if they had to take those routes, to look the other way until one was past the danger spot. Indeed, many people seem to have avoided even mentioning such addresses, as if, like evoking Monfaucon, they would bring bad luck. And it was some time before the Germans started covering the walls of Paris with the black and red posters of executions. In 1942 and in 1943, the Parisian Jews destined for the death camps were taken away to the Vélodrome d'Hiver and to Drancy in the familiar green buses of everyday usage, as if this too were but a routine journey on one of the usual routes; indeed, some of the poor children thus transported may have been under the impression that the journey would end at the Bon Marché or the Printemps, though their parents would have known better. The decision to use such transport seems, on the part of the prefecture of police and the prefecture of the Seine, like some hideous reminder of *les taxis de la Marne* of the summer of 1914. More likely, it was not deliberate, the buses simply being the only form of mass transport available. But the very familiarity of the means employed adds to the horror of the journey.

Of course, in the Nord, people would not have been fooled by this sort of thing, for they had been through the experience before and they were only too aware of a continuity of a very different kind, that of enemy exactions and brutalities, insensitivity, and that, too, of widespread physical destruction. But the Germans were not concerned to reassure people who knew what it was all about. The Parisians were new to the game. The white barriers must have come as a bit of a shock at first, forcing pedestrians to abandon familiar itineraries or to cross over to the other side of the street. But the *agents de police* looked much the same and wore familiar uniforms, like those British bobbies in the Channel Islands. There was a great chasm between 1939 and 1940; but it is in the nature of humble, comfort-loving and prudent people to avert their eyes from chasms, and to cling to the familiar calendar as a source of private strength. For some people, indeed, the world really did come to a sudden end in May/June 1940 – plenty of soldiers were killed, many civilians perished on the roads or in urban bombardments, and prisoners of war would have months, even years, to reflect daily on the gulf between freedom and captivity, between a private existence and the promiscuity of the prison camp. But here was Paris, as beautiful as ever, in its autumn glory, its gardens full of happy children, its monuments being admired by German soldiers, its *lycées* and schools disgorging their usual noisy, satchelled battalions late in the afternoon. No, the world had *not* come to an end; and life was still there to be lived.

Another reaction would be to seek refuge in the privacy of work and memory. The occupation years were years of stock-taking for many people, who turned to their diaries for comfort and who plunged themselves into academic work, completing their theses huddling in cold rooms. Nineteen forty-two and 1943 witnessed some celebrated *soutenances* both at the Sorbonne and in provincial universities. This applied as much to history as to medicine or law. To some extent at least, outside realities could be shut out, and many people must have followed the example of Proust in contriving for themselves cork-lined rooms. Indeed, some people even had constructed rooms within rooms, not so much in order to surround themselves in a double envelope of privacy as to conserve what little heat was available during the bitter winters of occupation.

For those who did venture out, or who had to venture out, what could be more reassuring than seeing all – or nearly all – the familiar names, and discovering that entertainment and leisure, social life, and literary and cultural occasions were being provided for as before, even if they had to end in the evening earlier than usual? The most valuable form of propaganda is the *acte de présence*, the reassurance of a daily roll call of neighbourhood, of sociability, and of the annual smart society calendar: the same postman delivers the same papers and reviews, in the same covers, though with subtly different contents. Most of the neighbours are now back from what has turned out in the end to have been an unusually prolonged and, indeed, unusual, holiday. There are the same faces at the local street market, though the market itself already has rather less to supply. Even the university term gets off at much the usual date – something that has never happened since 1968; and the well-known professors are back in their *amphithéâtres*. The intellectual establishment is more or less *au complet*. All that is being asked of most of the famous names is simply to be cited, to be noted down in the press: Gide, Sartre, MacOrlan, Aymé, Cocteau, Colette, Queneau, Simenon, all find their way into the pages of familiar reviews, even if they do not write anything that can be interpreted as political, as expressing an adherence to the new order of things. That is something that can be left to more committed writers and artists. All that is demanded of the great names is to be there, and to be seen to be there. *Acte de présence*.

Of course some writers, both living and dead, were misused. Some unpublished stories of Eugène Dabit, who had died in 1936, were reproduced in the collaborationist review, *Germinal*, in 1943, despite the protests of his widow. The dead could be annexed to the New Order, as well as the living, and the presence – hardly surprising – of the son of Péguy on an editorial board of a Parisian review might be seen as enlisting the pseudopeasant and the pilgrim to Chartres in the cause.

Literature, at least as viewed from Paris, or, for that matter, from the Guéret of Jouhandeau, from the Bordeaux of Mauriac, could offer at least the illusion of a continuity that tended to disguise the realities of national defeat and exploitation at the hands of a ruthless foreign power motivated by a detestable ideology. But, as Pascal Ory argues so convincingly, there was much more *political* continuity between 1934 or 1936 and the *années noires* than has generally been realized by historians, who were concerned to see 1940 as a break in French political narrative. There was a *pétainisme* before Vichy – Pétain himself had been a defeatist as early as 1917 – and, like so many old men who were childless, he had long been obsessed with what he saw as the related problems of youth, education and family. A new, more politically aware Pétain had come on the scene in about 1934, and the Marshal had acquired some highly dubious friends during his time as ambassador to Spain just before the outbreak of war. Neither Pétain nor *pétainisme* was born overnight. Other strands of collaborationism can be traced back to the various ex-service associations that grew up after the First World War; others again date from 6th and 12th February 1934, from the experience of the *Front Populaire* and of the Spanish Civil War; others from attitudes to Munich. France had lived in what seemed like an atmosphere of moral civil war and of approaching real civil war at least from 1934. The putschists of the *6 février* were later to turn up either in Vichy or in Paris – more often, first in Vichy, then in Paris. Most of those who had opted for Franco found their way early on to the Hôtel du Parc. The group that formed up round Abetz and Luchaire had long been associated with *les amitiés franco-allemandes* or with organizations deriving from the League of Nations (in which Luchaire had been a high-ranking official in the 1920s).

Among the first wave of *vichyssois*, there was a considerable contingent of *maurrassiens*. The anti-Semites of 1940 had been virulently anti-Semitic since 1924, some even longer; Drumont's widow was even enlisted in the occupation period in order to give anti-Semitism a more distant historical reference. Laval had been a defeatist in 1917 and had sought an alliance with Mussolini in 1935. Doriot had started on his sweaty journey towards the *PPF* and the *SS* as early as 1933; Déat, who had talked and written high-flown philosophical nonsense ever since his schooldays, had discovered in himself all the marks of a leader as early as 1934 and had been embittered by his inability to persuade others of his merits in this respect.

Indeed, in the second half of the thirties, just as there had existed a number of competing youth movements, not all of them composed of youths, unless it were in the sense that *la jeunesse réside dans le coeur*, there had arisen something of a plethora of *apprentis-dictateurs* and self-proclaimed saviours, a rivalry which split French fascism already into a number of competing splinter groups. Small clubs composed of technocrats had formed secret societies and conspiracies, for the purpose of subverting parliamentary democracy under the impact of the Stavisky affair, which had also caused the ruin of *l'inspecteur* Bonny, so that 1940 found him unemployed, available and ready to serve in the newly formed French *Gestapo* of the rue Lauriston. Even Petiot appears to have had several murders to his name, in the Auxerre region, before he had set up shop in the *quartier* Saint-Lazare and in the rue Lesueur; but these had been young peasant girls, including a female domestic. Jews were a new departure, resulting from the favourable opportunities offered by the chain of escape running from Antwerp, through Paris, to the Spanish frontier. And here too there is an obvious line of continuity from Landru to the mad doctor. The *sieur de Gambais* had specialized in elderly widows who were refugees from the occupied departments of the Northeast and who thus would not have any relatives close by to ask awkward questions. Both Landru and Petiot took advantage of the exceptional circumstances offered by a wartime situation to carry out, for a time with impunity, their private campaigns of extermination. Petiot, in the course of his trial, was even to refer to his ingenious predecessor. He may also have found inspiration in the example set by Eugène Weidmann, who killed a dozen people in the Paris region in the course of 1937, *l'année Expo*. A number of the killers recruited into the *Milice* had been killers, either on their own account, or in the service of *OVRA*, or in gangs operating in Marseille, throughout the second half of the thirties.

Perhaps such continuity should be sought both still further back and in regional and collective terms. Montherlant, Brasillach and Déat all had doting mothers who believed in their sons' genius, spoilt the little horrors, and indulged their cruellest fantasies. Brasillach constructed for himself a spurious Catalan ancestry and throughout his adolescence lived in a fantasy world of medieval troubadours. He was lonely and moody. Montherlant likewise turned to a self-invented Spain, indulging in dreams of aristocratic derring-do. All three seem to have discovered the artistic beauty of cruelty in adolescence, Déat even managing to induce one of his schoolfellows to commit suicide, in a sort of Gidean *acte gratuit*. All three could be described as adolescent nihilists of the right; at the same time, incapable of fully coming to terms with an adult world, they tended to cling to the inventions of a perverted childhood. Montherlant and Brasillach shared a delight in bullfighting and an obsession with virility. Believing that the English considered bullfighting a cruel and disgusting sport, they drew from this assumption – one very much to our credit, even if undeserved – a lasting anglophobia, directed, as in the case of de Maupassant's *Miss Harriet*, against the long-toothed Misses. Like Peyrefitte, another spoilt and very depraved boy, who majored in collaboration as a result of his active pederasty, they were both from the Southwest. Giono was from the Southeast. Darnand had spent most of his life in Nice, recruiting there the hard core of his killers. There were a great many southerners in the ranks of ultracollaborationism; most of them came from Catholic backgrounds, none was a Protestant. There were a great many Corsicans and North Africans among the killers; some of the latter were to graduate in the fifties to positions in the *FLN* in the Paris region.

Many were the sort of simple souls who were ready to invest in overall solutions and all-embracing definitions. Quite a few had early succumbed, in the thirties, to the pseudoscientific quackeries of eugenics and neopositivist biology of the type promoted so successfully by Dr. Alexis Carrel. Their vocabulary litanizes *l'élan vital*, their papers and reviews favour 'dynamic' and imperative titles such as *L'Elan*, they have a fondness for simple verbs of movement and action or of concrete engineering – *agir*, *construire*, *refaire*, and *repartir* – their treatises grope blindly towards simplistic solutions presented in messy imprecision. It is the journey that matters, getting there, rather than what is at the end of the road, because movement is the supreme, liberating action.

Energy is the thing, so there is a repetition of the vocabulary of mountain climbing: *pic, jalon, posons de nouveaux jalons*. And everything is new: *ancien* smells of the Third Republic; *vieux* and *vieille* hint at decay and corruption, doubt and indifference. Their speeches harp on virility ('élites viriles et scientifiques') and vitality ('. . . un univers tout physique, où triomphe une vitalité brute . . .', '. . . un lyrisme de l'énergie vitale . . .'). A strange choice of words for movements mostly concerned with death.

Their speeches echo 'energy', both human and scientific, 'loyalty', 'fidelity', both given solemn illustration by elaborate oath taking; and their programmes bear such energizing, and ultimately meaningless, titles as *Vouloir*. The adjectives most favoured are *net, sain, propre, franc, hardi*; their recruits, looking straight ahead towards a golden future yet to be revealed (and which will end up in the flooded tunnels of the Berlin subway) *ont le regard hardi, les yeux clairs*. All this implies a great deal of washing, preferably stripped to the waist, in freezing water. Fascism constantly emphasizes physical cleanliness and rippling muscles. The enemies of fascism are not only degenerate, but weak and, presumably, unwashed. It is a language of infinitives and of short, sharp adjectives borrowed as much from boy scoutism and from the on-your-toes literature of the *Auberges de la Jeunesse* (an ambience originally very *Front Populaire*, but easily transformed into healthy, open-air collectivism, former *ajistes* being numerous in all the youth movements of the Paris groups) as from the *presbytère* and the parish bulletin.

Perhaps, in the Vichy zone, there is rather more stress on moral qualities; but both sides agree in favouring cleanliness as a symbol of renewal and of the break with a dirty past: clean pants, clean bottoms, clean white socks, clean necks, scrubbed faces, clipped hair, chins up, the proud *béret*, the ideal covering for the French head, *le regard en avant*, and forward – no matter whither, but forward. It is also a vocabulary that puts much stress on leadership – there are *Grands* – and that makes reiterative use of the word *cadre*. In short, a language of 'doing' and 'being' rather than of 'thinking'; and 'doing' and 'being' in groups. How, one wonders, did the lonely, narcissistic, self-centred Drieu ever get into such a sweaty (but honest sweat, of course, the fruit of effort) collective *galère*? Perhaps with him, as no doubt with other intellectuals, it was all an exercise in fantasy, because it was in such marked contrast to the realities of their sybaritical daily manner of life.

So much of all this emphasis on 'doing' seems to echo a desperate need to escape from boredom and self-hatred. It is certainly pretty hard work reading this sort of stuff, though it is no worse than being subjected to long passages of equally 'joyful', equally 'energizing' Soviet uplift of exactly the same period, as if in illustration of the common theme of the two immense and rival pavilions of the 1937 *Expo*: Soviet youth, male and female and equally muscle-bound, hurling invisible javelins at Nazi youth, male and female and equally muscle-bound and similarly engaged. At the time, the *Canard* had joked about the similarity. The paper did not know what France would be in for three years later. Nothing is more revealing of the total indigence of fascism and collaborationism than a language constructed for cretins and scoutmasters.

A few years in a medical school or in the French navy could also offer a promising grounding in this or that form of Paris collaborationism. The cult of violence, apparently as appealing to former pacifists as to lifelong *truands*, could explain the ready transition from militancy in the ranks of the *PCF* to militancy in those of the *PPF*. In both, the faithful would have grown hoarse shouting simple slogans of hate; it was merely a matter of barking different words, it was still barking. *Apprentis-fascistes* were more likely to be practising Catholics than practising Protestants. Anglophobia could also be a common starting point, drawing recruits as much from the extreme left, from *munichois* pacifists and defeatists anxious to avoid war at any price, as from the old, italophil, fascist right. (The same was true – though, to a lesser degree – of americanophobia. It was typical of the confused thinking and inverted standards of these generally mediocre people, still set in an already irrelevant historical context, that they thought Britain still a much greater potential threat to French interests and ambitions than the United States; in this respect, Duhamel and Céline had been precursors, and it was *gaullisme* that would provide the new wave of americanophobes.) An almost congenital anglophobia could mobilize such enthusiastic adherents to the New European Order as admirals Platon and Auphan, the naval writer Paul Chack, the journalist Georges Blond, the author of the spiteful and childish *L'Angleterre en guerre* (Blond was later to write an enthusiastic account of D Day and the Normandy campaign, having adjusted himself to a new set of circumstances that had seemed highly unlikely in 1940), Jean Hérold-Paquis, Henri Béraud, and, any time between August 1939 and June 1941, Jacques Duclos, Marcel Cachin (who, in August 1940, called on the workers of Paris and its suburbs to fraternize with the German soldiers) and the other leaders of the clandestine Communist party. The England that they all so resolutely hated and so stridently denounced was a pretty amazing place, a land inhabited by T. E. Lawrence (apparently granted the gift of everlasting life), and run by a semioccult *cavalerie de Saint-Georges* that operated through a European network of Masonic lodges.

Of this mixed and very confused group, only Platon and one other French admiral had ever crossed the Channel. The two had stayed for some days, in June/July 1940, at the Randolph Hotel, Oxford, as guests of the British government; they had also been granted dining rights at All Souls College, the fellows of which they had endeavoured to persuade of the urgent need for Britain to conclude an honourable peace with a victorious Reich, while there was still time and while Hitler was willing to offer generous terms. Their advice had not been appreciated.

Anglophobia undoubtedly drew sustenance from the events of the summer of 1940. The French felt, not unreasonably, that we had let them down – a member of the Anglo-French Purchasing Commission, set up in London at the outbreak of war, himself an almost professional anglophil, wrote me a furiously anti-English letter in June 1940 on the subject of the young men whom he could see, from his office, exercising their dogs in St. James's Park, while the young men of France bled to death because Britain had denied them air cover, carried out Dunkirk and left the French on the beaches. (He had recovered his anglophilia when I met him by chance in the Paris *métro* in October 1944.) But perhaps a more important reason for anglophobia in 1940 was that the British had had the presumption not to have heeded the admirals' no doubt well-meaning advice and had gone on fighting after the French had opted for an armistice, a decision on our part that was an implicit condemnation of Vichy.

This was Britain's real crime, yet at the same time one that could not be openly stated. It was one that could unite in common hostility to the inconvenient, impossible and obstinate island such disparate elements as the French admirals and the officer corps of *la Royale*, nurtured in anglophobia from generation to generation, Paris ultracollaborationists, former pacifists, ambitious professional 'Europeans', Catholic admirers of Franco, anti-Semites and anti-Protestants and members of the Communist party. The very existence of Vichy and all the Paris forms of collaboration based their most convincing arguments on the assumption, shared by the majority of the French, and indeed by world opinion, that the war was all but over in the summer of 1940, and that it only remained now for Germany to get on with the constructive work of laying down the details of the New European Order, an Order in which France, by a display of willingness and good behaviour, could aspire at least to a subsidiary rôle. But if the war were to continue, if only for a few more months or another year, the bargain concluded in the summer of 1940 between Vichy and the Germans would have lost most of its value. The war *had* to come to a halt there and then, in order to justify Vichy's betrayal and to render complete the sense of relief felt by Parisian pacifists and nazis. Hence Jean Hérold-Paquis's cries of rage against a Britain that had to be destroyed, because Britain now remained the one obstacle to a German peace, was getting in the way, and was upsetting a timetable on which both the early *Vichyssois* and the Paris collaborationists had been counting. Britain's continued resistance threw all such long-lasting schemes completely out of joint, even lending to the future an inappropriate, annoying uncertainty. The French defeat had been so complete that it was inconceivable that it could not have been complete for Britain too. In the summer of 1940, a great many patriotic Frenchmen may have followed a similar line of argument. A year later, by June 1941, the situation had changed radically. Now, with Britain allied to the Soviet Union, both Vichy and the Paris groups could find a new moral argument for anglophobia, while the Communists might have been converted to a grudging admission that Britain had been right all the time and that the war which she had persisted in carrying on was indeed one directed against fascism. But, already in the summer of 1940, the decision taken by the British government to carry on the war alone, or with such allies as could be gathered together in Britain or overseas, had undermined the very *raison d'être* of Vichy, placing the southern government in the same invidious position as that adopted by Leopold III, the self-styled *roi prisonnier*, who had likewise calculated on the totality and permanence of German victory.

In the twenties, there had been more Latin fascists; even in the thirties the Italians had lavished more money on the venal right-wing Paris press – *Le Matin, Le Merle blanc, Le Jour, L'Ami du peuple*, and so on – than had the Germans, latecomers in this respect. But in the second half of the thirties, the *maurrassien*-type italophils were giving way to more Germanic fascists, especially among the very young. Hitler's Germany seemed the land of limitless energy, the regime of the future. Hitlerism also had a strong appeal to pederasts, practising or concealed, though many of these, once Vichy had been set up, gravitated towards movements such as *les Chantiers de la Jeunesse, Jeunes de France*, and so on. Homosexuals as a group had a built-in interest in a change of regime, though Paris offered them a more favourable climate than the clerical espionage of Vichy's New Moral Order.

Another way to define the mentality of the collaborationist would be to enumerate what he lacked, for, of necessity, he must have been either an amputated or an uncompleted individual. Goodness, sympathy, love, charity, compassion and doubt would be among the missing parts. Intelligence would rarely be there, save in a warped and twisted form. Pleasure – simple pleasure, based on common observation, on the movement of the crowd, or on the speckled skies of the Ile-de-France – would have been left out, pleasure being confined to boisterous collective occasions, marching songs, vast fascist family gatherings, the right-wing equivalent of the annual September *Fête de l'Huma*, and offering much the same emotional appeal. There would be no place at all for laughter, save in a cruel, mocking form at caricatures of Jews, Bolsheviks, and Anglo-Saxons. The enjoyment of one's own company would have been a crippling disqualification, though it failed to

Richard Cobb

disqualify the introverted Drieu and the narcissistic Brasillach and the silly, pretentious literary *gamin*, Cocteau, drawn to collaborationism as a form of *épater le bourgeois*. As Brasillach was to urge, perhaps in an effort to convince himself and to escape from the bitter loneliness of his own private fantasies, fascism was about being together, just like Communism. So loners should not apply to either.

Delight in female company, for its own sake, would be a serious disadvantage, for a 'virile' antifeminism was the mark of the hero, of *le Chef*, and Costals was as true, as integral a fascist as his creator, Montherlant. Drieu might be allowed the benefit of the doubt, for he had many lady friends, though he treated them all abominably. The rôle of women was to be the object of masculine conquest and to provide *le repos de guerrier*. Montherlant went even further, assigning to France a feminine rôle in a sexual relationship with a triumphant and virile Germany: a marriage that was a recurrent theme in collaborationist literature, and that had its parallel in the proposed alliance between a purely rural France and a highly industrialized Germany – the marriage of Ceres and Vulcan, another pipe dream of the Paris collaborationist press, but one that also had an increasing ring of truth as the occupying authorities set about pillaging France of her resources in food and drink. Indeed, Vulcan could be seen any day, *attablé*, in any of the smarter Paris restaurants, an immense napkin under his chin. A few favoured Parisians might even be invited to his table, to take part in this Franco-German communion.

In short, collaborationists were, by definition, by the mere fact of their choice, very nasty people; it was their sheer nastiness that had got them there, to the end of the journey, though they might combine nastiness and a taste for gratuitous cruelty with stupidity, a hatred of the truth, and an ability to succumb to lies and to slogans, if repeated enough. Some collaborationists were quite clever, though one should not make too much of the cleverness of people who had backed the wrong horse (in the case of Drieu, there seems to have been a positive exultation in having done just that; in that of Laval, it would have been more a matter of peasant obstinacy, a reluctance to admit that he had made a most appalling mistake). Others were stupid, muddled, misguided; a few may even have been victims of circumstances, of time, place and opportunity. It might have been just a matter of having been in Paris, rather than, let us say, in Lyon or Toulouse, in the autumn and winter of 1940 (and a great many early *gaullistes* owed their recruitment into the new movement to the fact that they had happened to have been already in London in June/July 1940). Often there is only a very thin line between commitment to collaborationism, to resistance, or to *gaullisme*; one should not exclude the elements of luck and of chance, especially in the lottery of wartime that puts a special premium on unpredictability and that may hand out, with equally blind impartiality, the winning number or the tarot card of death.

There is at least some satisfaction in the fact that so many of them got what they wanted: death. For the ultimate realization of fascism and Nazism, the one thing that they are good at, is death. In the midst of so much confused thinking, the one matter on which the French fascists displayed some lucidity, some awareness of reality, is when they described themselves as revolutionaries. Here indeed they could commune with the holy band of the saints and martyrs, of Saint-Just and the *communards*, of Robespierre and Babeuf, of Delescluze and Rigault. Indeed, we find both *Germinal* and Drieu drawing just such parallels, the latter, in his last work, evoking a reconciliation between Saint-Just and Charlotte Corday, and envisaging an eventual alliance between fascism and Communism. Indeed, why not? The cult of death has had many devotees in many places. After all, the last stage of commitment would be to be among the killers of the *Milice*, or fighting in the Berlin subway, in May 1945, alongside fifteen-year-old members of the *Hitler-jugend*. Drieu, always a loner, much attached to his privacy, and perhaps therefore not a real fascist but rather an aesthete who toyed with the dark beauties of fascism, took his own life, also in 1945.

These then were the *purs*, the fascists *à part entière*, who travelled the whole distance, whether to Sigmaringen or to Berlin, and who even seem to have taken a sort of perverted pride in the totality of their commitment, in the uniqueness of an experience that set them aside from the rest of the community, as self-appointed *exclus*, people who had burnt their boats, and for whom there could be no way back, only a way forward, to ultimate destruction, mercenaries in the armies of the night, still fighting for a regime that was already in an advanced stage of disintegration and in a cause that had totally failed. The awareness of their rejection seems to have strengthened their resolve to go on to the end, as if in fidelity to themselves and to illustrate the purity of their fanaticism. To have pulled out, in 1944 or 1945, would not merely have been a disavowal of everything that they had stood for since 1940, or even earlier; it would also have been an admission that the Third Reich did not represent the golden and joyous future, and that the Nuremberg rallies would end, not in a vast vista of architectural marvels, but on a scene of total destruction; and these totalitarians, like their Stalinist counterparts, had always been futurists. 'England shall be destroyed, like Carthage,' screamed Jean Hérold-Paquis, night after night, on *Radio Paris*. England had not been destroyed, or at least not in the manner that he had so joyously evoked, and Paquis had been shot.

Déat, on the other hand, accompanied by his wife Hélène, managed to get across the Alps, to be taken in by a monastery in the Dolomites. Thence he had made his discreet way to Turin, where he was to live a further twelve or thirteen years, undetected by the Liberation *Questura*, teaching French to the sons and daughters of pious Catholic families. One only hopes that the French he taught was not of the obscure, tangled and Germanic kind that had characterized his so-called philosophical writings and his vapid political manifestoes. At least, there is a fitting artistry in this transformation of the would-be *Chef* of the *parti unique* that never was – and, indeed, as far as the Paris Germans were concerned, never could be, because they were determined throughout that French political power should be dispersed over a wide spectrum of rival movements – into the bearded Monsieur Dubois, *professeur de français*, recommended from one family to another. For Déat was a *normalien type*, the lower-middle-class scholarship boy who had fought his way up through the French educational system, and who had excelled in that perverse and muddy discipline, *la philo*. Déat, who owed everything to a Third Republic that he set out, for once quite successfully, to subvert, should never have left the classroom in the first place; now he was back in it. He had not been made for a world of action, *agir* was not the right word for this verbose, confused and turgid hack-philosopher; *discourir, enseigner* – pointing the pedagogic finger – were verbs that would have suited him better. He had hardly been a success as a fascist; as a collaborationist, he had carried little weight, the Germans merely tolerating him and his movement, using them as counter-weights to the much more formidable Doriot and his *PPF*, a movement that had some genuine populist undertones. There was nothing populist about Déat, who had never felt at ease when confronted with a crowd. Now, in his Turin obscurity, this failed collaborationist and failed politician was granted the rare grace of retirement, was allowed to grow old – he died in his sixties – and old age is something that is generally denied, perhaps mercifully, to a committed fascist, for a true fascist must remain eternally young, fascism representing the forward march of virile youth, as they stride out shoulder to shoulder before clusters of flags blowing in the wind. It is just possible that, in this process of quiet, unruffled ageing, something of his fascism may have slipped away from him; it is even possible that the conversion of this convinced anticlerical, who had repeatedly condemned Christianity, along with most of his companions and rivals of the Paris group, as the religion of the weak and the defeated, the resigned and the slavish, may have been sincere, and that he had repented. One would like to think so, though the spectacle of a repentant fascist seems pretty improbable. He had certainly been very lucky. Whether he complained of his fate we do not know. What his widow has since complained of is the lack of interest shown, by subsequent generations, in her husband's political career. And so it was with excitement and a touching eagerness that she received the visit of a young English researcher, Dr. Clive Youlden, concerned to rescue Marcel Déat from obscurity.

Céline was also very lucky; but when the Danes put him in prison, he complained bitterly; he had previously complained about the remaining Hitlerites, and when de Gaulle pardoned him, he went on complaining. What Degrelle did with himself in Franco's Spain, we do not know. What is certain is that 'Rex' must have lost his virile good looks years ago, putting on weight, acquiring an un-Mussolinian chin, even if he managed to retain, in exile, the warmth, inventiveness and crudity of his Walloon *patois*, his most convincing passport to a fascist sort of populism which had earned for him the early admiration of the equally crude Doriot.

Any anatomy of a fascist must, of necessity, be a composite one. For there are many approaches to that totalitarian goal, many incidents on the way, revelation can take many different forms, and there is no iron law that prevents a fascist from turning himself into a Communist, though the reverse process seems to have been rather commoner, especially in 1940/1.

Fascism is always violent, indeed violence is its *raison d'être*, its alibi for an absence of any coherent doctrine. Yet collaborationism might spring initially from a horror of violence and from a rejection of war. There was a large contingent of lifelong pacifists in the ranks of Paris collaborationism, including such veteran campaigners as Félicien Challaye. So there could be a place for such people in the German system, at least in 1940, at a time when, as far as the Germans were concerned, the more pacifists there were in France, the better. They would show less tolerance of French pacifism after 1943; but that is to look ahead. Indeed, the Nazis had long taken an active interest in pacifist movements and declarations, especially in Denmark and in Britain, and conscientious objection, of course unthinkable in the Third Reich, was something to be encouraged among potential adversaries. As it turned out, the Germans were to become victims of their own propaganda, for, as Richard Griffiths has shown, they had greatly exaggerated the strength of the pacifist groups in Britain, convincing themselves that British opinion was totally hostile to the possibility of war, and that morale was so low that the country was like a rotten fruit, ready to fall to a determined aggressor.

In terms of individual commitment, too, there is no ready-made portrait of a fascist. The narcissistic and dandyish van Severen had little in common with the freebooting Staf de Clercq; van Severen had even come to accept the possibility of extending *Verdinaso* to include Walloons, while de Clercq remained in the stricter tradition of Flemish nationalism, treason and separatism. The very basic Degrelle is far removed from the conceited, cosmopolitan de Man, who, like many Belgians of the older generation, had been partly educated at German universities. Déat was the very opposite to Doriot. Bonnard was *sui generis*, illustrating his own extravagant form of fascism under his nickname of *gestapette*. Leopold III, certainly an *apprenti fasciste*, and anything but a constitutional monarch, had seen himself, in the summer of 1940, as a Belgian Pétain, a view, however, not shared by most of his subjects. Then there were the separatists among the national minorities. Members of the *PNB*, the pro-German Breton movement, closely linked to the *PPF*, reached fascism through anti-Parisian fanaticism, using the admirable opportunity afforded by the circumstances of occupation to mark out the 'foreigners', the *mocos*, that is to say Frenchmen, who had reached positions of influence in the peninsula. Both Breton and Flemish fascists tended to identify the hated democratic foe with southerners. For *moco*, read *méridional*. At the lower échelons, there are plenty of people who embraced fascism for what they could get out of it: power, a sense of self-importance, dressing up, loot, revenge, killing.

But each, at some stage, had made the choice, had opted for fascism and collaborationism, often for what looked like a going concern, the politics of the future, something certainly worth getting in on, and as soon as possible. (One indication of the firmness of collaborationist stances would be the speed with which one returned to a Paris left open to all manner of personal initiatives, a conquered city indeed, wide open not just to the conquerors, but to ingenious Frenchmen who, in the course of *l'Exode*, perhaps as early as mid-June, had realized that the empty capital was beckoning them and that no time was to be lost in getting back there, *à contre-courant*, before the population as a whole started flowing back.) For, in the summer and autumn of 1940, it would have been quite apparent to those back in Paris, or to those who had never left, that the Germans had a great deal to offer: money power, influence, free travel, lecture tours in the Reich, flattery, applause, agreeable social engagements, grand lunches and dinners, elaborate parties, access to editorial chairs, even the possibility, hitherto undreamt of, of publication. The opportunity would seem all the greater because Vichy had drained away most of the official organizations and higher échelons of a truncated French state. Here then was an unprecedented opportunity for the new men, the true revolutionaries. In this respect, early Paris collaborationism represented a vast new deal, in terms of jobs, money and influence. First come, first served. Commitment to collaborationism could be commanded quite as much by self-interest and conceit as by fanaticism. Probably, in most cases, it would have been a bit of both. The Germans, on their part, were keen to set up as soon as possible an alternative personnel that could be used to circumscribe Vichy, possibly even to replace it; so they would naturally most favour those who approached them first. All the ultracollaborationists were already in place and active by the autumn of 1940. With the implementation, in the Occupied Zone, of Vichy anti-Semitic legislation, collaboration would offer more solid inducements, in the form of the confiscated flats and property of leading Paris Jews.

Fascism and collaborationism are not diseases of the blood, nor are they hereditary, though, in Catholic or autocratic circles, it might have been quite possible to have been born with *maurrasisme*, a virus that had been spreading its ravages now for forty years, not merely in France, but also in Belgium, where it had provided the point of departure of both Degrelle and van Severen, and in French Canada, where it had been a powerful stimulus to *Québecois* neutralism and ultraclericalism. In the second generation, *maurrasisme* might develop into something even worse: from *la France seule* to *l'Europe nouvelle*. (The Paris collaborators would refer to *la France seule* derisively, but not inaccurately, as *la Provence seule*, though Maurras had in fact set up *l'Action Française* in Lyon. And, in any case, *la France seule* was hardly a programme for 1940, when France, far from being alone, found herself saddled with one powerful, and one ignoble, neighbour indeed sharing in her national territory.) Let us say that, given a certain family background and a certain regional upbringing, some might be more predisposed to the disease than others. There were other external influences, including age, class background, and the experience of the previous years. Those who had made a mess of their careers in the 1930s, and who had blamed anyone but themselves for the fact, those who had gone bankrupt, had been caught with their hand in the till, had been condemned for minor sexual offences, or had been involved in something disgraceful and had been found out would naturally welcome the opportunity to make a fresh start and to avenge themselves on a social system and on a political regime that, as they would see it, had let them down. Tiffauges, the resourceful hero of *Le Roi des Aulnes*, would have done well in the Paris of collaboration; as it was, he was spared that temptation by being taken off as a prisoner of war to East Prussia, where he readily acclimatized to an entirely new situation in a totally alien environment. There were no doubt armies of unknown Tiffauges hanging about outside the Majestic, or the Meurice, craning over the white barriers, pleading with the German sentinels to let them in, in the summer of 1940. Certainly a great many of these early recruits to Paris collaborationism possessed *casiers judiciaires* that had seen better days and that were far removed from virginity. But people like Déat, whose political career during the thirties had limped from failure to failure, from miscalculation to miscalculation, no doubt represented a more typical example of this form of *ratisme*.

Paris collaborationism, even at its prime, in 1940 and 1941, when it drew much strength from the likelihood of the war soon being over with the imposition of a German peace, represented a series of minority movements that involved only a small proportion of the population. In 1940 and 1941, it was unable to draw in large crowds, and meetings, however well publicized, seem to have been ill attended. Later, after 1942, *any* public meeting was likely to be ill attended, especially by young people, who stood in fear of being caught in a joint Franco-German police operation designed to net recalcitrant conscripts for the *STO*. Any exact statistics as to membership are impossible to come by, the collaborationist groups being already very secretive at the time, no doubt in order to conceal their pitiful resources and their lack of appeal, while membership lists, both for Paris and for other towns, have had a habit of disappearing from the records since the Liberation. But it seems certain that collaborationism represented a movement involving less than ten percent of the population of the capital. The appeal of Vichy, at least between the summer of 1940 and the spring of 1941, was much wider; but, after 1942, the divergence between the Parisian and the Vichy forms of collaborationism became less marked, with the leaders of the Parisian movements moving into official positions of power within the *Etat Français*, which was increasingly taken over by personalities such as Henriot and Darnand.

There seems to exist some sort of historical law, if indeed one believes in such things, as a consequence of which regimes that owe their existence to a combination of treason, sabotage and conspiracy (to the quick seizing of the opportunity presented, all at once, by a total military collapse, by the failure of military leadership, and by an unprecedented national humiliation) show an almost hysterical, querulous concern for the outward trappings and panoplies of nationalism. From the start, both Vichy and the German-controlled movements in Paris draped themselves in the French flag – later there was even an abortive *légion tricolore* – their numerous, and rival, youth organizations starting and closing the day with elaborate ceremonies centred on the raising or the lowering of the *tricolore*. Old emblems, such as Joan of Arc and Bayard, Sully and Henri IV were trundled out, to witness whether for the New Moral Order or for the New European Order. And great ingenuity and silliness were deployed in the invention, or the alleged reinvention, of new symbols of *la francité*, an ugly word that in *pétainiste* usage, seems to have owed something to Franco's equally spurious and clumsy *la hispanidad*. As the stress on atonement and redemption became more abject, as the insistence on the renewing virtues of national socialism became more compelling, so attachment to the manifestations of *la francité* became more inane. Perhaps these did not in fact amount to very much; if it were merely a matter of wearing a *francisque* in one's button hole in order to express one's new orthodoxy, it was small enough a price to pay. And the *francisques* were both cheap and mass-produced (in small towns like Thiers and Riom). So Vichy might have been described as the first of the 'button regimes', a variety later to be annexed by a wide range of organizations committed to the ostentatious, plastic display of the new orthodoxies of the far left.

La francité also had to be decently, even dowdily clothed, though in a variety of uniforms – in these years of military collapse and national disgrace, there never had been so many uniforms – all of them healthy-looking, displaying less leg above the knee in the Vichy area, more leg above the knee in the German-occupied area, though, in both zones, skirts would remain equally long. Fine marching legs and knobbly knees would be masculine legs and knees. Women were not expected to do much marching, though they could be expected to salute. And there were even new forms of saluting, Frankish forms as befitted young people who were to grow up *franc* and *loyal*.

Whatever the variations of the uniforms, all had in common a headdress, the *béret*, though, even here, size and shape could

indicate a wide range of commitment, from fussy Vichy orthodoxy to the madder fringes of ultracollaborationism. It was
generally agreed that the beret was the proper headgear of the
true Frenchman and Frenchwoman but there was considerable
disagreement as to size and shape; and there were after all a
great many forms of berets from Borotra-style Basque variety, to
prewar *ligue* Alpine style, as favoured by the *Jeunesses Patriotes* (as
it turned out, a double misnomer, as they were pro-Italian and
contained in their ranks quite a number of old men). Nor could
the beret, in its simplest form, be wholly disassociated from the
hateful memory of the *Front Populaire*. Close-fitting, covered in
grease, and worn almost over the ears, it might even have protected the heads of an engine-driver and his fireman. Let then
such memories be erased. Now, at least, there could be no ques-
tioning the fact that the beret was the proper *couvre-chef* of *la
francité*. Nor could there be any doubt that its only acceptable
colour was dark blue. White would be fey, hinting of the *gar-
çonnes* of the disgraceful 1920s, green might do for Dorgère's
rural fascists but it was not sufficiently austere, purple, lilac, and
lie de vin were yet to come, following the formation of paratroop
regiments. A dark blue beret was now the national headdress of
the rejuvenated, regenerated French; it could match a light blue
shirt and dark blue trousers or ample skirt, or shorts worn with
white stockings. Vichy could be both a blue-and-white regime
(*les couleurs de la santé*) or a clerical harmony of blues and blacks.
Red was out of the question, harking back as it did to the red ties
of the *faucons rouges* of the *Jeunesses Socialistes* that were worn
with light blue shirts. Dark blue also hinted at sobriety, the colour of the uniforms of those who attended Juilly or Stanislas. It
was also the colour of the navy. But later, Darnand, emulating
no doubt the *SS*, imposed a black beret on *la Milice*.

One sees a multitude of berets when one looks at group
photographs dating from *les années noires* – and there were of

course quite an unusual number of these: back rows standing, middle rows seated, with the important figures in the middle, their rank indicated by their long Alpine walking sticks (*la cordée* was another key word in the Vichy vocabulary, which made much of the invigorating tonic of mountaineering), front rows cross-legged on the ground, arms folded over knees and covering long white stockings, as one would expect of a regime that had put a whole population back to school in order to relearn the simple rules of simple living and 'togetherness'. One is confronted with rows of heads all topped with berets, pushed over the eyes, forcing up the chins and obliging the wearers to look downwards, *le regard clair* (and preferably blue) and, of course, *franc* (this regime of hypocrisy and *double-entendre* made much of its frankness and its crisp, plain speaking) as they stare resolutely into whatever gleaming future – perhaps *bleu azur*, or, in the case of Paris, brown or black – their particular organization might be peddling: *Travail, Famille, Patrie*, or *le Nouvel Ordre Européen*. Young girls, future mothers (one *hopes* – anyhow one can make it jolly difficult for them not to be), look out confidently, yet wistfully, under their berets, placed at an angle, not rakish, but giving a very slight suggestion of chic; for the new Frenchwoman, while destined for maternity, is not a prude. And so the snapshot of Yvette Marie, somewhat gawky in her dark blue jacket and long black skirt, her beret apparently very insecure on top of her corn-coloured hair, stares at me, with the hint of a smile, across the abyss that separates 1942 from July 1944. Is she witnessing fervently for the Marshal, as she stands rather uncertainly to attention? Or is she merely doing what the others do? It is hard to say. What is certain is that, after June 1944, the beret would be hidden away in a drawer, as if, poor thing, it had been an active participant in the inanities and the equivocations of a recent regime now rejected with contumely. Yvette could now display her Norman hair uncovered or with a silk foulard tied round it.

The *Chantiers de la Jeunesse* favour the beret worn straight; but some of the Vichy Ministers stare out dolefully (they would have been even more doleful if they had known what was coming to them), as if they were already in some doubt about the golden future, from under a floppy beret worn at a rakish angle and giving hints of a buccaneer disposition, however incongruous in an ageing *académicien*. Priests and monks, generally visible, hovering in the middle distance, as if anxious not to push themselves forward too obviously but rather to maintain a discreet presence as guarantors of the moral order, in photographs of Vichy ceremonials, have likewise caught the prevailing message, discarding their shovel hats for tight-fitting berets which will stay on while they play volleyball, their *soutanes* tied up, or while they stride up mountains; their berets sit awkwardly on their round heads, suggesting a rather recent conversion to a vestimentary *francité*. But members of the hierarchy retain their furry black hats; the purportedly classless beret, Vichy's rather obvious claim to a populist base, was perhaps too egalitarian for the princes of the Church. Hospital nurses, on the other hand, wear berets, pulled well back, like dark blue haloes, when they are walking out. Under Vichy rules of fashion and deportment, berets are not to be pushed insolently and provocatively forward, over freckled snub noses, an angle suggestive of the frivolity of the previous regime. Nor are they to dangle just above the Gauloise stuck to the lower lip, a position more suited to louche characters in René Clair films of the thirties. As the Marshal of France, wearing a homburg hat and carrying a walking-stick, goes on his progresses through small provincial towns, their fine avenues of peeling plane trees throwing deep shadows on the ground, and emphasizing the southernness of the truncated kingdom that had fallen to this Picard peasant, he is greeted by young girls and boys, by municipal authorities and by high officials of *la Révolution Nationale*, all wearing the national beret (perhaps it was the *only* thing that was national about a revolution that was in fact a counterrevolution?). At larger gatherings, as witnessed from a rostrum or a balcony, a position favoured by newsreel cameramen in order to indicate massive attendance and enthusiasm, one is confronted with an immense sea of eddying berets, like some strange form of cultivation, a mushroom farm in which the mushrooms have turned blue, or like the much magnified pullulations of corpuscles. In a disarmed and defeated nation, in which a large section of the population has taken to wearing a variety of uniforms belonging to rival or parallel youth movements, the beret has become the common emblem of French alertness. *Toujours prêt!*

Indeed, as little was left to chance, once the regime had been set up in Vichy, one suspects that one of the Vichy leaders with strong southern connections – Laval seems the most likely candidate, even though himself far too attached to the vestimentary traditions of the old Chamber of Deputies ever to have worn a beret – must have hit on the fact that berets are made of a particular sort of resistant and moisture-absorbing felt, one of the rare products of an underprivileged Midi dotted with small, semirural industries, situated in the foothills of the Pyrenees.

The beret seems actually to have made its first appearance among the shepherds of the Basque country and of the sandy, watery Landes – of the Alps or the Massif Central. (Among its increasingly rare wearers at the present day, one would still find a faithful clientèle in the supporters of the rugby clubs of the Southwest.) Some time in the second decade of the present century, the beret had started to travel northwards, from its homelands in the Mediterranean strip or along the Spanish frontier, to cross the Loire, and invade Paris, capping first of all schoolboys and schoolgirls, displacing sailor hats with long ribbons, then moving on to crown adult heads, depriving them of bowlers, boaters and panamas. It would be interesting to discover at what date the beret first appeared on the counters of the Bon Marché or the Samaritaine and when it gained *droit de cité* in their catalogues. But, certainly, by the 1920s, it had conquered Paris – had indeed become the very emblem of francophilia on unsuitable Anglo-Saxon heads and thus was the surest way of drawing attention to the possession of a British or an American passport – ousting, in the quartier du Montparnasse, the wide-brimmed black hats previously favoured by poets, painters and writers. Only the *ceinture rouge* remained impenetrable to the dark blue invasion from the south, the *salopards en casquette* remaining faithful to the proletarian cap right up to the outbreak of the Second World War. The *milieu*, equally conservative, stuck to the long-peaked variety of cap that had been rendered fashionable by the bad boys of the rue de Lappe and of *la Bastoche*. The beret, apostle of the Midi, in its northward march never really penetrated the wool towns of the Northeast, nor indeed Belgium. But now, with France, or the least significant part of France, subjected to a southern regime, with Vercingétorix and the *paysans du Cantal* rediscovered, along with many other Gaulish oddities, it was appropriate that the beret should at last be awarded official national status, the visible affirmation of *la francité*, in the form of an exemplary, and no doubt profitable, *revanche du Midi*.

Who supplied the suddenly immense needs for this new emblem of moral regeneration? Were they made in humble workshops in hill villages of the Pays Basque or of the Haute-Provence? Did they emerge, in shoals, like jellyfish in a warm Mediterranean Sea, from some pious *oeuvre* – Bon Pasteur, Notre Dame du Puy – run by nuns, well-pressed and in soft resistant felt, their linings in brightly coloured silk, the work of girls recently fallen and already working their way up the slow ladder of moral regeneration, in fact just the sort of *oeuvre* to find favour in the clerical circles of Vichy? Or were they made in the prisons

Richard Cobb

of the Southern Zone, Roanne, Saint-Joseph, les Baumettes? Was there even some central organization, patronized by the primate of the Gauls: *l'Oeuvre Nationale du Béret*? Was their manufacture subjected to state planning? Did Borotra or Taittinger set the operation in motion? Or was it due to the initiative of a retired officer of the *Chasseurs Alpins*, a regiment that was closely involved with the early ethos of the new regime? These are all questions for the eager, enquiring social historian.

One thing that is evident, even to the eye, is that Vichy and Paris collaborationism, for once in agreement in promoting an emblem that both reassured as a reminder that one could still be French, and even more French than ever, despite national humiliation, and that represented the quintessence of *la francité*, eventually finished the beret off, not all at once, but on a steadily declining course. The beret had somehow lost its innocence, it had become politically contaminated, it could no longer perch on the awkward, gawky head of Monsieur Hulot, who would have to wear a little hat instead, nor on that of poor Bourvil, his inane, moonlike countenance and bovine expression so well attuned, however, to such a covering, especially in its pancake version. There was nothing clownlike any more about the beret, henceforth associated with organized killing and violence, in dubious causes, the wine-coloured emblem of *les paras*, and the badge of other young men who were neither comedians, nor eccentrics, nor private, retiring individualists, hiding in the shade of its modest blueness. Nowadays, in Paris at least, it is rarely seen, save on the heads of aged and tottering canons of the chapter of Notre-Dame, in stained cassocks and black boots, figures from a very distant past, as they emerge from matins in the cathedral. Washed out, its colour going under the impact of rain and of a boiling sun, it may have managed to survive, in a few remote villages, protecting the heads of elderly smallholders dressed in faded blue smocks; but, nowadays, even Pagnol's *joueurs de pétanque* would have adopted a different headgear, perhaps even the peaked cap of pseudosailors, while the new fascists of the left would publicize their bloody convictions under Castro-style bush-hats.

In a new history of contemporary France, the volume for the period 1930 to 1944 could be described, and effectively terminated, under the title: '*L'Age du Béret*', each period having to be the age of something, preferably something simple and easily identifiable. This would be the final word on the subject of a form of headgear that had much to recommend it, because it was cheap, waterproof, convenient and very fetching when placed above a freckled nose; it could be stowed away in a pocket; and it had, for forty or fifty years, served to distinguish Frenchmen and Frenchwomen – not least of its merits was that it was common to both sexes – from other Europeans, to give them an unassertive, sensible national identity, starting from the top.

Its undeserved history could be interpreted as an allegory on the theme of lost innocence and on that of a false continuity, abused in a public effort to reassure, to make people believe that nothing much had changed, that things were much as they had been before (barring a few minor amputations such as the discreet removal of the Jews, the persecution of the Freemasons, the stealthy handing over of Luis Companys to the Franco authorities), that France had indeed survived, a France of a sort, barely recognizable in terms of the much decried and relatively decent Third Republic. What a shame that the sneaking crimes of Vichy, and those – at least more obvious, more brazenly advertised – of Paris, should have been given this banal and sensible cover!

Would it not be much the same in England under a foreign occupation? Would not bowlers and umbrellas survive in the City? Would not school caps still perch on the round heads of schoolboys? Would not schoolgirls still wear straw hats or amazing boaters with red bands around them? Could not blazers be accommodated to the needs of collaborationism (when, after all, they have done years of yeoman service in the cause of apartheid)? Would not cricket caps, along with the game itself, be encouraged, even patronized, by *l'occupant*, in an effort to prove that things were much as usual, that the county matches would still go on (and the counties would be given their old names back), and that there would always be a Fourth of June? Would not a separatist Scotland, set up by *l'occupant*, impose the wearing of the kilt and penalize those who persisted in sticking to trousers, in an effort to affirm a national identity acquired as a consequence of defeat and as a fringe benefit of occupation? Would there not be morris dancers on every village green? Would not a truncated Wales be given over to harp playing and ancient song? I leave these hypotheses to novelists such as Kingsley Amis and Len Deighton. But let us not be deceived into believing, in terms of our fortunate past, that the history of Vichy, especially in its insistence on an apparent, but in fact contrived, continuity, has nothing to teach us.

Bibliography

Bibliographical Note

In the course of the last five years, Anglo-Saxon historians have displayed a sustained interest in the study of the second occupation, collaborationism, Vichy, and the Resistance. Much of this preoccupation with the subject as displayed by British, American and Canadian historians can no doubt be attributed to its unfamiliarity in their own national terms. Nor is there any sign of any falling off of research and secondary works devoted to France during this period, though, recently, British historians – as they have done with regard to the study of the French Revolution – have come to address themselves to all these related problems in a more local context, probably the only one, such is the extreme diversity both of collaborationism and resistance, to provide new approaches and valuable reassessments. In the last year I have reviewed Marrus and Paxton's invaluable and deeply researched indictment, *Vichy France and the Jews*, Halls's quite as significant and as deeply researched *The Youth of Vichy France* (which has, among other qualities, a great deal of unpublished material relating specifically to the Nord), David Pryce-Jones's *Paris in the Third Reich*, a work perhaps rather too severe on the Parisians as a whole, but offering new material mostly from interviews with surviving German occupation officials (it also provides first-rate visual evidence of the Franco-German mingling in public and on social occasions, horse races and other leisure activities, a constant and useful reminder of the sheer 'everydayness' of the German presence), and, finally, Herbert Lottman's *The Left Bank*, a somewhat gossipy account of literary frequentations, who met whom and where, between about 1933 and 1956, which nevertheless provides some quite new material derived from personal interviews. During the same period, I have had occasion to review Richard Griffiths's excellent *Fellow Travellers of the Right*, a related subject in that it offers an account of those in Britain who might have become our own *vichyssois* and our own collaborationists, had circumstances turned out differently. As it was, most of those in this very disparate group – the only thing that they have in common is a varying degree of germanophilia, or, more rarely, of italophilia – were happily preserved from the temptation of having to make a choice that might have brought them into disrepute and disaster. Richard Griffiths's book certainly helps us to bring a sense of proportion to the study of each of the personal case histories of those in France who took the one choice or the other, as well as of those who refused to make a choice at all. His book is, in this respect, a logical step forward from his previous study, his sober and fair-minded biography, *Pétain*, written over ten years ago, and still the best account of Pétain *avant pétainisme*, and of the formation of a Pétain party and a Pétain myth between 1934 and 1939. A few years earlier, I had read for review Roderick Kedward's *Resistance in Vichy France*, a magnificent study based on original work on sources in the Southern Zone, as well as on interviews, particularly valuable for its treatment of the terrible choices facing *PCF* militants in the (for them) extremely difficult period of 1939–41. Anyone who tends to think of the *PCF* as a monolithic party, minutely controlled from the top, and responding with alacrity to orders from Paris – or from Brussels – should read this invaluable corrective: a description of bewildered individuals, isolated and left to their own devices, often cut off from even local fellow militants, and reduced to acting on instinct or impulse rather than on a 'party line' which often failed to express itself clearly. At about the same time, I reviewed David Weinberg's compassionate and minutely researched *Les Juifs à Paris*, now published in English in the United States, a book that is a necessary prelude to the work by Marrus and Paxton that takes the dreadful story to its tragic, and, in so many cases, definitive, conclusion. Earlier still, I reviewed Pascal Jardin's delightful account of his childhood in Vichy at a time when his father,

Jean Jardin, was *chef de cabinet* of Pierre Laval, before fleeing to Switzerland in 1943. A few years after that, I wrote a review – which was never published – of Georgette Elgey's diary as a schoolgirl, between the ages of 9 and 13, in English translation, under the title, *The Open Window*. Finally, I have had the pleasure of reviewing M. R. D. Foot's account of resistance movements, a subject with which he was intimately connected, having accomplished several missions in occupied France; for myself, his book provided me with all the excitement of several dips into occupied France, a flirtation with resistance tourism, without any of the risks involved, risks which I would have been quite unprepared to incur had I been given the chance to do so at the time. I have also had three encounters with Malraux, one of them echoed four years ago in *Le Canard enchaîné* in his much inflated (indeed largely self-imagined) rôle as a resistance leader, in my reviews of Lacouture's biography, Max Hastings's recent study of the SS Division, *Das Reich*, and Herbert Lottman's series of literary reminiscences. I have benefited, in different degrees, from all these books, so that, although I have never undertaken any personal research on the occupation period, I have felt that I did not come to the subject as a total stranger. As is the case with Bill Halls, I left just before Act One, and came back just after Act Five, leaving France in the late summer of 1939 and returning to it in midsummer 1944, so that I often had the impression that I had come in just after the end of the play. For someone in my position, Vichy would seem both very close and very distant, almost palpable and quite unattainable. Indeed, I *had* actually seen Admiral Platon, his colleague and their two aides-de-camp, two elegant *lieutenants de vaisseau*, during their stay at the Randolph Hotel, in June 1940, just as I had seen trainloads of French sailors as they passed through Oxford station on their way to Aintree – the very opposite direction to Vichy – at much the same time. It was pretty obvious even to an observer as ill informed as myself that the British authorities did not know what to do with these unwanted visitors (the sailors as unwanted as the admirals) and that they had left them entirely to their own devices, that is, to the blandishments of their officers, so that only a tiny proportion of them were to opt to remain in England and in the war, a golden opportunity that was missed by default and from lack of imagination (or, possibly, francophobia, for there was as much of that about in Britain in the summer of 1940 as there was of the counterproduct the other side of the Channel). Again, at much the same time, I had a long conversation with a French army evacuee from Dunkirk who was wounded and in hospital at Aylesbury. He told me that he was from the Pas-de-Calais and that his one idea was to get back there, to his family and his butcher's shop. I hope that he did, though, by the time of his recovery, that would have been extremely difficult. Much later, in 1943/44, I had the fairly regular, and very moving, experience of broadcasting into occupied France and Belgium. I often wondered about my listeners, trying to give them individual identities, faces, names, professions. Was I heard in Paris? Later, in Roubaix, I encountered a number of people who had recognized my voice. This, too, provided a bridge over the years of enforced absence and separation.

I have tried to make up for these by an exhaustive gutting of literary material, novels and memoirs. I have drawn heavily on the diary of Barthas, on the *Liller Kriegszeitung* (discovered in the Bodleian) and on *Invasion 14*, as well as on the memoirs of General Spears, for the First World War. For the second occupation, I have found Guéhenno's moving *Journal des années noires* much the most illuminating, though the novels and short stories of Marcel Aymé and Jean Dutourd have provided me with insights similarly intimate, even to the extent that many of their characters can actually make themselves heard to me, often in entirely familiar Paris slang, across the gap of years and the Channel. As a portrayal of the banality and everydayness of the German presence in a small provincial town, over the period of four years, the first volume of the *Carnets* of the Breton novelist, Louis Guilloux provides a testimony that offers a valuable antidote to overdramatic descriptions of the relations between *occupants* and *occupés*. In his daily observations, Guilloux introduces individual Germans of quite convincing human proportions, providing them with names, even accents and places of origin. Reading his muted account, one begins to realize that the Germans, in their regular daily occupations and in their as regular hours of leisure, come more and more to blend with the activities of the inhabitants and with the steady breathing of the coastal cathedral town, through the hours of daylight and darkness and through the seasons.

When I had my first conversation with an inhabitant of l'*Hexagone* – the first Frenchman I had met in four years who was not a Free Frenchman – an elderly Lower Norman peasant with a straggling sandy moustache, in July 1944, I felt that I was taking up a conversation that I had left off the day before. The years of severance disappeared overnight, I was back where I had started from. And yet, of course, I was not. Experience not shared is an almost uncrossable barrier. So I have tried to cross it above all by addressing myself to works of literature, rather than to historical studies. But probably the best bibliography of all has been supplied by so many of my French friends, both prewar and postwar, and in a few cases – the most interesting – both.

On the everyday administration of a great and complex city such as Paris, and on the daily cooperation between French and German technical services – power, public health, transport – Henri Michel's latest work, *Paris allemand* has been a mine of information. Drawing mostly on the *Bulletin municipal* as a primary source, his account of these years of Parisian administrative history is likely to be definitive. I have also used Amouroux's four volumes of material concerning the occupation years, a veritable ragbag of miscellaneous and often unrelated information, derived from a variety of sources that seem to constitute a private archive: *document inédit en la possession de l'auteur* is often the only indication of provenance, though there is no need to doubt the authenticity of a *fonds* that seems to have been collected in rather a haphazard manner. As a general rule, when all other sources are silent, it may be assumed that Amouroux will have the answer. He is particularly informative on the accidents and intimacies of personal relationships, especially between French and Germans, some of these even stretching back to the First World War and to the French occupation of the Rhineland, an event that produced its long-term results in the birth of a number of Franco-German children. It is only from Amouroux that one can discover that some of the conquerors of 1940 were themselves half French, or that some of the *occupés* of the same year had German daughters. Amouroux is a masterful observer of encounters of such an intimate and unexpected kind. He depicts an elderly Breton peasant resolutely refusing to open her door to a German soldier whom she recognizes as her son, a man who had deserted to the Germans in 1917 and who had returned to his former country in 1942. I have myself met the illegitimate daughter of a German admiral in command at Brest and a local prostitute from the rue de Siam.

Pascal Ory offers an admirable record on the political origins of the various forms of collaborationism. For the first occupation, apart from Barthas and van der Meersh and the German soldiers' newspaper in Lille, I have made use of the official Michelin guide for Lille published in 1920, as well as a number of articles devoted to Lille, Douai, Valenciennes and Roubaix in the *Revue du Nord* and the *Revue d'histoire moderne et contemporaine*. I have also drawn on the childhood recollections of two of my friends, Arthur Birembaut and Emile Auvray, the former from Hénin-Liétard, the latter from Lens. I have also found much useful material in Perreux's book on civilian life during the First World War. Finally, I examined the thesis devoted to Marcel Déat presented at Oxford for the D.Phil. by Clive Youlden. A detailed list of works consulted appears below.

Bibliography

Amoretti, Henri. *Lyon capitale 1940–44*. Paris, 1946.

Amouroux, Henri. *Le Peuple du désastre*. Paris, 1976.

——. *Quarante millions de pétainistes*. Paris, 1977.

——. *Les Beaux Jours des collabos*. Paris, 1978.

——. *Le Peuple réveillé*. Paris, 1979.

——. *Les Passions et les haines*. Paris, 1981.

Aron, Robert. *The Vichy Régime*. Philadelphia, 1966.

——. *Léopold III ou le choix impossible*. Paris, 1977.

Aymé, Marcel. *Le Vin de Paris*. Paris, 1947.

Barthas, Louis. *Les Carnets de guerre de Louis Barthas, tonnelier, 1914–1918*. Paris, 1979.

Céline, Louis-Ferdinand. *D'un château l'autre*. Paris, 1957.

Cobb, Richard. 'The Anatomy of a Fascist'. In *A Second Identity*. Oxford, 1969.

——. *Promenades*. Oxford, 1980.

Dabit, Eugène. *Journal intime 1928–1936*. Paris, 1939.

Dejonghe, Etienne. 'Aperçus sur la zone réservée'. *Revue du Nord*, 1978.

——. 'Aspects du régime d'occupation dans de Nord et le Pas-de-Calais pendant le seconde Guerre mondiale'. *Revue du Nord*, 1978.

Delarue, Jacques. *Trafics et crimes sous l'Occupation*. Paris, 1968.

Drieu la Rochelle, Pierre. *L'Homme couvert de femmes*. Paris, 1925.

——. *Mémoires de Dirk Raspe*. Paris, 1966.

Ducasse, André, Meyer, Jacques, and Perreux, Gabriel. *Vie et mort des Français 1914–1918*. Paris, 1959.

Dutourd, Jean. *Au Bon Beurre*. Paris, 1964.

Duvertie, Dominique. 'Amiens sous l'occupation allemande 1940–1944'. *Revue du Nord*, 1982.

Elgey, Georgette. *The Open Window*. London, 1973.

Fabre-Luce, Alfred. *Journal de France 1939–1944*. Geneva, 1964.

Field, Frank. *Three French Writers and the Great War: Barbusse, Drieu la Rochelle, Bernanos*. Cambridge, 1975.

Foot, M. R. D. *Resistance: European Resistance to Nazism 1940–1945*. London, 1976.

Galtier-Boissière, Jean. *Mon journal pendant l'occupation*. Paris, 1944.

——. *Mon journal dans la drôle de paix*. Paris, 1947.

Gascar, Pierre. *Les Bêtes*. Paris, 1958.

Gordon, Bertram M. *Collaborationism in France during the Second World War*. Ithaca, 1980.

Griffiths, Richard. *Pétain*. London, 1970.

——. *Fellow Travellers of the Right: British Enthusiasts for Nazi Germany 1933–1939*. London, 1980.

Guéhenno, Jean. *Journal des années noires 1940–1944*. Paris, 1947.

Guilloux, Louis. *Carnets 1921–1944*. Paris, 1978.

——. *Carnets 1944–1974*. Paris, 1982.

Halls, W. D. *The Youth of Vichy France*. Oxford, 1981.

Hamilton, Alastair. *The Appeal of Fascism: A Study of Intellectuals and Fascism 1919–1945*. London, 1971.

Hastings, Max. *Das Reich: Resistance and the March of the 2nd SS Panzer Division through France, June 1944*. London, 1981.

Jardin, Pascal. *La guerre à 9 ans. Récit*. Paris, 1971.

Kedward, Roderick. *Resistance in Vichy France*. Oxford, 1978.

Lageat, Robert. *Robert des Halles.* Paris, 1980.

Le Roy Ladurie, Emmanuel. *Paris-Montpellier PC-PSU, 1945–1963*. Paris, 1982.

Lille Before and During the War. Clermont-Ferrand, 1919.

Liller Kriegszeitung. 1915–1918.

Marrus, Michael, and Paxton, Robert. *Vichy et les Juifs*. Paris, 1981. (*Vichy France and the Jews*. New York, 1981.) The French edition contains a full set of documents concerning anti-Semitic legislation.

Meyers, W. 'Les Collaborateurs flamands de France et leurs contacts avec les milieux flamingants belges'. *Revue du Nord*, 1978.

Michel, Henri. *Paris allemand*. Paris, 1981.

Moulin de Labarthète, Henri du. *Le Temps des illusions. Souvenirs (juillet 1940–avril 1942)*. Geneva, 1946.

Ory, Pascal. *Les Collaborateurs*. Paris, 1976.

Paquis, Jean Hérold. *Des illusions . . . Désillusions (15 août 1944–15 août 1945)*. Paris, 1948.

Paxton, Robert. *Vichy France: Old Guard and New Order*. New York, 1972.

Perreux, Gabriel. *La Vie quotidienne des civils en France pendant la Grande Guerre*. Paris, 1966.

Peyrefitte, Roger. *Les Amitiés particulières*. Paris, 1943.

——. *Manouche*. Paris, 1972.

Plumyène, J., and Lasierra, R. *Les Fascismes français*. Paris, 1966.

Pryce-Jones, David. *Paris in the Third Reich: A History of the German Occupation 1940–1944*. London, 1981.

Rousseau, M. 'Douai 1939–1945'. *Revue du Nord*, 1979.

Sicard, Maurice-Yvan, under the pseudonym Saint-Paulien. *Histoire de la Collaboration*. Paris, 1966.

Spears, Edward. *Two Men Who Saved France: Pétain 1917. De Gaulle 1940*. London, 1966.

——. *Liaison 1914*. London, 1939.

——. *Assignment to Catastrophe*. London, 1955.

Teissier du Cros, Janet. *Divided Loyalties. A Scotswoman in Occupied France*. London, 1962.

Trouillé, Pierre. *Journal d'un préfet pendant l'Occupation*. Paris, 1972.

Vandenbussche, R. 'Le Pouvoir municipal à Douai sous l'occupation 1914–1918'. *Revue du Nord*, 1979.

Van der Meersch, Maxence. *Invasion 1914*. Paris, 1935.

Vidalenc, Jean. *L'Exode de mai-juin 1940*. Paris, 1957.

Warner, Geoffrey. *Pierre Laval and the Eclipse of France 1931–1945*. New York, 1968.

Weinberg, David. *Les Juifs à Paris de 1933 à 1939*. Paris, 1974. (*A Community on Trial: The Jews of Paris in the 1930s*. Chicago, 1977.)

White, Ralph, and Hawes, Stephen, eds. *Resistance in Europe 1939–1945*. London, 1979.

Translations

1. Good morning, Fritz – Good morning, sir – Cold – Yes, not warm – And your officers? – When it's cold, the officers are not here; they drink champagne. – Evil war! – And not over!

2. I must have been six years old, this is in 1917. I am with Roger, my big brother. Men wearing blue, nothing but blue, soldiers, a regiment passing by, thud! thud! their boots on the cobblestones. I take Roger's hand, he squeezes my small hand tightly. We follow the soldiers to the houses over there, thud! until they disappear into the distance. Never to come back, thud thud thud! with their little rifles they surrounded those poor men.

   Roger and I gave a final wave, and along tree-lined roads, empty once again, we went home.

3. . . . the regiment headed towards Noyelles-sur-Mer to board a train there to a destination officially unknown, but everyone had the feeling that we were going to Verdun . . . at seven o'clock in the morning, we passed through Bourget. At midday, we were at Sézanne, in Champagne, and we were still travelling towards the east. At four o'clock in the afternoon, the train pulled into the station at Vitry-le-François. At this point, we still did not know our destination but soon our course would be set if the train went in the direction of *Châlons*, we were going into Champagne very calmly at this moment; if we were to continue eastward, without a shadow of a doubt, we were going to Verdun. Alas! It was definitely there that we were going and at nightfall we boarded a train at Revigny station . . .

4. . . . two kilometers past Lamotte-Buleux, the railway forks in one direction towards Noyelles-sur-Mer, our station of departure, and in the other direction towards the Ponthieu plains; the efforts that we made the next day to keep an eye on the direction that the head of the train would take at this junction will be explained. We let out a sigh of relief on noticing that the vanguard was turning its back on Noyelles; we were not therefore going to board, we were not leaving for Verdun, the name of which alone froze us with horror. We were indifferent to every other destination and immediately joy and cheerfulness spread through the ranks in the form of songs, laughs, taunts and animated conversations . . .

5. . . . In the silence, in the middle of a fleeting nocturnal peace, grew a muffled rumbling, still more tragic than all the others, the rumbling of trams, lorries, trains going towards the front, carrying their loads of men or taking back the injured and the dead while Roubaix slept. The Germans hid the movements of the troops from the population. We listened anxiously to all this . . .

6. My dear little *friends*, at this time of the year, and each year you are in my thoughts. My best years were those that I spent on the school benches. My dear little friends, do not copy, do not cheat, nominate from among yourselves a class leader, establish in each class an honour committee

7. The *soldaten*, he said . . . there aren't any good ones. The Krauts, they are a little too damn good for me . . .

8. . . . Later a Kraut asked me for directions in the street. He wanted to go to Etoile. I sent him to Bastille . . .

9. don't worry, we are going to survive, tear up this letter, goodbye . . .

10. When I gave myself to Europe, I had no political ideas yet. I was offered two posts: either a bodyguard or a pedlar of beauty products . . . Among Fantin's staff, we were resisting . . . If I had chosen salesman . . . I would be on the Tricolour with a ministry job, well paid, eating well, with government typists and smoking American cigarettes.

11. They give us wine, I can't anymore . . . I used to be as robust as the Pont-Neuf, never a day of illness . . . Like the Pont-Neuf, yes, I

carried myself. The Pont-Neuf, good God . . . Enough, that's fine, but too much, it's too much. The Pont-Neuf . . . If it's not revolting. The Pont-Neuf . . . A litre a week. A litre. No, *one* litre. I can't anymore . . .

12. . . . The chap wears short trousers from which emerge skinny thighs and the greenish legs of an old man. His smooth knees, appearing out of thick woollen stockings, suggest something weak and tired that doesn't go with the warlike appearance of the rest of his attire . . .

13. . . . A band was marching, playing *The Allobroges* in the most warlike way. Behind the band, some civilians wearing berets, loaded with crosses and sat atop a broad tricolour flag like a brigantine sail, were walking to the beat. The onlookers took off their hats . . .

Index

JOURNEY INTO FEAR

Eric Ambler

It is 1940 and Mr Graham, a quietly spoken engineer and arms expert, has just finished high-level talks with the Turkish government. And now somebody wants him dead. The previous night three shots were fired at him as he stepped into his hotel room, so, terrified, he escapes in secret on a passenger steamer from Istanbul. As he journeys home – alongside, among others, an entrancing French dancer, an unkempt trader, a mysterious German doctor and a small, brutal man in a crumpled suit – he enters a nightmarish world where friend and foe are indistinguishable. Graham can try to run, but he may not be able to hide for much longer . . .

'One of the best stories you'll ever read' *New Yorker*

ORIENTALISM

Edward W. Said

In this highly acclaimed work, Edward Said surveys the history and nature of Western attitudes towards the East, considering orientalism as a powerful European ideological creation – a way for writers, philosophers and colonial administrators to deal with the 'otherness' of eastern culture, customs and beliefs. He traces this view through the writings of Homer, Nerval and Flaubert, Disraeli and Kipling, whose imaginative depictions have greatly contributed to the West's romantic and exotic picture of the Orient. Drawing on his own experiences as an Arab Palestinian living in the West, Said examines how these ideas can be a reflection of European imperialism and racism.

'Stimulating, elegant and pugnacious' *Observer*

GOODBYE TO ALL THAT

Robert Graves

'There has been a lot of fighting hereabouts. The trenches have made themselves rather than been made, and run inconsequently in and out of the big thirty-foot-high stacks of bricks; it is most confusing. The parapet of a trench which we don't occupy is built up with ammunition boxes and corpses . . .'

In one of the most honest and candid self-portraits ever committed to paper, Robert Graves tells the extraordinary story of his experiences as a young officer in the First World War. He describes life in the trenches in vivid, raw detail, how the dehumanizing horrors he witnessed left him shell-shocked. They were to haunt him for the rest of his life.

'One of the most candid self-portraits of a poet, warts and all, ever painted' *The Times Literary Supplement*

HERZOG

Saul Bellow

Is Moses Herzog losing his mind? His formidable wife Madeleine has left him for his best friend and he is left alone with his whirling thoughts, yet he still sees himself as a survivor, raging against private disasters and those of the modern age. His head buzzing with ideas, he writes frantic, unsent letters to friends and enemies, colleagues and famous people, the living and the dead, revealing the spectacular workings of his labyrinthine mind and the innermost secrets of his troubled heart.

'A masterpiece . . . Herzog's voice, for all its wildness and strangeness and foolishness, is the voice of a civilization, our civilization' *The New York Times Book Review*

BREAKFAST AT TIFFANY'S

Truman Capote

'What I've found does the most good is just to get into a taxi and go to Tiffany's. It calms me down right away, the quietness and the proud look of it; nothing very bad could happen to you there, not with those kind men in their nice suits . . .'

It's New York in the 1940s, where the martinis flow from cocktail hour till breakfast at Tiffany's. And nice girls don't, except, of course, Holly Golightly. Pursued by Mafia gangsters and playboy million-aires, Holly is a fragile eyeful of tawny hair and turned-up nose, a heartbreaker, a perplexer, a traveller, a tease. She is irrepressibly 'top banana in the shock department', and one of the shining flowers of American fiction.

'One of the twentieth century's most gorgeously romantic fictions'
Daily Telegraph